God and Caesar

God and Caesar

Biblical Faith and Political Action

JOHN EIDSMOE

Crossway Books • Westchester, Illinois
A division of Good News Publishers

To my parents,
Russell and Beulah Eidsmoe,
who taught me good citizenship;
and
to my children,
David Christopher Eidsmoe
and
Kirsten Heather Eidsmoe,
in the hope that
their generation
will more fully implement
biblical norms and standards
than ours has done.

Bible quotations are taken from the King James Version of the Bible.

Copyright © 1984 by John Eidsmoe. Published by Crossway Books, a division of Good News Publishers, Westchester, Illinois 60153.

First printing, 1984

Printed in the United States of America

Library of Congress Catalog Card Number 84-71423

ISBN 0-89107-313-2

Contents

Introduction

"This is a Christian country!"

"Don't mix religion and politics!"

"The church should save souls, not get involved in politics."

"The gospel should transform institutions as well as men."

"Separation of church and state."

"One nation under God."

In nearly every discussion of religion and politics, slogans like these abound. What do they mean? How do they relate to each other? Can America be a Christian country and still practice separation of church and state?

American Christians are rethinking their role in American politics. Many who stayed on the sidelines in the past are now entering the political arena. Around 1976 many Christians seemed to realize that a "born-again" Christian could be elected to public office. Large numbers of evangelicals voted for Jimmy Carter because he was born again, but many gave scant attention to whether or not Carter's stand on the issues was compatible with their own.

By 1980 the evangelical community was more sophisticated. They were largely disappointed with the position and performance of President Carter, and they had come to realize that being born again was not in itself enough of a reason to vote for a candidate. They remained interested in the candidate's spiritual status, but they also wanted to know whether his stand on the issues was compatible with the Christian viewpoint as they saw it. Groups such as the Moral Majority and Christian Voice were formed to articulate the concerns of conservative evangelicals, and support of the Christian Right undoubtedly contributed to the election of Ronald Reagan and the conservative gains in Congress.

Reaction came quickly. The secular media were especially vitriolic in their criticism of the Christian Right, often to the point of distortion. They portrayed Moral Majoritarians as a modern-day Inquisition seeking to impose its will upon others, violently if necessary. And voices of protest arose within Christendom as well. Liberal Christians attacked the Christian Right as a dangerous fusion of religion and politics which threatened the very basis of religious liberty—apparently forgetting their own crusades on behalf of racial equality, peace, and ecology only a few years earlier.

Dissent existed even among evangelicals. Stan Mooneyham, head of World Vision, declared, "I sense the mood of some of my fellow-evangelicals in 1980, and it scares the daylights out of me. . . . I am as scared of an evangelical power bloc as I am of any other."[1]

The one-time champion and standard-bearer of the conservatives, Senator Barry Goldwater, put it more bluntly:

> And I'm frankly sick and tired of the political preachers across this country telling me as a citizen that if I want to be a moral person, I must believe in "A," "B," "C," and "D." Just who do they think they are? And from where do they presume to claim the right to dictate their moral beliefs to me?
>
> And I am even more angry as a legislator who must endure the threats of every religious group who thinks it has some God-granted right to control my vote on every roll call in the Senate.[2]

It is easy to dismiss the Christian Right by caricaturing its adherents as religious bigots and transplanted Puritans. Ridicule is always more effective than straightforward refutation. But what, really, is wrong with the Christian Right?

"It's obvious," someone may answer. "They're crackpots! They claim to be God's spokesmen! They say God told them how to vote on every issue, and they're trying to cram their religion down my throat. I don't think God told them how he stands on abortion or anything else. I don't think God is even a registered Republican!"

Perhaps not. But even if God hasn't made Jerry Falwell his political mouthpiece for America, can we assume that God isn't interested in politics and go our merry way without him?

Or is it possible that the almighty and omniscient God, the God who is concerned about the fall of a sparrow and who has numbered the very hairs on our heads, does know what is going on in American politics and is interested in our affairs of state? Is it possible that the God whose prophets of old thundered against the abuses of the kings of Israel and Judah, who warned of the evils in Assyria and Babylon, is also concerned about the rulers of America? Could it be that the God of whom Daniel declared that "He removeth kings, and setteth up kings," is actively involved in this nation's electoral process?

More to the point: could it be that God, if he does have opinions about American political affairs, has revealed his opinions to men in some way—for example, in his revealed word, the Bible?

You can search the Bible from cover to cover (even the Bible "The Old-Time Gospel Hour" offers to send you!), and you won't find any verse which tells you how to vote. But you will find much in God's Word that speaks about government and citizenship. God's Word is a treasure-house of wisdom on economics, military power, war and peace, international relations, social reform, social welfare, crime and punishment, capital punishment, church and state—just about every issue you can imagine. While God's Word is not primarily a political textbook, it does frequently touch upon political matters; and when it does so, it is just as inspired and accurate as when it addresses any other topic. The Christian who refuses to preach on such matters, when God's Word plainly addresses them, is not presenting the "whole counsel of God."

I believe the entry of evangelicals into the political arena is a positive step. And in one sense I find it encouraging that evangelicals are not united in their political beliefs. One of the great strengths of Christianity is that it can function under any political system—capitalist, Socialist, monarchist, even Communist. This certainly does not mean that all or any of these systems are in conformity with God's Word, but God's people exist in all of them. And it is also encouraging that Christians in this country adhere to all parties and all ideologies. There are Christian Republicans, Christian Democrats, Christian independents, Christian conservatives, Christian liberals, and even occasionally a Christian Socialist! It is good, and in accordance with God's plan, that Christians should make their influence felt in all of these camps.

But this does not mean that all of these groups are equally right. Truth cannot contradict itself. Who is right, the capitalist or the Communist? The conservative or the liberal? The Republican or the Democrat?

My major criticism of the Christian Right—and it is constructive criticism, for I am largely in agreement with them—is that they talk too much in general terms about the "moral view," the "Christian position," "God's answer," etc. Too little attention is given to the basic question, "What saith the Scriptures?"

Christians must remember that our source of authority is God's Word, the Bible. A political position is neither Christian nor moral unless it can be supported, directly or indirectly, with God's Word.

And that is the purpose of this book—to examine Christian citizenship from God's standpoint, the Bible.

Part I   The Biblical View of Government

1   Why Do We Need Government?

"Why do we need government?" one is sometimes inclined to ask. "All it ever does is take our money and boss us around!"

It is easy to think that way. And in a society in which the state has exceeded its legitimate bounds and intruded into areas in which it has no business, such a statement has more than a little truth.

But the state was founded, by God, for a legitimate purpose. "There is no power but of God: the powers that be are ordained of God" (Romans 13:1).

Why did God establish government?

To Restrain Sin

The most basic reason God ordained human government has to do with the spreading cancer of human sin.

> For rulers are not a terror to good works, but to the evil. Wilt thou then not be afraid of the power? do that which is good, and thou shalt have praise of the same; for he is the minister of God to thee for good. But if thou do that which is evil, be afraid; for he beareth not the sword in vain; for he is the minister of God, an avenger to execute wrath upon him that doeth evil. (Romans 13:3, 4)

We do not know what type of human government existed before the time of Noah and the Flood. We do know that Cain built a city (Genesis 4:17), and we may presume that city must have had some form of leadership and organization. But what it was—monarchy, tyranny, democracy, or Communism—is pure conjecture.

After the Flood, God entered into a covenant with Noah (Genesis 9). By the Noahic covenant God delegated to man the power to preserve order in society by restraining and punishing crime: "Whoso sheddeth

3

man's blood, by man shall his blood be shed: for in the image of God made he man" (Genesis 9:6). This covenant, by which human government is given divine legitimacy, is not limited to Noah and his time. The covenant is with "you (Noah), and with your seed after you" (9:9) and with all creation (9:10). It is an "everlasting covenant" (9:16) that endures for "perpetual generations" (9:12). In other words, it is valid today, it covers us, and it applies to every society on the face of the earth.

God gave human government the authority to restrain and punish crime, because the root of crime is the sin nature of man (James 4:1-3; Romans 1:28-32; Galatians 5:19-21). By holding before men the threat of temporal punishment, government can hold man's sin nature in check and can compel men to refrain from criminal acts. But that is all government can do. Government can only restrain sin and promote civil righteousness—and that with only partial success. Government cannot eradicate the sin nature or cleanse men from their sins. Only the finished work of Jesus Christ on Calvary's cross can do that.

To Preserve Order

There is another reason for human government. Even if man had no sin nature, he would need leadership and organization. (Even the elect angels of God have the same.) Someone would still have to make rules as to speed limits, who stops for whom at intersections, and countless other matters.

For both of these reasons, then, God established human government—to restrain sin, and to organize society. Augustine stressed the role of government in restraining sin; Aquinas emphasized the role of government in promoting man's innate social structure and needs.[1] Sharing his emphasis on the sin nature of man, I agree with Augustine that the first purpose is primary. But I believe Paul had both purposes in mind when he admonished Timothy to give prayer and thanks to God "for kings, and for all that are in authority; that we may lead a quiet and peaceable life in all godliness and honesty" (1 Timothy 2:1, 2).

2 Applying the Bible to Modern Government

Righteousness exalteth a nation: but sin is a reproach to any people. (Proverbs 14:34).

Today it is common to hear people say that America needs to turn back to God, to reassert the biblical heritage upon which this nation was founded.

But how does a nation apply the Bible to government? Do we simply petition Congress to codify the Pentateuch and make it the law of our land? Or do we pick and choose which portions of the Bible to enforce today? If we follow and apply the Old Testament laws against murder and stealing, must we also stone to death homosexuals, Sabbath-breakers, and blasphemers?

Most American Christians, while holding the Bible to be God's inspired and inerrant Word, would not apply every single facet of its teachings literally to government. But if we do not apply it literally and completely, we need a basis for determining when to apply the Bible literally, when to apply it less than literally, and when not to apply it at all. We cannot do this on a piecemeal basis, taking whatever we like out of the Bible and passing over whatever is disagreeable or inconvenient. We need some sound principles for applying the Bible to modern government. Let me suggest several.

Use Sound Principles of Hermeneutics
Before we can apply the Bible to contemporary situations, we must first interpret it correctly. This is not the place for a complete course on hermeneutics (the science of Bible interpretation), but let me suggest several basic principles:

(1) A literal meaning is to be preferred unless the context clearly

5

indicates otherwise. This does not mean that everything in the Bible is to be taken literally. Even the most extreme fundamentalist does not believe the beast of Revelation 13 is a literal monster with seven literal heads and ten literal horns, or that when Jesus called Herod a fox he meant a four-legged animal with a reddish-brown coat and a bushy tail. But if the average "man on the street" of biblical times would have understood a passage of Scripture in a literal sense, that is probably the way we should understand it today.

(2) If the language used in a Bible passage is not clear by itself, consider the intent of the human author. Consider the historical setting, the purpose of the writing, the audience, and the author's other writings.

(3) Look at the context. Sure, Psalm 14:1 says, "There is no God," but it really says, "The fool hath said in his heart, There is no God."

(4) Apparent conflicts in the Bible should be harmonized wherever possible. That is, if two problem passages could be interpreted in one way by which they contradict each other, and in another way by which they agree, the latter interpretation is preferable.

(5) Apparent conflicts should be resolved by letting the latter passage control the earlier passage. If the Old Testament and the New Testament conflict, the New Testament should be regarded as the more applicable expression of the mind of God.

(6) If one passage is clear, and another is ambiguous, let the clear passage control the interpretation of the ambiguous one.

(7) Let God the Holy Spirit guide you, both through prayer and through the application of your God-given power of reason, as you seek the meaning of the Scriptures.

Distinguish Law from Gospel
Law is not limited to the Old Testament, and gospel is not limited to the New Testament; each has much law and much gospel. The law is what God demands of us; the gospel is what God offers to us. The law says, "This is what you must do for God." The gospel says, "This is what God has done for you." Gospel is for individuals and has little application to governmental entities. Law, on the other hand, does relate to government responsibilities.

Distinguish Uses and Categories of the Law
Luther and Calvin both distinguished three uses of the law:

(1) The social or political use: to constrain people to do good by punishing those who do evil. This is primarily the role of civil government, a task given to government by God.

(2) The pedagogical use. "Pedagogue" means schoolmaster, and in Galatians 3:24 we are told that "the law was our schoolmaster to bring

us unto Christ." That is, the law convicts us of our sins by showing us the perfect and holy standards of God, and thereby convincing us that we need forgiveness for our sins through faith in Christ's finished work on the cross.

(3) The didactic use. This describes the process by which God uses the law to teach believers to conform their lives to the will of God— not as a means of salvation, but as a means of spiritual maturity.

Of these three uses, the first clearly is the province of civil government. The latter two are more the responsibility of the individual and the church.

We today are not accountable to the letter of Old Testament law (ceremonial law). But we are responsible to observe God's moral law, for it shows the holiness, justice, and righteousness of God (Romans 7:12). The moral law of God is an eternal reflection of God's absolute standards, a means by which we may know how God would have us live. We can look to the moral law for guidance in the ordering of society.

Apply Scripture Differently to Government Than to Private Individuals

Some say the Bible has no application to government. I emphatically reject this view. The Old Testament prophets preached to their rulers, and sometimes they emphatically condemned them for their violation of God's law.

However, God's law applies differently to government than to private individuals, because the civil ruler has privileges and responsibilities that the private citizen does not have.

Romans 12 and 13 are a good illustration. In the last five verses of Chapter 12 Paul admonishes individual Christians to not recompense evil for evil (v. 17), but to live peaceably with all men inasmuch as possible (v. 18); to not avenge themselves (v. 19), but rather to forgive their enemies (v. 20) and overcome evil with good (v. 21).

But in 13:1-7 he draws a sharp contrast between the individual believer and the civil ruler. Unlike the individual believer, the ruler is a terror to evil works (13:3); he bears not the sword in vain, for he is the minister of God, an avenger to execute wrath upon evildoers (13:4). Why? He is ordained by God (13:1) for this very purpose. God has delegated to civil rulers the authority to punish evildoers and avenge crimes; God has not delegated this power to private citizens.

The ruler therefore has responsibilities both to God and to his subjects; he must execute God's justice and protect his subjects from criminals. There is a Latin maxim that expresses it well: *Minatur innocentibus qui parcit nocentibus* (He threatens the innocent who spares the guilty). This does not mean that mercy has no place in the criminal justice system, but it must be exercised with due concern for the rights and safety of innocent citizens.

God's Word Must Often Be Applied as Principle Rather Than as Law

As I examine the Scriptures I find no precise verse that tells me exactly what the speed limit ought to be on Lewis Avenue, or how long the moose hunting season ought to be in North Dakota, or whether the investment credit ought to be continued or repealed. But as we search the Scriptures we find many principles that apply to such situations.

Take hunting laws, for example. Does the Bible say anything about hunting? Let's go back to the Noahic covenant. In that covenant God specifically gave men authority to use animals for food:

> And the fear of you and the dread of you shall be upon every beast of the earth, and upon every fowl of the air, upon all that moveth upon the earth, and upon all the fishes of the sea; into your hand are they delivered. Every moving thing that liveth shall be food for you; even as the green herb have I given you all things. (Genesis 9:2, 3)

Man, then, has authority from God to hunt animals, at least for food. But this doesn't give man the right to engage in mass and wanton slaughter of the animal kingdom. God placed man in the Garden of Eden, not to destroy it, but to "dress it and to keep it" (Genesis 2:15). So God also requires man to exercise wise stewardship in his use of the animal kingdom and of natural resources in general.

We see, then, a dominion mandate (by which man has the right to use natural resources) and a stewardship mandate (by which man has the responsibility to use them wisely). Putting these mandates together, we can formulate a principle about hunting: God has given man authority to hunt animals to the fullest extent consistent with sound conservation practices.

The application of that principle will produce different results at different times and in different jurisdictions. North Dakota has only a limited moose hunting season, and only in a few northeastern counties where sufficient numbers of moose live, whereas Minnesota and Canada both have longer seasons. It is not that different principles apply in Minnesota and Canada than in North Dakota, but that the circumstances are different—Minnesota and Canada have more moose, and therefore sound conservation practices allow a longer moose hunting season there than in North Dakota. If the moose population in North Dakota continues to grow, it may be that North Dakota can expand its hunting season. (Not long ago moose were so scarce that North Dakota didn't allow them to be hunted at all.) Same principle; different circumstances; different application.

**God's Word Must Be Applied According to the
"Two Kingdoms" Concept**

In deciding whether to make such crimes as murder and blasphemy illegal—remember that both were capital offenses in Old Testament times (Exodus 21:12; Leviticus 24:16)—we must examine whether the offense is prohibited by God's law.

But we must go further than that. We must ask whether God has given to civil government the authority to punish this violation of his law.

God has established two kingdoms on this earth, the church and the state. He has given certain authority to each, and he has also placed certain limitations upon each. But the precise relationship between God's law and these two kingdoms will be covered in the next chapter.

3   *The Two Kingdoms: Church and State*

Throughout most of human history, God has divided authority between two kingdoms, the church (or its Old Testament predecessors) and the state.

Today many of the most strident advocates of separation of church and state are strongly anti-Christian. They often fail to realize that separation of church and state, and the entire concept of limited government, is a uniquely Judeo-Christian idea. Even though many civil libertarians have left the traditional faith, their views on church-state relations have developed out of the very Judeo-Christian culture they now reject.

In most pagan cultures, church and state are or were one. The king was not only head of the state but also head of the church, with no distinction in these offices. The unity of the state was founded on a common religion, and the king was frequently considered to be either a demigod or a descendant of a god or a god himself. Emperor-worship and state-worship were the order of the day. Not all pagans took this view, nor did they all accept it absolutely. Some of the ancient Greeks and Chinese recognized that if the ruler abandoned the gods, the gods could turn against him.

This was particularly true of ancient Rome. As Waring notes,

> In the history of Rome there was a time when the word of Caesar was the law and the worship of Caesar was the religion of the world. As Pontifex Maximus he was the high priest of the national religion. He held control of both church and state in his own person. Indeed, in a large sense, he was the state, and he was the church.[1]

Other religions received a considerable measure of toleration. People could generally worship whatever additional gods they wished, so long as they worshiped the emperor and gave their supreme allegiance to the state. If Christians could have proclaimed Christ as just another god, they would have had little opposition from Rome. The anger of the authorities was aroused by the exclusiveness of their claim: "Thou shalt have no other gods before me" (Exodus 20:3).

In a world accustomed to Caesar-worship, the Christian view sounded very strange indeed: a kingdom that is not of this world, a God who had ordained Caesar but given him only limited authority, a suffering Servant who died on a cross but who will come again in glory as King of kings and Lord of lords to rule all nations with a rod of iron. But the view spread, and Hegel has noted that the spread of freedom is coterminous with the spread of Christianity. Let us examine its biblical and historical basis.

The Biblical Background

Old Testament Israel was a theocracy. That term is commonly used today to refer to a society in which the church rules the state, but that is not its true meaning. The word actually comes from two Greek words, *theos* meaning God and *kratos* meaning ruler. A theocracy, then, is a society ruled by God.

Old Testament Israel did not practice separation of church and state as we practice it today. When Elijah slew the priests of Baal (1 Kings 18:40), he didn't worry about their right to free exercise of religion! But the concepts of separation and limited government have their roots even in the Old Testament.

Before the time of King Saul, Israel was governed by judges. The office of judge was distinct from the offices of prophet and priest. The priests, it will be recalled, came only from the tribe of Levi, but the judges came from various tribes. On rare occasions the same individual held both offices (priest and judge) and possessed the gift of prophecy as well. But these were exceptions (Moses and Samuel being the only two), and the situation seems to have occurred only in times of dire need in Israel. And even then the offices were distinct. The situation might be analogous to a person serving as a minister of a church and the mayor of a city at the same time. The offices are distinct, even though the same individual holds both offices.

After the establishment of the monarchy, the distinction becomes even clearer. The kings always came from the tribe of Judah, while the priests continued to come from the tribe of Levi. A king could not be a priest, and a priest could not be a king. On at least two occasions Israel's king tried to usurp the functions of the priesthood—and was severely punished by God. Saul offered a peace offering himself, and as a result God cut Saul's line off from the kingship of Israel (1 Samuel 13). Later King Uzziah became proud and tried to burn incense on the altar. In punishment, God smote him with leprosy for the rest of his life (2 Chronicles 26:16-21). In these passages God seems to be telling the civil rulers: keep your hands off my kingdom!

Jesus shed further light on the "two kingdoms" concept when he answered the Pharisees' question about paying tribute to Caesar. Even their question, "Is it lawful for us to give tribute unto Caesar, or no?" (Luke 20:22) seems to imply that there is a higher standard—God's law—by which Caesar's demands are to be judged. And while Jesus confirmed that the requirement of tribute was within Caesar's jurisdiction, he declared that there are some things which are beyond Caesar's control: "Render therefore unto Caesar the things which be Caesar's, and unto God the things which be God's" (Luke 20:25). Lord Acton has recognized in this charge a clear declaration of the authority of the state but also of its limits:

> . . . when Christ said "Render unto Caesar the things that are Caesar's and unto God the things that are God's," He gave to the State a legitimacy it had never before enjoyed, and set bounds to it that had never yet been acknowledged. And He not only delivered the precept but He also forged the instrument to execute it. To limit the power of the State ceased to be the hope of patient, ineffectual philosophers and became the perpetual charge of a universal church.[2]

The "Two Kingdoms" Concept in Church History

The relationship of church and state has received much attention throughout history. Many different perspectives on the subject have arisen, but let us identify four basic positions.

The Catholic view. Catholic theologians have generally recognized the two kingdoms and the distinct role played by each. But they have usually considered the church to be the greater kingdom and the state to be the lesser, because the church is eternal while the state is only temporary (Augustine's explanation), and because the church must answer to God for the conduct of the state (the explanation of Pope Gelasius I). Some have argued that the power of the keys given to Peter in Matthew 16:19 gave the church the authority to control the state. Many medieval theologians saw the church's authority in the two swords of Luke 22:38. One of these swords is the sword of the church, to be wielded by the church, and the other is the sword of the state, to be given by the church to the state. As Pope Boniface VIII decreed in his papal bull, *Unam Sanctum*, in 1302:

> We are told by the word of the gospel that in this His fold there are two swords,—a spiritual, namely, and a temporal. For when the apostles said "Behold here are two swords"—when, namely, the apostles were speaking in the church—the Lord did not reply that this was too much, but enough. Surely he who denies that the temporal sword is in the power of Peter

wrongly interprets the word of the Lord when He says: "Put up thy sword in its scabbard." Both swords, the spiritual and the material, therefore, are in the power of the church; the one, indeed, to be wielded for the church, the other by the church; the one by the hand of the priest, the other by the hand of kings and knights, but at the will and sufferance of the priest. One sword, moreover, ought to be under the other, and the temporal authority to be subjected to the spiritual. For when the apostle says "there is no power but of God, and the powers that are of God are ordained," they would not be ordained unless sword were under sword and the lesser one, as it were, were led by the other to great deeds.[3]

Still others looked to a medieval document known as the Donation of Constantine, by which the Roman Emperor Constantine I supposedly gave much of the Western Roman Empire into the hands of Pope Sylvester I. For centuries popes and other officials relied upon this document, but today even Catholics generally regard it as a forgery.[4]

In this view, the relationship of church to state and to believers and unbelievers could be conceptualized with the following diagram:

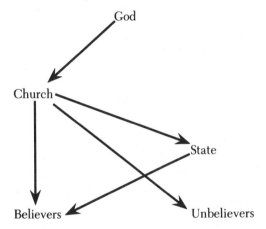

The Anabaptist view. We must be careful to distinguish the Anabaptists of the Reformation, led by men such as Menno Simons, from today's Baptists. The former are in many ways the spiritual ancestors of today's Baptists, but like many families they have undergone many changes over the generations. In their views of church-state relations, most Baptists in America today would find themselves closer to Luther and Calvin than to the early Anabaptists, though there are many strains of opinion among Baptists and Anabaptists then and now.

Many (but by no means all) of the early Anabaptists believed that the state was part of the evil world-system from which believers were to separate themselves. If Satan were not actually the founder of the state, he had at least taken control of it. Consequently believers were to separate themselves from the state as much as possible; they were not to vote; hold public office, serve in the armed forces, or involve themselves with government in any other way. They were to obey the state generally, but the state had no real authority over believers, nor did the church have any authority over unbelievers. There were many variations in Anabaptist thought, but in the extreme Anabaptist model the lines of authority could be conceptualized as follows:

The Calvinist view. Unlike many Anabaptists, Calvin recognized that the authority of the state comes from God. Unlike many Catholic theologians, Calvin believed that authority came directly from God to the state rather than through the church. The believer was a citizen of both kingdoms and under the authority of both the state and the church. However, the state's authority over the believer is limited to that which God has given to the state; if the state steps beyond that authority, it acts without legitimacy, and believers are to resist it.

Furthermore, the mission of the church is to renovate the world, including the state, according to Christian concepts. And the state is to assist the church in Christianizing the world. Consequently Calvin served as a political leader as well as a church leader in Geneva, and he saw no problem in using the machinery of the state to further his version of Christianity by punishing heretics, etc. Here is the Calvinist model:

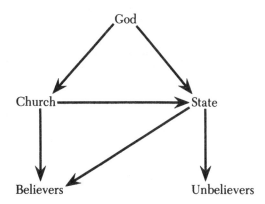

The Lutheran view. Of the three views just discussed, Luther's view was closest to that of Calvin. Luther had been an Augustinian monk. He had made Augustine the subject of special study for many years, and he was greatly influenced by Augustine's view that the purpose of the state was to restrain man's sin nature. Like Calvin, he recognized that the church and the state are each ordained by God. Like Calvin, he recognized that believers belong to both kingdoms, the church and the state, and have responsibilities to each. Unlike Calvin, he hesitated to impose Christian precepts upon an unbelieving world. Luther distinguished between faith and reason, and he believed that Christians relate to the first kingdom (the church) primarily by means of faith in divine revelation, and to the second kingdom (the state) primarily by means of reason. In theology he emphasized reason less strongly than did Calvin, but in politics he emphasized reason more strongly than did Calvin. Luther even went so far as to say that if he were faced with the choice between a ruler who was prudent and bad and another who was good but imprudent, he would choose the prudent and bad, because the good by his imprudence would throw everything into disorder, whereas the prudent, however bad, would have enough sense to restrain evil. This does not mean Luther wanted immoral rulers. He would have preferred a ruler who was both prudent and good.

Luther's primary difference with Calvin, then, would be that he did not believe Christians had the right to use the state to promote Christianity and to Christianize the world. Christians in government could invoke Christian principles in the affairs of state, only to the extent that those Christian principles could be defended and justified by natural reason. The Lutheran model would look like this:

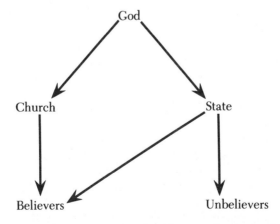

Modern evangelicalism. Where should evangelicals stand today? I believe the best position is somewhere between Luther's and Calvin's. Luther probably drew too sharp a distinction between faith and reason, for the two need not be incompatible. Faith may transcend reason, but faith need not contradict reason. One need not apologize for appealing to scriptural authority in the political arena.

At the same time, Christians today should not expect the state to advance the work of the church. God ordained the state for a different purpose. But Christians may expect the state to provide the church with the same protection it gives other persons and institutions—police and fire protection, protection of the constitutional right to free speech and free exercise of religion, etc. And Christians have every right to expect the state to not take positions which are hostile to Christianity. Recent attempts by schools and universities to deny Christians the same right to meet in school facilities which is routinely granted to non-Christian and anti-Christian groups are certainly contrary to the true "two kingdoms" concept. One of the greatest dangers in America today is the establishment of a religion of secular humanism in American government, particularly in the public schools. Unfortunately, our courts and legislatures have mistaken secularism for neutrality.

The Division of Authority

As we apply God's Word to modern society in light of the "two kingdoms" concept, (the key point to remember is that while God has ordained the state, he has given it only limited authority.) In Deuteronomy 17:14-20 Moses prophesied that the day would come when the people of Israel would demand a king. Moses therefore commanded that the monarchs of Israel were to observe limits: (1) they were not to take to themselves excessive wealth or wives (vv. 16, 17); (2) they were subject to the laws and precepts of God (vv. 18, 19); and (3) their hearts were not to be lifted up above their brethren (v. 20)—that is, they were not to become proud.

Those were unusual commandments to give a king. Could you imagine Moses saying that in any other culture? If Moses had told Nebuchadnezzar of Babylon that he was not to take excessive wealth or wives, Nebuchadnezzar would have laughed in his face (at least before his apparent conversion). "What do you mean, I can't take wealth or wives?" he would have asked. "I'm going to be the richest king in the world!"

Or picture Moses telling Sennacharib of Assyria that his heart should not be lifted up above his brethren. "I'm the king!" Sennacharib would have snorted. "Those peasants aren't my brethren!"

Or what if Moses had tried to tell Caesar he should be under the law of God? "Nonsense!" Caesar would have shouted. "I am God!"

Why limit governmental power? Remember the basic purpose of government, which is to restrain human sin. We must remember that if all have sinned and come short of the glory of God, then rulers are also sinners. Excessive power concentrated in the hands of sinful men is a formula for tyranny and disaster. As Lord Acton noted, "Power corrupts; absolute power corrupts absolutely." We therefore must avoid concentrating too much power in the hands of any one man or any group of men, lest they become proud and corrupt and abuse their power.

But in order to restrain sin effectively, government needs considerable power. And this has been one of the principal problems facing political theorists for thousands of years: how to make sure government has enough power to function effectively, yet enough limits on its power to avoid tyranny and corruption. Lord Acton commented that America's founding fathers, at the Constitutional Convention of 1787, solved that problem with amazing ease, by a system of separation of powers among legislative, executive, and judicial branches of government, with checks and balances, a division of powers between federal, state and local officials, and constitutional protections of individual rights so that even majorities must respect the rights of minorities. I have previously said that one of the strengths of Christianity is its ability to function and flourish under any political or social system. But it must also be said that a system of constitutional republicanism seems most consistent with the biblical view of the nature of man and the danger of power.

Principles for Dividing Authority Between the Two Kingdoms

As we determine whether to make a particular act illegal, whether it be murder, failing to offer sacrifice or blasphemy, we must ask three questions: (1) Is the act a violation of the law of God? (2) Does that portion of God's law apply today? (3) Has God given to civil government the authority to punish that violation of God's law? The questions become progressively more difficult; the last is one of the most difficult facing Christians today.

I do not claim to have a definitive answer to that question, but I offer several guidelines:

Actions v. thoughts. Does the offense against God's law involve actions or words, or does it involve thoughts only? The state has some jurisdiction over actions and words, but thoughts are beyond its authority. One's thoughts can violate the laws of God. Proverbs 6:16-19 tell us pride and wicked thoughts are abominations before God. Yet no one in the Bible was ever punished by the civil authorities for pride or for the thoughts of his heart. Jesus declared that anyone who looks upon a woman with lust has already committed adultery in his heart (Matthew 5:28), but no one in the Bible was ever stoned to death for lust, nor did Jesus say they should be. John said that whosoever hates his brother is a murderer (1 John 3:15); Exodus 21:12 commands that a murderer be put to death. But no one was ever put to death for hatred. Why? Because even in the Old Testament theocracy, the civil rulers had only limited authority. Thoughts were beyond their jurisdiction. That is even more true today.

Believers and unbelievers, or believers only? Does the offense against God's law affect believers and unbelievers alike, or does it affect believers only? Matters concerning doctrine, church practices, etc. only affect believers and therefore are reserved to the church or to God himself. Other matters such as property and contracts apply to believers and unbelievers alike, and therefore are within the jurisdiction of the state.

Vertical or horizontal? Man's responsibilities under the law of God may be roughly divided into two categories: his horizontal responsibilities to other men, and his vertical duties to God. The former are within the jurisdiction of government; the latter are not. For example, "Thou shalt have no other gods before me" is a vertical command involving man's duty to God; no state may enforce it or enjoin it. But "Thou shalt not steal" is a horizontal command involving man's duty to respect the property of his neighbor, and the state may enforce it.

Force or nonforce? So far we have been discussing limits upon the state; here is a limit on the church. Generally speaking, the church is not to use force in accomplishing its goals. When the rich young ruler came to our Lord, Jesus preached the Word to him. But when that man went away sorrowful, Jesus let him go. Jesus didn't force the young man to accept Christianity at sword point; he respected the young man's volition.

This does not mean the Christian should not fight in legitimate self-defense, nor does it mean a Christian should not serve his country in time of war. When the Christian serves his country in the military or as a policeman, he acts not as an agent of the church but an agent of the state—ordained by God to do so pursuant to Romans 13. That issue is covered in Chapter 9.

But generally speaking spiritual goals should not and usually cannot be achieved by force. It may be that the Crusaders had a legal and moral right to invade Palestine to protect the safe conduct of pilgrims to the Holy Land. But when they forced Moslems to accept Christianity or die, they went beyond the authority of God had given them.

The above principles are only guidelines. One can probably imagine many exceptions to each of them, and there are many gray areas as to what is primarily a duty to God and what is primarily a duty to other men. For example, the duty to refrain from blasphemy is primarily a duty to God, but in a public place where others may hear and be offended it may also involve a duty to other men. We will employ these guidelines as we examine the biblical view of Christian citizenship on various national issues.

4 Church and State in America: The First Amendment

Most of America's early settlers crossed the Atlantic because they wanted the freedom to worship God according to the dictates of their own consciences. However, most of them were not particularly interested in granting religious liberty to others. Most of them came, not to find religious liberty, but to establish a state church that was more to their liking than that which they left in England. Consequently Puritan Congregationalist establishments arose in Massachusetts, Connecticut, and New Hampshire, and Anglican establishments in Virginia, North Carolina, South Carolina, and Georgia. The Anglicans were the established church in Maryland, but because the founder of Maryland (George Calvert, known as Lord Baltimore) was Catholic, there was a strong policy of toleration for Catholics. Rhode Island and Pennsylvania, because of the convictions of their founders (Roger Williams and William Penn), were much more tolerant than most other colonies; yet even in these colonies Catholics were at times disenfranchised. New York allowed each township to determine its own religion, and New Jersey and Delaware seem to have practiced full religious toleration.

After the War for Independence, there were thirteen states, each with its own religious groups and many with their own established state churches. Each was afraid of the other. The Anglicans in the southern states were concerned that the Puritans in New England would seek to make Congregationalism the national religion of the United States. New Englanders were afraid of the Anglicans. The Baptists and Quakers didn't want any established national church, and the Congregationalists and Anglicans didn't want the federal government interfering with the established churches in their respective states.

The result, after much deliberation, was the First Amendment:

"Congress shall make no law respecting an establishment of religion or prohibiting the free exercise thereof. . . ." It is significant that the founding fathers regarded religion as being so important that when they passed the Bill of Rights, religious liberty was the very first right they safeguarded—even ahead of freedom of speech and freedom of the press.

Note that the First Amendment restricts only the *federal* government. "Congress shall make no law," it says; it doesn't prohibit the states from doing so. The founders intended to prohibit two things: (1) any attempt by the federal government to establish a national religion; and (2) any attempt by the federal government to interfere with the various state churches.

But the Fourteenth Amendment changed all of that. Adopted in 1868, the Fourteenth Amendment provides in part that no state may "deprive any person of life, liberty, or property, without due process of law. . . ." In the 1940 case of *Cantwell* v. *Connecticut*,[1] the U.S. Supreme Court held that the word "liberty" in the Fourteenth Amendment embraces all of the guarantees of the First Amendment. Hence, any establishment of religion prohibited on the federal level is now equally prohibited on the state level. Neither states nor local communities could any longer maintain establishments of religion.

So what does the First Amendment mean today? Let's examine both what it means and how it has been distorted.

What the First Amendment means. The First Amendment divides into two clauses dealing with religion: the establishment clause ("Congress shall make no law respecting an establishment of religion . . .") and the free exercise clause (". . . or prohibiting the free exercise thereof. . . .").

In the 1971 case of *Lemon* v. *Kurtzman*,[2] the Supreme Court set forth a three-prong test that is still used by the courts today to determine whether government activity constitutes an establishment of religion: (1) Does the activity have a secular purpose? (2) Does the primary effect of the government activity either advance or inhibit religion? (3) Does the activity constitute excessive government entanglement with religion? If a particular government activity, such as school prayer, fails any one of these tests, it must be struck down as an unconstitutional establishment of religion. An establishment of religion, then, might be defined as an activity by which the government sponsors a religion or religious belief or activity, or shows a preference for one religion over others.

The free exercise clause protects the right of the individual believer to believe, preach, and practice his religion as he sees fit. Since the right to freely exercise one's religious beliefs is a fundamental right, the government may interfere with that right only if it has a very strong, compelling reason for doing so, and even then only if the government cannot fulfill its purposes by any less restrictive means.

The difference between the two clauses might be summarized this way: If government were to require everyone to attend a Baptist church, that would violate the establishment clause. If government were to prohibit people from attending a Baptist church, that would violate the free exercise clause.

At times tension arises between the establishment clause and the free exercise clause. One such area of tension concerns the use of government facilities for religious purposes. Suppose a Christian group wishes to meet on a college campus. Some might argue that to allow them to use government facilities at taxpayers' expense constitutes an establishment of religion. But others might argue that to refuse them the right to do so, especially when secular groups are allowed to meet, violates their right to freely exercise their religion. If the groups cannot work out an agreeable solution, the courts have to resolve the tension.[3]

What the First Amendment does not mean. The First Amendment is a healthy concept of religious liberty and is very much in accord with the biblical concept of the two kingdoms. Unfortunately it has been grossly distorted in recent years, both by enemies of religious liberty and by enemies of Christianity. We have seen what it means; now let's look at what it does not mean.

To begin with, the First Amendment does not mean total separation of church and state. The words "separation," "church," and "state" aren't even mentioned! The phrase "wall of separation," so often used by the courts, comes not from the First Amendment but from the pen of Thomas Jefferson. Jefferson was in France when the Constitution was drafted, and while he had some influence upon those who wrote the First Amendment, he was not a member of the Congress that passed the First Amendment, nor of any state legislature that ratified it. His "wall of separation" statement comes from his address to the Danbury Baptists in 1802, thirteen years after the passage of the First Amendment and eleven years after its ratification. In no way should this phrase of Jefferson be considered the definitive interpretation of the First Amendment.[4]

Far from intending such total separation of religion from government, Congress called upon the President to declare a day of public thanksgiving and prayer the very day after Congress passed the First Amendment.[5]

When James Madison offered the First Amendment in its original form to Congress in 1789, he was asked what it meant.

Mr. Madison said, he apprehended the meaning of the words to be, that Congress should not establish *a* religion and enforce the legal observation of it by law, nor compel men to worship God in any manner contrary to their conscience.[6]

Considering the frequent references to God and Christianity in the Continental Congress, and Madison's statement quoted above, it is clear that while the founders wanted to protect individual freedom of conscience, they had no intention of separating religion from government.

Second, the authors of the First Amendment did not intend to separate religion or religious thinking from public life or public thought. Many of the most strident advocates of separation of church and state seem to believe Christians have no right to participate in government at all, or if they must participate they have to leave their religious beliefs behind them. Whenever the biblical view or the Christian view is mentioned in public debates on national policy, someone screams that the "wall of separation" has been breached. Biblical Christianity, it seems, must be confined to the walls of the church, and possibly the home. Under no circumstances may it enter public life. Advocates of this radical separationist view are free to believe as they wish, but they are wrong to invoke the First Amendment in support of that view, for that is not what the authors of the First Amendment meant.

Our first President, George Washington, greatly feared the rise of a godless, secular state. In his farewell address on September 17, 1796, President Washington warned America,

Of all the dispositions and habits, which lead to political prosperity, religion and morality are indispensable supports. In vain would that man claim the tribute of patriotism, who should labor to subvert these great pillars of human happiness, these firmest props of the duties of men and citizens. The mere politician, equally with the pious man, ought to respect and cherish them. A volume could not trace all their connexions with private and public felicity. Let it simply be asked, Where is the security for property, for reputation, for life, if the sense of religious obligation desert the oaths, which are the instruments of investigation in courts of justice? And let us with caution indulge the supposition, that morality can be maintained without religion. Whatever may be conceded to the influence of refined education on minds of peculiar structure, reason and experience both forbid us to expect, that national morality can prevail in exclusion of religious principle.

It is substantially true, that virtue or morality is a necessary spring of popular government. The Rule, indeed, extends with more or less force to every species of free government. Who, that is a sincere friend to it, can look with indifference upon attempts to shake the foundation of the fabric?[7]

God's Word has a lot to say about politics, and Christians who believe God's Word are duty-bound to proclaim God's truth in the political arena. Nothing in the Constitution or in the American tradition prevents them from doing so. Christians must speak and act with due regard for the rights of others, but they must not let the enemies of Christianity misuse the First Amendment to intimidate Christians into silence.

Third, the First Amendment does not mean that laws and policies may not reflect the Christian tradition. If it did, America would rapidly become a lawless society, because our nation has very few laws that do not have their ultimate roots in religion. Rushdoony put it well:

> Behind every system of law there is a god. To find the god in any system, locate the source of law in that system. If the source of law is the individual, then the individual is the god of that system. If the source of the law is the people, or the dictatorship of the proletariat, then these things are the gods of those systems. If our source of law is a court, then the court is our god. If there is no higher law beyond man, then man is his own god, or else his creatures, the institutions he has made, have become his gods. When you choose your authority, you choose your god, and where you look for your law, there is your god.[8]

Many secularists would dismantle every law that has any connection with Christianity, but fortunately the Supreme Court has not been willing to go that far. In 1980 the Supreme Court decided *Harris* v. *McRae*,[9] a case involving a challenge to the Hyde Amendment, that restricted federal funding for abortions. Plaintiffs had argued that the Hyde Amendment was unconstitutional because the restriction on abortion funding coincides with the teachings of the Roman Catholic Church. But the Court rejected that argument. As Justice Stewart said in the majority opinion, ". . . we are convinced that the fact that the funding restrictions in the Hyde Amendment may coincide with the religious tenets of the Roman Catholic Church does not . . . contravene the Establishment Clause." That was a most fortunate decision; a ruling to the contrary would have required the dismantling of Western civilization. Even our laws against murder and stealing have their roots in the Ten Commandments and in the Judeo-Christian view of life and property.

Fourth, the First Amendment does not require a secular humanist state. The U.S. Supreme Court declared in *Abington Township* v. *Schempp*[10] that ". . . the State may not establish a 'religion of secularism' in the sense of affirmatively opposing or showing hostility to religion, thus 'preferring those who believe in no religion over those who do believe.' " Yet through the teaching in the public schools and in many other ways, the United States seems to be moving toward a secular humanist state. As I will demonstrate in Chapter 15, this is not required by the First Amendment and is itself an unconstitutional establishment of the religion of secular humanism.

Fifth, the First Amendment does not require that Christianity be excluded from the public schools or from public life. Justice Clark said in *Abington Township* v. *Schempp*,[11] the famous decision that appeared to prohibit Bible reading in the public schools, "Nothing we have said here indicates that such study of the Bible or religion, when presented objectively as part of a secular program of education, may not be effected consistently with the First Amendment." While the schools may not dogmatically indoctrinate students with Christianity, they need not exclude the Christian viewpoint in science classes, religion classes, health classes, values clarification classes, or any other subject in which the Christian view is relevant. There is no reason the Christian view cannot be presented as one of several alternative positions.

Properly construed, the First Amendment is an excellent expression of the "two kingdoms" concept and an excellent means of preserving the religious liberty God has given us. Unfortunately, many would distort the First Amendment to require the suppression of Christianity and the establishment of secular humanism. That is not the purpose of the First Amendment, and that interpretation must be resisted at all costs.

Part II *The Biblical View of Our Duty to Government*

5 Prayer

Not everyone can serve in Congress or lead troops into battle for his country. Not everyone can organize political campaigns or lobby for important issues. But there is one thing every Christian can do for his country—pray.

> I exhort, therefore, that, first of all, supplications, prayers, intercessions, and giving of thanks, be made for all men; for kings, and for all that are in authority; that we may lead a quiet and peaceable life in all godliness and honesty. (1 Timothy 2:1, 2)

Paul uses four different words for prayer, each with a slightly different meaning. The first, "supplications," is the type of prayer that springs from a feeling of want and may include asking God to help a ruler avert a specific evil. The second term, "prayers," is a more general word for petitions to God and may refer to requests for positive good that God could perform through rulers. The third, "intercessions," refers to prayers uttered in close intimacy with God and often includes requests to God on behalf of others, such as the ruler himself. The last, "giving of thanks," is the gratitude we express to God for having given us the protection of civil rulers.

Paul asks for such prayers on behalf of all men, but especially for leaders in government: "for kings, and for all that are in authority." This is not limited to kings or presidents; it includes congressmen, state respresentatives, judges, city councilmen, school board members, and policemen. They all are in positions of authority, they all are ministers of God, they all face difficult decisions, and they all need our prayers.

Why pray for government officials? Because they are ministers of God (Romans 13:1-4), and God works through them to restrain sin in the world. Proverbs 21:1 tells us that "The king's heart is in the hand of the Lord, as the rivers of water: he turneth it whithersoever he will." I am convinced that in answer to prayers of believers, God speaks to the hearts of government officials, gives success to their efforts, and leads them to correct decisions.

The Hon. Wyatt Lipscomb, a leading Christian judge in Texas, has proposed the "Key-16" concept. "Key-16" means that there are sixteen key government officials who are in authority over each believer in the United States. These are the President, the nine U.S. Supreme Court Justices, your state's two U.S. Senators, your local congressman, your state's governor, your local state senator, and your local state representative.[1] Think of the changes that could take place in this country if every believer would pray daily for these sixteen key leaders! But it doesn't stop there. There are a host of other leaders at all levels of government who need our prayers.

One final thought: we should not pray only for those whom we like. It is easy to pray for the leader whom we respect or with whom we agree. It is much harder to pray for the leader whose personality is offensive, whose ethics are questionable, who takes the "wrong" position on every issue, or who is in the "wrong" party. Yet these leaders are also ministers of God. They don't necessarily deserve our votes, but they do deserve our respect and prayers. And they need our prayers—perhaps more than those we like.

6 Obedience and Disobedience

When God established civil government, he empowered the state to punish people for violating its laws.

But the government can't put everyone in jail. Society cannot function effectively amid widespread lawlessness; it degenerates into chaotic anarchy, a totalitarian police state, or both. Government needs the willing obedience of most of its citizens.

That is one reason God commanded believers to obey government. In Romans 13:1, 2 Paul directed,

> Let every soul be subject unto the higher powers. For there is no power but of God: the powers that be are ordained of God. Whosoever therefore resisteth the power, resisteth the ordinance of God: and they that resist shall receive to themselves damnation.

Paul, it is generally believed, wrote Romans around A.D. 56, and he directed the book to the Christian community at Rome. At this time, the emperor of Rome was Nero. While Nero's most severe persecutions had not yet begun, Nero was already hostile to Christianity and soon to be one of the most vicious persecutors of Christianity of all time. He even held garden parties at which Christians wrapped in oil-soaked rags were set afire to serve as torches! Yet Paul calls Nero a "minister (*diakonos*, servant) of God" and declares that Nero has been "ordained of God." If Christians were obligated to respect Nero as the minister of God and to obey his commands, think how much greater duty we owe to our government today.

Peter gave similar direction to believers. He wrote 1 Peter around A.D. 64, again while Nero was on the throne. Since Paul was already in prison by this time and James had already been killed, Peter must have sensed the coming persecution. Nevertheless, he exhorted his readers:

> Submit yourselves to every ordinance of man for the Lord's sake: whether it be to the king, as supreme; or unto governors, as unto them that are sent by him for the punishment of evildoers, and for the praise of them that do well. For so is the will of God, that with well-doing ye may put to silence the ignorance of foolish men: as free, and not using your liberty as a cloak of maliciousness, but as the servants of God. Honor all men. Love the brotherhood. Fear God. Honor the king. (1 Peter 2:13-17)

Those who say that civil government has no authority over believers should remember that Paul and Peter were writing to Christians. They strongly command believers to obey the laws of the government, for several reasons: (1) to avoid punishment (Romans 13:3, 4); (2) to avoid divine discipline (Romans 13:2); (3) because it is the right thing to do (Romans 13:5—"not only for wrath, but also for conscience' sake"); (4) to provide a Christian testimony—"that with well doing ye may put to silence the ignorance of foolish men" (1 Peter 2:15).

On the other hand, sometimes our duty to God requires us to disobey government. The very writers who exhort us to obey government—i.e., Peter and Paul—both collided with government from time to time. Paul was jailed several times for preaching the gospel, and eventually he was executed by Rome. Peter was also imprisoned and executed for the faith; and earlier, when the authorities did not allow him to preach the gospel, he and the other apostles declared, "We ought to obey God rather than men" (Acts 5:29).

In the Old Testament we see two clear examples of this very thing. When the Egyptian pharaoh commanded the Hebrew midwives to kill newborn baby boys, they refused to do so: "But the midwives feared God, and did not as the king of Egypt commanded them, but saved the male children alive. . . . Therefore God dealt well with the midwives: and the people multiplied, and waxed very mighty" (Exodus 1:17, 20). The midwives' disobedience was motivated by their fear of God, and God rewarded them for their disobedience to the king.

The Book of Daniel gives additional insight. Daniel is an excellent model for Christians living in a non-Christian society. Taken from his homeland to Babylon as a youth, educated in the philosophy, science, religion, and culture of pagan Babylon, Daniel remained true to God in every respect, yet was also able to serve his king. He served as ruler of a province of Babylon and "chief of the governors over all the wise men of Babylon" (like chief of staff of Nebuchadnezzar's cabinet), and also "sat in the gate of the king"—like being Chief Justice of the Supreme Court (Daniel 2:48, 49). Yet he probably also succeeded in winning King Nebuchadnezzar to the Lord. As a man who could function effectively in the government of a pagan country and still remain completely faithful to God, Daniel deserves the careful study of civic-minded Christians today.

In Chapter 1 Daniel had his first conflict with the Babylonian authorities. Ashpenaz, the master of the eunuchs, was responsible for the care of Daniel and his fellow-captives, and he insisted that Daniel and his friends eat the king's food and drink the king's wine. Daniel refused, putting God first.

Daniel didn't get all geared up for a hunger strike, a confrontation, or martyrdom. He didn't scream at Ashpenaz, "I'm not eating this heathen junk!" Rather, he spoke respectfully to Ashpenaz, asking that the menu might be altered for him and his companions.

Ashpenaz liked Daniel personally, and that made it easier for Daniel to reason with him. But Ashpenaz was concerned that if Daniel and his friends did not eat the king's diet, they wouldn't be healthy, and he (Ashpenaz) would be in trouble with the king.

Instead of drawing the lines of battle, Daniel offered a solution that would satisfy the concerns of Ashpenaz and at the same time relieve Daniel's problem with the food. And at the end of a ten-day test, Daniel and his friends were healthier than the youths on the king's diet; consequently Ashpenaz allowed Daniel and friends to continue with their own vegetable diet.

Too many Christians seem to be itching for a confrontation with the state. Daniel spoke respectfully to those in authority over him and tried to work out conflict whenever possible.

The crisis in Daniel 3 involved Daniel's friends, not Daniel himself. King Nebuchadnezzar had made an enormous gold image and commanded everyone to fall down and worship it. This time there was no room for compromise; either you worship the image, or into the fire you go. Shadrach, Meshach, and Abednego didn't try to slink away into the background or call in sick that day. They respectfully but firmly declared that they would not worship the golden image and were willing to take the consequences of their civil disobedience. They expressed confidence that God was able to deliver them, and they expressed a belief that God would deliver them; but they went on to declare that even if God chose not to deliver them from the furnace, they would remain faithful to him.

After the Medo-Persians took over Babylon, Daniel became a provincial ruler under Darius, and Darius decided to make him prime minister. But the other provincial rulers were at odds with Daniel, perhaps because of jealousy, perhaps because he was Jewish. They tricked the king into signing a decree that no one could ask anything of any man or god for the next thirty days, except of the king himself. In effect, they prohibited prayer. This clearly conflicted with Daniel's religious life, a part of which was daily prayer.

Again there was no possibility of compromise. Under Persian law, once a decree had been issued, even the king himself could not change it. Daniel recognized that he had to obey God or obey man, and he chose to obey God. He wasn't secretive about it either. Just as before the decree, he knelt and prayed in front of his open windows, undoubtedly knowing that the other rulers would be watching his every action, so they could report him to the king. They did just that, and the king had to enforce the decree, reluctantly casting Daniel into the den of lions. Of course the Lord delivered Daniel from the lions, and as King Darius released Daniel from the lions' den, Daniel continued to address the king with respect: "O king, live for ever" (6:21). And he continued to serve the king after that.

What principles about civil obedience and disobedience can we learn from Daniel? Several, and they are very important:

(1) Normally we should obey, respect, and do our best to please those in authority over us in civil government.

(2) We should resist and disobey government only when that government commands us to do something the Word of God forbids, or forbids us to do something the Word of God commands—either directly or by clear implication.

(3) Even when government and the Word of God conflict, we should not disobey government unless and until we have done everything possible to try to work out the conflict and effect a suitable accommodation of our religious beliefs. In a system of representative government like ours, we have a great responsibility to use the courts and the political process to try to get the law changed.

(4) When it is necessary to disobey government, we should be willing to suffer the necessary civil or criminal punishment for our act. If the principle is not worth being punished for, it is not enough of a principle to justify civil disobedience.

(5) Even while disobeying government, and even while being punished for our disobedience, we should at all times be respectful to the civil authorities. Even though they have misconstrued God's will, they are still God's ministers—whether they know it or not!

What About Revolution?

Our perspective on revolution varies with the situation. Rebels who meet with our approval are called "patriots" and "freedom fighters"; those of whom we disapprove are "subversives" and "insurrectionists."

The terms "rebel," "rebelled," "rebellest," "rebellion," "rebellious," and "rebels" are found approximately one hundred times in the Bible, and almost without exception they are used disapprovingly. Usually they connote rebellion against God; sometimes they connote rebellion against his civil servants.

If civil disobedience is wrong, rebellion is even more wrong. For civil disobedience is an attack against one law or one policy (though it can undermine confidence in the entire legal system), while rebellion is an attack against the entire governmental system. And rebellion usually doesn't work. Usually it fails, and simply brings disorder and bloodshed. If it succeeds in overthrowing the government, it usually replaces that government with another government that turns out to be just as bad or worse—witness the French Revolution and the Russian Revolution. Rebels usually come to power promising freedom, justice, prosperity, and equality; but shortly after they take power they usually become just as totalitarian, just as unfair, and just as inept as their predecessors. Every Communist government in the world today is proof of that.

Nevertheless, there may be circumstances in which revolution is the only alternative. If a government becomes so totally corrupt, so totally repressive, and so totally unjust as to destroy rather than promote the legitimate ends of government, revolution may then be justifiable either as a necessary good or as the lesser evil.

But before deciding upon that course of action, would-be revolutionaries should carefully consider what they are doing. Is the government really so totally destructive of the legitimate ends of government that revolution and all its attendant evils are justified? And am I really sure that if the revolution succeeds, I have a plan for a new government that will ensure a better government than we have now?

I can recall, during the late 1960s, listening to a revolutionary speaker at the University of Iowa answering questions from his audience. One student asked what type of government he and his comrades planned after the revolution succeeded. His answer was, in effect, "Let's not worry about that for now. Right now let's concentrate on the revolution, and we'll worry about that afterwards." The reason for his evasion was that he faced an audience of revolutionaries with widely different ideas. They knew what they were revolting *against*, but they disagreed on what they were revolting *for*. Some were Communists, some were Socialists, some were anarchists, some were trade-unionists, and many had other ideas. If he had revealed his plans, he would have lost much of his support. Cunning, but totally irresponsible! If his revolution had succeeded, there would have been nothing but civil war between the competing factions.

But, it is often argued, what about the American Revolution? How can you be so negative toward revolution when America's founding fathers were revolutionaries?

I believe that is a misnomer. The American "Revolution" was not a revolution at all; it was a war for independence. That's not just word-playing; there's a vital difference. The American colonies were a continent to themselves, they were an ocean away from England, they had their own colonial governments, and with the exception of Georgia and possibly New York they had received no financial assistance from England.[1]

Furthermore, they had every legal right to break away from England. For in asserting its authority over the colonies, England sought to deny to the colonists many basic rights which were not only God-given but which had been expressly recognized by the English Crown when King John signed the Magna Carta in 1215 A.D. and by Parliament when it passed the Petition of Right in 1628 and the English Bill of Rights in 1689. The English government went far beyond its authority when it tried to force its will upon the colonists.

Legal authority in England is vested in two institutions, Parliament and the Crown. The colonies received their charters from the Crown, not from Parliament, because Parliament had no authority in the New World. Around 1649 Parliament tried to assert its authority over the colonies, after King Charles I had been executed,[2] but Parliament had no authority to do so and the colonies never acquiesced to Parliament's claim. For when the Crown granted the initial charters to the colonies, the Crown gave the colonies full legislative authority. The Charter of Maryland of 1632, for example, gave the colony of Maryland

> free, full and absolute Power . . . to ordaine, Make, and Enact LAWS of what kind soever, according to their sound discretion.

The charters of other colonies contained similar provisions.

Furthermore, Parliament was to have representatives from all areas over which it exercised jurisdiction. The colonies had no representatives in Parliament. This is the legal significance of the colonists' slogan, "Taxation without representation is tyranny!"

And what of the king's authority? The king, as we have said, had gone far beyond whatever limited authority he had over the colonies, for he tried to violate basic rights which the Crown had recognized as belonging to Englishmen in the Magna Carta. The colonists were careful to document those violations in the Declaration of Independence. The legitimate authority of the Crown over the colonies was further placed in doubt in 1688, when the Stuart kings who had granted the initial charters to the colonies were forced from the throne in the Glorious Revolution. If any British authority over the colonies remained after that, it evaporated on December 22, 1775, when Parliament (which after 1689 had gained supremacy over the king) passed the Prohibitory Act which removed the colonies from the king's protection and declared that they were to be treated as foreign enemies. The basic principle of authority in British feudalism was that a king or lord provided protection for his subjects, in return for his subjects' allegiance. When the protection was removed, the duty of allegiance was removed also. Many in Britian, including Edmund Burke, recognized the validity of the colonists' case.

Our founding fathers, then, were not rebels or anarchists. They strongly believed in the divine institution of government, but they also believed that government must be founded upon the law of God rather than the caprice of man. Their colonial governments were the true authority in their territories, and the colonies had a moral and legal right to be independent. At Independence Hall on July 4, 1776, they did not rebel against England; they simply declared that which was already an established fact—their independence. The War for Independence took place because the English government refused to recognize the colonies' rightful claim to independence. It was really a war of foreign (British) aggression.

The Key—Limited Authority

(The basis for any claim that Christians have the right to civil disobedience rests on the fact that government has only limited authority, and that men have certain God-given rights which government cannot violate.)

The humanist would remove this concept. He would deny that government derives its authority from God. But in doing this, he also denies the source of government's limitations and the source of human rights. If government does not depend upon God and his law for its authority, it is not bound to respect the limits God has placed on its authority, and it becomes a monster unleashed to do whatever it pleases. Under this concept there can be no such thing as an unjust law, for there is no higher standard by which man's law can be judged. If government is the highest authority, then all laws are just because government has said they are just; government becomes the arbiter of right and wrong as well as of legality.

That is why humanists, when they try to destroy the biblical foundations of government (in the name of liberty yet!), end up creating a tyranny far worse than even they had ever imagined. The very word *tyranny*, in its early Greek root *tyrannos*, means "one who rules without the sanction of religious law."[3]

William Penn summarized it well when he said, "Men must choose to be governed by God or condemn themselves to be governed by tyrants."[4]

7   Taxation

Nobody likes to pay taxes. The less you earn, the harder it is to make ends meet after taxes. The more you earn, the greater bite the tax-collector takes out of your paycheck.

But taxes are an economic and social necessity. God has authorized government to collect taxes, and he has commanded Christians to pay them.

When the Pharisees tried to trap Jesus with their questions, they asked him, "Is it lawful to give tribute unto Caesar, or not?" Jesus asked to see a coin, showed them Caesar's image on the coin, and answered, "Render therefore unto Caesar the things which are Caesar's, and unto God the things that are God's" (Matthew 22:17-21).

Again we see the "two kingdoms" concept in action. God has given certain authority to the state and has withheld other authority from the state. Money is minted by Caesar and bears Caesar's image; therefore taxation is within Caesar's God-given jurisdiction. The state has a right to collect taxes, and believers are directed to comply.

Some have used Matthew 17:24-27 to justify not paying taxes:

And when they were come to Capernaum, they that received tribute money came to Peter, and said, Doth not your master pay tribute? He saith, Yes. And when he was come into the house, Jesus prevented him, saying, What thinkest thou, Simon? of whom do the kings of the earth take custom or tribute? of their own children, or of strangers? Peter saith unto him, Of strangers. Jesus saith unto him, Then are the children free. Notwithstanding, lest we should offend them, go thou to the sea, and cast a hook, and take up the fish that first cometh up; and when thou hast opened his mouth, thou shalt find a piece of money: that take, and give unto them for me and thee.

This, however, was not a tax paid to civil government; it was the atonement money of Exodus 30:11-16 (also described in 2 Chronicles 24:4-14 and Nehemiah 10:32) and which apparently was sporadic and voluntary. In Jesus' time, it was used for maintenance of the temple at Jerusalem and consisted of half a shekel. Since this was an offering to God, and since God the Father would not require an offering from God the Son, Jesus was exempt from the atonement money. Since Jesus was the founder and head of a new temple, He was not obliged to maintain the old temple.[1] Nevertheless, Jesus paid the tribute (for himself and Peter) to avoid giving offense to others.

Lest there be any doubt that Christians are required to pay taxes, Paul reiterates in Romans 13:6, "For, for this cause pay ye tribute also: for they are God's ministers, attending continually upon this very thing."

Why do we pay taxes? Because government needs money to operate. The policeman needs to be paid, the judge needs to be paid, the clerks and secretaries need to be paid. It costs money to build and repair roads, erect courthouses, buy and maintain typewriters, and conduct the essential business of government. As citizens of both kingdoms, we must do our part to support both.

Many will protest that the taxing system is unfair, or that tax money is wasted for immoral or unnecessary purposes. I won't argue that. I personally believe much of our present tax structure penalizes property owners and stifles incentive. In particular, the graduated income tax penalizes the person who works extra hard or takes extra risks or does an extra-good job, by placing him in a higher tax bracket. The Old Testament system of an across-the-board 10 percent—a common ancient practice and one that predates the Mosaic law (Genesis 14:17-20; 28:22) and is therefore of legitimate application today—is much more fair, makes far more sense, and would probably result in increased revenue. And I too dislike seeing my tax dollars wasted by government or spent on projects in which government has no legitimate business being involved.

But the same was true in Jesus' and Paul's time. The Roman government of Paul's day deified Nero, ran a welfare state, and sponsored many pagan practices, Rome certainly did not use its tax money as Christians would desire. The tax-collectors of Jesus' time, who usually were paid no salary but rather became rich by overcharging and cheating people, certainly did not employ fair methods of taxation. Yet Jesus and Paul both spoke very clearly on the subject: the Christian ought to pay his taxes.

This does not mean, however, that the Christian needs to pay more than his fair share of taxes. Nor does it mean that Christians should not take advantage of honest and legitimate tax shelters such as charitable deductions, trusts, etc. Our government has specifically written these "loopholes" into the tax laws so that Christians and other persons may use them to support religious and charitable causes the government wants to encourage. The government not only allows you to use these tax shelters; it expects and encourages you to use them.

There is a difference between tax evasion and tax avoidance. Tax evasion is dishonestly not paying taxes you legally owe, perhaps by failing to report income that should be reported. Tax avoidance, on the other hand, is arranging your income and assets so that you do not legally owe as much in taxes. Robert F. Sharpe has compared tax evasion and avoidance to a man wanting to cross a river but not wanting to pay to use the tollbridge. He could try to sneak past the tollgate, but that would be evasion and would be wrong. Or he could go out of his way and use the free bridge a few miles upstream, or swim or row across. That's avoidance, and there's nothing wrong with that.[2]

In short, you may save taxes in every legal way you can, but you must pay that which you legally owe. It is your civic and Christian duty.

8 Patriotism

We have examined the Christian's duty to obey his government and to pay taxes to support his government. We need to remember that the Christian should perform these duties, not out of a sullen or grudging obedience, but out of true love and devotion—in other words, in a spirit of patriotism.

Some Christians are troubled by patriotism. They wonder, Can I love God and love my country too? Doesn't patriotism border on idolatry? How can I love my country when it has so many faults?

Many non-Christians have felt this way for years. The signers of *Humanist Manifesto II* "deplore the division of humankind on nationalistic grounds" and "reaffirm a commitment to the building of world community. . . ."[1] In the media and in the intellectual community, patriotism is commonly put down as old-fashioned and unsophisticated.

God, however, is not known to be an avid follower of all the latest trends. I believe God wants us to be patriotic, and I believe he has commanded patriotism in his word.

God possesses infinite glory, but he has sovereignly bestowed glory upon civil rulers and, by implication, upon the governments and nations they represent. In Daniel 2:37 the prophet told Nebuchadnezzar, "Thou, O king, art a king of kings: for the God of heaven hath given thee a kingdom, power, and strength, and glory." Incredible! A Jewish believer, speaking by divine inspiration, tells a pagan ruler of a pagan empire that God had given him glory!

In the New Testament we are likewise commanded to give honor to civil rulers, and by implication to the country they represent. Among the various forms of prayer we are to render on behalf of civil rulers, according to Paul in 1 Timothy 2:1, 2, is "giving of thanks." This implies appreciation and gratitude for our nation and the protection it affords us.

Paul concludes a passage on obedience to civil rulers (Romans 13:1-7) with the words, "Render therefore to all their dues: tribute to whom tribute is due; custom to whom custom; fear to whom fear; honor to whom honor." Peter concludes his dissertation on obedience by saying, "Honor all men. Love the brotherhood. Fear God. Honor the king" (1 Peter 2:17). In both passages the word for "honor" is *time*, which is variously translated respect, value, honor, worship, or esteem. The Greek Septuagint uses the same word, *time*, to translate the commandment, "Honor thy father and thy mother" in Exodus 20:12, as well as to translate the word "glory" mentioned above in Daniel 2:37. Our duty to government, then, is more than grudging submission; it includes love and devotion for our nation.

We can find many examples of patriotism in the Bible. Esther, even while she was a Persian queen, remembered her Jewish heritage and loved her people so much that she risked her life to save them. Nehemiah apparently had a very good position with the Persian government, yet was so depressed by the chaos and disrepair in his Jewish homeland that he sought and received permission from the Persian king to return to Palestine and rebuild the walls of Jerusalem. The aging Jacob, living with his sons in Egypt, commanded that his body be taken back to the land of Canaan to be buried with his ancestors (Genesis 49:29—50:14). Joseph commanded likewise, and the Israelites kept his body in a coffin throughout four hundred years of slavery in Egypt until his wish could be carried out (Genesis 50:22-26; Exodus 13:19; Joshua 24:32).

The Old Testament prophets were patriots who loved their country dearly. Read the book of Jeremiah, the Lamentations of Jeremiah, or the book of Hosea, and see how the pages almost come aflame with love of country. The Lord Jesus loved Jerusalem so much that he wept over the city (Luke 19:41). In one sense these examples are unique because of God's special relationship with Israel and Israel's special relationship with its land. But as we have seen from Daniel 2:37, Romans 13:7, 1 Peter 2:17, and 1 Timothy 2:2, the responsibility to love and appreciate our country applies not just to the Jews but to believers and unbelievers of all nations.

Why does God want us to be patriotic? I believe God has placed patriotism in men's hearts because God knows a nation cannot survive without it. Patriotism is the bond that unites a nation into one people and holds them together. Patriotism is the spark that makes people willing to place their country above themselves, to sacrifice for their country, even if that sacrifice means their lives. Patriotism is the spirit that gives a special flavor to a nation and which enhances our appreciation for that which is our own. The spirit of patriotism has enabled Americans to unite and struggle through every crisis in our nation's history—until the opinion-makers taught the post-World War II generation that patriotism is neither necessary nor chic.

Almost everywhere else across the world, feelings of patriotism and nationalism are on the rise. How strange it is that only in America and western Europe is patriotism considered passe! I believe, however, that the last few years have marked the beginning of a rebirth of patriotism. Part of this is due to an implicit realization that without patriotism America cannot survive.

While patriotism is necessary for national survival, and while God has commanded us to love our country, patriotism can certainly be abused. Instead of loving our country because God has directed us to do so, it is possible for love of country to take the place of love for God. The flag should symbolize God's love for America; but it is possible to get so wrapped up in the flag that we can no longer see God. When that happens, we have rejected the Christian view of patriotism and have embraced the pagan view of the state—that the state *is* god!

Misguided patriotism can also blind us to our country's shortcomings. It can stifle criticism and cause us to regard dissent as unpatriotic.

But that's not true patriotism. The true patriot sees his country's faults and works to correct them. As the patriot sings that great hymn,

> O beautiful for patriot dream
> That sees beyond the years,
> Thine alabaster cities gleam
> Undimmed by human tears. . . ,

he sees even more clearly that America's cities are not all gleaming alabaster and are not entirely undimmed by tears. And he strengthens his resolve to do what he can to improve them.

Still, even while criticizing his country, the patriotic Christian does not adopt a sour negativism. His criticism is constructive, not destructive. He never loses sight of the many positive things about his country. That is especially true of a country like ours, in which we have so much to be positive about: religious and civic liberty, courts that are for the most part just, technological advances, material prosperity, abundant resources, gorgeous scenery, and above all a heritage based on the Bible.

> Righteousness exalteth a nation: but sin is a reproach to any people. (Proverbs 14:34)

> Be watchful, and strengthen the things which remain, that are ready to die. (Revelation 3:2)

9 *Military Service*

War!

There is probably no subject that has aroused more controversy throughout two thousand years of church history than the Christian attitude toward war.

Christians follow the Lord Jesus Christ, who is described in Isaiah 9:6 as the "Prince of Peace" but in Revelation 19:11-21 as the "King of Kings and Lord of Lords" who slays the armies of the wicked with a sword that proceeds out of his mouth. Christian martyrs have included pacifists and warriors alike. Maximilian the Martyr, who at Carthage around A.D. 295 accepted death by execution rather than service in the army of Rome, declared, "I cannot serve as a soldier; I cannot do evil. I am a Christian."[1] On the other hand, Archbishop Turpin of Reims around A.D. 778 fought valiantly on behalf of Charlemagne and the forces of Christendom against the Saracens, slaying hundreds after having been mortally wounded. He was eulogized in the *Song of Roland:* "In great battles and in beautiful sermons, all his life he was a champion of Christendom against the pagans. May God grant him His holy blessing!"[2]

Why so much confusion? Partly because war necessarily involves strong emotions of fear and anger, loyalty and love. Partly because war involves strong and conflicting loyalties: respect for life, concern for suffering, devotion to country, preservation of honor. And largely because too many Christians approach the question from human viewpoint rather than from God's viewpoint, asking "What do we think?" instead of "What saith the Scriptures?" One believer will say, "A Christian shouldn't engage in bloodshed!" while another will just as adamantly argue that "A Christian must serve his country!" All too often both sides fail to look to the Scriptures for guidance.

In dealing with a topic as important and controversial as this, I must remind the reader once again that a position is neither Christian nor moral unless it is supported directly or indirectly by the Scriptures. I believe this analysis will demonstrate that the Scriptures do justify war and military service, at least under some circumstances.[3]

Just Warfare Is at Times a Legitimate Exercise of National Policy

King Solomon tells us in Ecclesiastes 3:8 that there is "a time of war, and a time of peace." Certainly it is wrong to make war when it is time for peace, but it is just as wrong to insist upon peace when it is time for war.

Isaiah spoke longingly of a time when "they shall beat their swords into plowshares, and their spears into pruning hooks" (Isaiah 2:4). But he wasn't speaking of his day or of ours; he was speaking of the Millennium when Christ himself shall rule. Joel said just the opposite in Joel 3:10—"Beat your plowshares into swords, and your pruning hooks into spears." But he, too, was speaking to a particular people at a particular time and place. There is a time of war, and a time of peace. Considering the "wars and rumors of wars" (Matthew 24:6, 7) that are to plague the world up through the end of the age, we must recognize this age as potentially a time for war and prepare accordingly. The false priests and prophets who cry "Peace, peace; when there is no peace" (Jeremiah 6:14; 8:11) do a disservice to themselves, to the nation, and to God.

A Strong Defense Deters Aggression and Helps to Preserve Peace

When a strong man armed keepeth his palace, his goods are at peace: but when a stronger than he shall come upon him, and overcome him, he taketh from him all his armour wherein he trusted, and divideth his spoils. (Luke 11:21, 22)

In this passage, Jesus was not speaking primarily about war. Rather, he was speaking about demon possession and the power of God through Christ to cast out demons. The "strong man" of verse 21 is Satan and/or a demon, and the "stronger" in verse 22 is the Lord Jesus Christ. When the "stronger" (Jesus) overcomes the "strong" man (Satan), Satan is driven out and defeated.

But to illustrate his point, Jesus used an analogy. He employed a commonly understood principle of deterrence—that military strength deters aggression and prevents war. An aggressive nation, like a neighborhood bully, is likely to attack someone who is weak and vacillating rather than someone who is strong and capable of using his strength. By keeping its defenses strong, a nation is more likely to deter warlike aggressors and enjoy peace.

The principle of deterrence is illustrated in the book of Nehemiah. Nehemiah, a Jew in the palace of the Persian king, returned to Jerusalem after the exile to inspect the condition of the city (Nehemiah 2). Finding its walls in disrepair, Nehemiah organized the people for the purpose of rebuilding them. But as they did so, several hostile kings from the surrounding area plotted to stop their work:

> But it came to pass that, when Sanballat, and Tobiah, and the Arabians, and the Ammonites, and the Ashdodites, heard that the walls of Jerusalem were made up, and that the breaches began to be stopped, they were very wroth, and conspired all of them together to come and to fight against Jerusalem, and to hinder it. . . . And our adversaries said, They shall not know, neither see, till we come in the midst among them, and slay them, and cause the work to cease. (Nehemiah 4:7, 8, 11)

So after prayer (4:9), Nehemiah mobilized his forces and prepared them for war:

> Nevertheless, we made our prayer unto our God, and set a watch against them day and night, because of them. . . . Therefore set I in the lower places behind the wall, and on the higher places, I even set the people after their families with their swords, their spears, and their bows. (vv. 9, 13)

With all his forces on alert and ready to defend Jerusalem against attack, Nehemiah addressed his people:

> Be ye not afraid of them: remember the Lord, which is great and terrible, and fight for your brethren, your sons, and your daughters, your wives, and your houses. (v. 14)

And the enemy was deterred! Because of Nehemiah's military preparedness, the enemies saw that the Israelites were ready for battle, so they called off their attack:

> And it came to pass, when our enemies heard that it was known unto us, and God had brought their counsel to nought, that we returned all of us to the wall, every one unto his work. (v. 15)

But Nehemiah was not lulled into a false sense of security. He kept half his troops on alert, while the remainder were on standby reserve, working at their civilian occupations (construction) but keeping their weapons ready in case they should be needed for battle:

> And it came to pass from that time forth, that the half of my servants wrought in the work, and the other half of them held both the spears, the shields, and the bows, and the habergeons; and the rulers were behind all the house of Judah. They which builded on the wall, and they that bare

burdens, with those that laded, every one with one of his hands wrought in the work, and with the other hand held a weapon. For the builders, every one had his sword girded by his side, and so builded. And he that sounded the trumpet was by me. (Nehemiah 4:16-18)

Note that the entire crisis passed without the shedding of a single drop of blood. It could easily have been otherwise. Had Nehemiah not been prepared, the enemy would have attacked. A strong defense deters aggressors and helps to preserve peace. As Jesus said in Luke 14:31, 32:

Or what king, going to make war against another king, sitteth not down first, and consulteth whether he be able with ten thousand to meet him that cometh against him with twenty thousand? Or else, while the other is yet a great way off, he sendeth an ambassage, and desireth conditions of peace.

Refusing to Fight for One's Country Can Be a Sin Against God

Preachers commonly thunder, "Be sure your sin will find you out!" The last time you heard your preacher use that phrase, what sin was he rebuking? Drinking? Smoking? Promiscuity? Very likely he was not referring to a refusal to fight. But let's look at the way the phrase is used in the Bible.

Before they crossed the Jordan and entered the Promised Land, the Israelites fought many battles against their enemies, usually at the Lord's command (Numbers 31:1-3, for example). As the Israelites prepare to cross the Jordan, the tribes of Reuben and Gad saw the fertile lands they had conquered east of the Jordan, and they decided these lands would make excellent pasture for their cattle. So they asked Moses if they could stay there and make that land their inheritance (Numbers 32:1-5). Moses at first understood them to say that they did not want to join the other ten tribes in the battle for the Promised Land. Disturbed, he challenged them: "Shall your brethren go to war, and shall ye sit here?" (Numbers 32:6). Moses compared their attitude to that of the spies who discouraged Israel from conquering the land at Kadesh-Barnea, which resulted in forty more years in the wilderness.

However, the children of Reuben and Gad assured Moses that they were indeed willing to cross the Jordan and fight for Israel; they asked only for the right to return to these lands after the entire conquest was completed. Moses found this agreeable:

And Moses said unto them, If ye will do this thing, if ye will go armed before the Lord to war, and will go all of you armed over the Jordan before the Lord, until he hath driven out his enemies from before him, and the land be subdued before the Lord: then afterward ye shall return, and be guiltless before the Lord, and before Israel; and this land shall be your possession before the Lord. (Numbers 32:20-22)

But Moses added a stern warning.

> But if ye will not do so, behold, ye have sinned against the Lord: and be sure your sin will find you out. (Numbers 32:23; cf. Jeremiah 48:10)

That phrase, "Be sure your sin will find you out," may have many legitimate applications today. But in its original context it refers to the sin of refusing to fight for one's country.

Neither the Ten Commandments Nor the Sermon on The Mount Prohibits Just Warfare

When asked to justify their position with Scripture, those who believe a Christian should not engage in military service cite Exodus 20:13 more frequently than any other passage. But if "Thou shalt not kill" prohibits all forms of killing, then there is a contradiction in Scripture, for many other passages of Scripture justify or even command killing. Exodus 21:12, for example, commands that a murderer be executed. In Exodus 32:27 God commanded the sons of Levi to slay many of the Israelites because they had turned to idolatry while Moses was on Mt. Sinai. And in 1 Samuel 15:3 God commanded Saul and the Israelites to go to war against the Amalekites and "slay" them. How could God give these commands if he had previously forbidden all killing?

An examination of the original languages clearly shows that there is no such contradiction. In the Hebrew language there are at least nine words which roughly mean "kill," and each has a slightly different shade of meaning. *Muth* and *qatal* are very general terms for killing, and *nakah* is used in Numbers 35:15 for an accidental killing. Terms such as *harag* (Exodus 32:27) and *chalal* are frequently used for killing in war. Still others, like *zahvagh*, *tabach*, and *shachat* are commonly used for animal sacrifice. But the word used in Exodus 20:13 for "Thou shalt not kill" is *ratsach*, a very strong verb indicating an intentional and unjustified act of murder. This is not the same word as is used for killing in war, and thus killing in war is not covered by that commandment. The *New American Standard Bible* has translated Exodus 20:13 "You shall not murder," as has the *King James II Version*. *The Living Bible* renders the passage, "You must not murder," and both J. N. Darby's translation and Scofield's edition contain notes to the effect that the literal translation is "murder."[4]

The same distinction appears in the New Testament Greek. Whenever the commandment is reiterated in the New Testament (Matthew 5:21; 19:18; Mark 10:19; Luke 18:20; Romans 13:9; James 2:11), the Greek word is *phoneuo*, which normally means "to murder," though it can involve acts which are the moral equivalent of murder even though they do not involve violence or killing. But when the New

Testament speaks of killing in war, it uses different words: *apokteino*, a more general word for killing (Revelation 9:15, 18; 11:7; 19:21); and *sphatto*, meaning "slay" or "slaughter" (Revelation 6:4; 13:3).[5] All murder is killing, but not all killing is murder. The Decalogue pertains only to murder. In fact, the Old Testament seems to justify self-defense:

> If a thief be found breaking up, and be smitten that he die, there shall no blood be shed for him. If the sun be risen upon him, there shall be blood shed for him; for he should make full restitution: if he have nothing, then he shall be sold for his theft. (Exodus 22:2, 3)

Some might argue that these Old Testament concepts are modified or updated by Jesus' words in the Sermon on the Mount:

> Ye have heard that it hath been said, An eye for an eye, and a tooth for a tooth: But I say unto you, That ye resist not evil: but whosoever shall smite thee on thy right cheek, turn to him the other also. (Matthew 5:38, 39)

Jesus did not contradict the Old Testament law; rather, he corrected a contemporary Jewish distortion of it. The *lex talionis*, or law of like punishment, was an enlightened principle that limited the authority of government to punish criminals; it provided that the punishment must fit the crime. Jesus did not contradict this. But the Jews of his day had distorted this principle, so as to justify taking the law into one's own hands and taking personal revenge upon one's enemies, or punishing alleged criminals with a "lynch mob" mentality, as seems to have been the case with the woman taken in adultery (John 8:3-11). Jesus inveighed against individuals taking personal revenge, not against government punishing offenders.

There is also a difference between returning insult for insult, and legitimate self-defense. As the *Interpreters' Bible* explains, "A blow on the right cheek was an insult—with the back of the hand, so that the palm of the hand could return with a blow on the left cheek."[6] The *International Standard Bible Encyclopedia* adds,

> The oriental guards with jealous care his cheek from touch or defilement. Therefore a stroke on the cheek was, and is to this day, regarded as an act of extreme rudeness of behavior, a deadly affront. Our Saviour, however, teaches us in Matthew 5:39 and Luke 6:29 that even this insult is to be ignored and pardoned.[7]

The blow on the cheek was an insult, not an injury. It did not place one in danger of death or serious bodily harm. Jesus simply says that Christians are not to return insult for insult; he does not prohibit

Christians from defending themselves when under genuine physical attack.

One might also distinguish between the individual right of resistance and the collective right of resistance. A person under attack might personally choose not to resist the attack and thus expose himself to danger. For the reasons stated above, I do not believe the Scriptures command him to do so, but that is one option for him. But what if the attack is directed, not against him personally, but against his loved ones—his wife or children? Must he—indeed, may he—then opt for nonresistance and thus expose them to danger? Furthermore, if a person may defend himself or his loved ones from physical attack, then may not a nation defend its citizens from attack through the collective use of force? I believe a nation which fails to do so has betrayed its responsibility to its citizens.

War and Military Service Are Not Incompatible with the Words and Character of Jesus Christ

I served in the Air Force during the close of the Vietnam war years. During that time someone asked me, "Can you imagine the Lord Jesus Christ wearing a military uniform and carrying an M-16?

Over the years I have reflected a great deal on that queston, and after careful study of the Scriptures my answer is an unhesitating "Yes"—though he would probably wear the uniform of a general rather than that of a private.

Near the opening of Jesus' public ministry, shortly after he had changed water to wine at the wedding feast at Cana, Jesus cleansed the temple with a strong display of force:

> And when he had made a scourge of small cords, he drove them all out of the temple, and the sheep, and the oxen; and poured out the changers' money, and overthrew the tables; and said unto them that sold doves, Take these things hence; make not my Father's house a house of merchandise. (John 2:15, 16)

The scourge *(phragellion)* was a whiplike device with a handle and several cords attached to it, often with jagged pieces of bone or metal affixed to the cords. It was often used by the Romans for severe bodily punishment. Lenski demonstrates that the tenses of the Greek verbs accentuate the decisiveness of the action:

> The aorists of the narrative are impressive; they state what was done, done in short order, done decisively and completely, begun and finished then and there. . . . Tender souls have imagined that Jesus only menaced with the scourge, at least that he struck only the animals. They are answered by *pantas ekebalen*, and *pantas* is masculine, its antecedent being *tous po-*

lountas and *tous kermatistas,* the men who were selling and the money-changers. With fiery indignation Jesus applied the scourge right and left to these men. Then also to the sheep and oxen.[8]

Mayfield adds,

What Jesus did here is entirely in keeping with His nature and character. There are some who think that all that can be said about Him is "gentle Jesus, meek and mild." It is true that He is loving and forgiving. He does describe Himself as "meek and lowly in heart" (Matt 11:29). But there is more than that, and in this incident one sees another aspect of His nature. He does not deal easily nor light-handedly with evil. . . . He took the scourge of small cords and drove them all out of the temple. The word translated "drove" is a strong term that means "He threw them out of the Temple." This has been described as a "wild scene, with cowering figures clutching desperately at their tables, as these were flung here and there: or running after their spilled coins, as these rolled hither and thither; or shrinking from the lash that had no mercy till the holy place was cleansed.[9]

And Jesus cleansed the temple again toward the close of his public ministry, as recorded in Matthew 21:12, 13; Mark 11:15-17; and Luke 19:45, 46.

At his Second Coming, the Lord Jesus Christ will return to the earth with another display of force. At that time he will appear mounted on a white horse, clothed in a vesture dipped in blood, with a sharp sword going out of his mouth, leading the armies of heaven behind him. It appears these armies are composed of both angels (Matthew 25:31) and deceased believers (Jude 14). He will slay armies of the wicked, and he will consign the beast and false prophet to the lake of fire (Revelation 19:11-21). Undoubtedly many pacifists today are true Christians and will be in heaven when Armageddon takes place. One cannot help wondering whether they will ask to be excused as conscientious objectors!

Certainly Jesus promised peace (John 14:27). But the peace he promised was a spiritual peace with God, not a worldly peace in the sense of absence of physical warfare. It is a peace one can have in one's heart even under heavy fire on a battlefield. Jesus also said that the gospel would at times cause conflict and division: "Think not that I am come to send peace on earth; I come not to send peace, but a sword" (Matthew 10:34-36). The "sword" here does not necessarily mean physical violence, but it certainly indicates conflict.

In another passage Jesus commanded military preparedness:

Then said he unto them, But now, he that hath a purse, let him take it, and likewise his scrip: and he that hath no sword, let him sell his garment, and buy one. . . . And they said, Lord, behold, here are two swords, And he said unto them, It is enough. (Luke 22:36, 38)

Some have tried to spiritualize the sword as the "sword of the Spirit." But if we spiritualize the sword, we must also spiritualize the purse, the scrip or bag, and the garment. There is no warrant for such an exegesis other than an aversion to the plain meaning of the Word of God. Nor does it make sense to make "sword" refer to a dinner-knife to be used during the Passover feast. The word is *machaira*, which everywhere else in Scripture refers either to a weapon or to violent death by the sword, and which is used in the Septuagint to translate the Hebrew word for sword, *herebh*. Furthermore, such a translation would render Christ's words to Peter later that evening an absurdity: "All they that take the dinner-knife (*machaira* again) shall perish by the dinner-knife" (Matthew 26:52).[10]

The plain meaning of Jesus' order in Luke 22 was that the disciples were to carry swords for self-defense. The obvious reason is that it was dangerous to travel in those days, and especially dangerous for those who were followers of Jesus.[11]

The Bible Tells of Many Among God's People Who Were in Military Service

Many of the great spiritual giants of the Old Testament were soldiers and military commanders: Moses, Joshua, Caleb, Jonathan, Gideon, Nehemiah, Josiah, and many others. In Genesis 14:14-17 we read that after Lot had been taken captive by Chedorlaomer and three other kings, Lot's uncle Abraham organized a daring commando raid and successfully rescued his hostage nephew. For this he received a blessing from Melchizedek, king of Salem (Genesis 14:17-24), who is later described as a type of Christ (Psalm 110:4; Hebrews 5:6, 10; 6:20; 7:1-22).

David is described in Scripture as a man after God's own heart. Yet the Israelites lauded him as having slain ten thousand while Saul had only slain thousands (1 Samuel 18:7; 21:11; 29:5). David himself attributed his skill in battle to the Lord: "He teacheth my hands to war, so that a bow of steel is broken by mine arms" (Psalm 18:34; cf. 2 Samuel 22:35). And, "Blessed be the Lord my strength, which teacheth my hands to war, and my fingers to fight" (Psalm 144:1).

In the New Testament at least two centurions became followers of Christ. (A centurion served as a soldier in time of war and as a soldier-policeman in time of peace. His title was derived from the fact that he commanded approximately one hundred soldiers.) One such centurion is found in Matthew 8:5-13. Jesus commended the centurion for his great faith, a contrast to the unbelief and half-belief that Jesus found around him:

Verily I say unto you, I have not found so great faith, no, not in Israel.
(Matthew 8:10)

Perhaps because of his military training and experience, this centurion
was able to understand better than most people the absolute authority
of Jesus Christ over sickness. He knew that his ailing servant did not
have to touch the hem of Jesus' garment or even be within seeing
distance in order to be healed. Just as the centurion could simply
command his soldiers and expect instant obedience, he knew that the
Son of God could command disease to leave his servant: "Speak the
word only, and my servant shall be healed." And unlike many of the
self-righteous Jews, the centurion was well aware of his unworthiness
before Christ: "I am not worthy that thou shouldest come under my
roof." Augustine says of this centurion,

> . . . counting himself unworthy that Christ should enter into his doors, he
> was counted worthy that Christ should enter into his heart. . . . He did not
> receive him into his house, but he had received him already into his heart.[12]

The second centurion was Cornelius, described in Acts 10:1, 2 as "a
devout man, and one that feared God with all his house, who gave
much alms to the people, and prayed to God always." God founded
the first Gentile church in this centurion's home (Acts 10, 11).

There was also a centurion who crucified Christ, thus (perhaps
unknowingly) playing a role in God's plan for the salvation of the
human race. Unlike the contemptuous religious leaders and the de-
spairing faithful remnant, this hardened centurion seems to have recognized Jesus Christ for who he really was. Luke tells us that the
centurion "glorified God, saying, Certainly this was a righteous man"
(Luke 23:47); and Matthew records him as saying, "Truly this was the
Son of God" (Matthew 27:54).[13]

To these might be added a fourth centurion, one who is not recorded
as having trusted in Christ but who is commended in Acts 27:43 for his
willingness to save Paul's life in the face of shipwreck.

The significance of these centurions is this: at no time was any of
them ever told by Jesus or any man of God that his participation in
military service was wrong. The harlot was told to "Go, and sin no
more" (John 8:11). Thieves are told to steal no more (Ephesians 4:28).
The publican who had enriched himself by cheating others showed his
repentance by promising restitution to those whom he had wronged
(Luke 19:1-10). Yet nowhere do we read any similar condemnation of
military service, and so far as we know all of these centurions remained in military service after they were converted. Military service
is an honorable profession in which a Christian can proudly engage.

The Best Way to End a War Is to Win It Decisively

The unpopularity of the Vietnam war was due largely to the indecision and irresolution of American leadership. America couldn't decide whether it wanted to be in or out; whatever force was applied was always too little and too late. When, in 1972, President Nixon finally ordered large-scale B-52 bombing raids against North Vietnam, the Communists quickly began serious negotiations at the conference table. But on the verge of victory, America accepted a peace treaty that not only fell short of ultimate victory but even allowed the Communists to keep their troops in the south. The result, as many predicted, was that the Communists gathered strength for a few years and then began a final offensive that overran not only South Vietnam, but Laos and Cambodia as well. There followed a horrid bloodbath, a mass exodus, the "boat people," and the rest. The final chapters have yet to be written.

That's not the way wars were fought in the Bible. As the Israelites took the Promised Land, they had a well-planned strategy, and they pursued it vigorously. As Leon Wood writes,

> Moses' strategy for taking Canaan, no doubt revealed to him by God, clearly had been to attack the land at its approximate midpoint, coming in from the east, and divide it into a south and north section, that each might be conquered separately. We may assume that Moses had shared this thinking with Joshua, so that the new leader had the plan in mind as the people prepared for crossing the Jordan.[14]

The Israelites went forth in battle after battle, attacking swiftly, fighting fiercely, winning decisively, and usually utterly destroying their enemies (Joshua 6:21; 8:25; 10:28, 30, 32, 33, 35, 37, 39, 40; 11:12)—all by the Lord's command (Joshua 8:1, 2; 11:20). The biblical account of the conquest of Canaan closes with these words:

> So Joshua took the whole land, according to all that the Lord said unto Moses; and Joshua gave it for an inheritance unto Israel according to their divisions by their tribes. And the land rested from war. (Joshua 11:23)

And the land rested from war! Peace came at last, but only through military victory. Not a permanent peace, of course—there is no permanent peace in this world short of Christ's return—but a temporary peace at least. In the Book of Judges we twice find the phrase, "And the land had rest forty years" (Judges 3:11; 8:28)—each time following a decisive military victory.

Military Service Is Not for Everyone

Before you rush down to your local recruiter, consider this: military service is not for everyone; military service may not be right for you. Old Testament Israel granted certain exemptions from military service:

> And the officers shall speak further unto the people, and they shall say, What man is there that is fearful and faint-hearted? let him go and return unto his house, lest his brethren's heart faint as well as his heart. (Deuteronomy 20:8)

The "fearful and faint-hearted" were not conscientious objectors; they were persons whose temperament was such that they simply would not make good soldiers, and their fearfulness would affect others and hinder good discipline. Exemptions were also granted to newlyweds (Deuteronomy 20:5; 24:5), engaged persons (Deuteronomy 20:7), and persons in certain occupations (Deuteronomy 20:6). These persons had their minds on other things besides fighting, and their inattentiveness could be a danger to others in the ranks.

Every believer must seriously consider military service, but he must consider whether his country needs him in military service, and whether he is "right" for the military. In peacetime, when there is no draft, it may be that the armed forces have all the personnel they need, and you can serve your country better in another capacity. If you are handicapped, or if you have serious emotional or psychological problems, military service might not be right for you. If you are highly individualistic and don't submit well to authority or work well with others, you may have problems in the service—although military training and discipline might do you a world of good! You will have to determine whether military service is God's plan for you, and this is a decision to be made with much thought and prayer.

In time of war or national need though, you should willingly serve unless you are physcially or mentally unable to do so. It is your civic and Christian responsibility.

10 Political Participation

[Christians love to talk about how degenerate society is becoming. They point to immorality in the schools, corruption in the courthouse, crime in the streets. Yet, when an opportunity arises to do something about it, Christians are strangely absent.]

Of all of the obligations to government that I have discussed—prayer, obedience (and disobedience), taxation, patriotism, military service—political participation is the most neglected. Until recently at least, evangelical Christians all too often tended to shy away from political participation. Some of this may have been due to apathy, but often there has been a negative undercurrent of thought that Christians shouldn't be involved in anything like politics.

There is no biblical support for this idea. Some of the greatest believers in the Bible were kings and judges of Israel. Can you imagine David saying, "No thanks, Samuel, I don't think a believer should be involved in politics"?

Some will object to examples taken from the Old Testament Israelite theocracy, which they feel are not applicable to politics today. All right then, let's go outside the theocracy and look at Daniel, a Jewish believer who was faithful to God while serving as a prime minister in Babylon and again as a prime minister in Persia. Can you imagine Daniel telling Nebuchadnezzar that politics is too dirty a business, or telling Darius he didn't want to get involved? Or consider Esther, a Jewish believer who became a Persian queen and used her position and influence to save her people. Or Ezra, the priest and leader of the Jews after the Babylonian exile. Or Joseph, who became prime minister of Egypt. They didn't shrink from political involvement.

Going to the New Testament, there are intimations of believers within Caesar's household, and "household" probably refers to the

Roman civil service (Philippian 4:22). In Romans 16:23 Paul mentioned "Erastus the chamberlain" who sent greetings to the Christians at Rome. A chamberlain was a city treasurer. The post of treasurer of a city the size of Corinth (the probable place from which Paul wrote the Book of Romans) was definitely a highly political position. Other followers of Jesus, such as Joseph of Arimathea and Nicodemus, probably sat on the Sanhedrin, the political and ecclesiastical court and governing body of Israel.

The duty of the believer who finds himself thrust into a secular society such as ours is well stated in the prophet Jeremiah's advice to the Jewish exiles in Babylon:

> Thus saith the Lord of hosts, the God of Israel, unto all that are carried away captives, whom I have caused to be carried away from Jerusalem unto Babylon; Build ye houses, and dwell in them; and plant gardens, and eat the fruit of them; take ye wives, and beget sons and daughters; and take wives for your sons, and give your daughters to husbands, that they may bear sons and daughters; that ye may be increased there, and not diminished. *And seek the peace of the city whither I have caused you to be carried away captives, and pray unto the Lord for it: for in the peace thereof shall ye have peace.* (Jeremiah 29:4-7, emphasis added)

The word for peace in verse 7 is *shalom*, which does mean peace but also means welfare or prosperity. The Jews who were exiled in Babylon had a civic duty to work for the welfare of Babylon. We as Christian citizens are to seek the welfare or betterment of the secular society in which we live.

Common Arguments Against Christian Political Involvement

"I believe Christians should be out saving souls, not politicking. After all, the Bible says we shouldn't be entangled in the affairs of this world." Certainly there is much truth in this statement. The primary mission of the church is and always will be to win souls for Jesus Christ and to guide them to Christian maturity through the faithful teaching of the Word of God. The social gospel of the late 1800s and early 1900s was largely a rejection of the Word of God and an attempt to find salvation through social and political action rather than through faith in the Lord Jesus Christ. The fundamentalist reaction against the social gospel was largely justified. No one ever has been or ever will be saved through political activity. We are saved *only* by believing on the Lord Jesus Christ.

But in their justifiable reaction against the social gospel, many fundamentalists went too far, refusing to touch politics or anything remotely political with a ten-foot pole. This is also an error, for it deemphasizes or eliminates much of the Word of God. God's Word has a lot to say about government, about crime and punishment, about abortion, about national defense, about war and peace, about the many political issues that face us daily. Paul declared that he had "not shunned to declare unto you all the counsel of God" (Acts 20:27). The fundamentalist who refuses to preach or consider what God's Word has to say about politics is not declaring the whole counsel of God and has a serious gap in his ministry. R. J. Rushdoony put it well when he said,

> Man must exercise dominion in the name of God, and in knowledge, righteousness, and holiness. . . . The world, moreover, cannot be surrendered to Satan. It is God's world and must be brought under God's law, politically, economically, and in every other way possible. The Enlightenment, by its savage and long-standing attack on Biblical faith, has brought about a long retreat of Christianity from a full-orbed faith to a kind of last-ditch battle centering around the doctrines of salvation and of the infallible Scripture. The time has come for a full-scale offensive, and it has indeed begun, to bring every area of thought into captivity to Christ, to establish the whole counsel of God and every implication of His infallible word.[1]

Second Timothy 2:4 does tell us, "No man that warreth entangleth himself with the affairs of this life; that he may please him who hath chosen him to be a soldier." This simply means that we do not let frivolous pleasures and distractions keep us from our mission. But transforming the world with the savor of God's Word, bringing Christian principles to bear in the political realm, is part of our mission.

"I don't know anything about politics." Let me answer this argument in two ways.

First, you may be astonished at how much you really know, compared to many who do participate. Many of those who occupy relatively high positions in politics get there because of their personalities, money, or contacts, and really know very little about the issues. I have been to many political conventions at which many delegates came only because a candidate promised them a free keg of beer in return for their votes. Many didn't even know who the other candidate was.

Second, you may be ignorant, but you don't have to stay ignorant. You can and should start becoming informed. Watching the news helps, but I certainly wouldn't rely on that alone. In fact, I wouldn't rely on any single source. Get your news from a variety of sources: television, newspapers, magazines, books.

"Politics is dirty." Yes, it is. So is business, law, labor, education, sports, and just about every other activity you can imagine. It's part of the human condition known as sin.

Think about it. How can you really expect politicians to be any better than the people who elect them? I believe the moral standards of politicians are no worse than those of society at large. In fact, they may be slightly better. With all their public exposure, they are forced to keep their act somewhat clean.

But if politics is dirty (and it is), is that any reason not to get involved? If Christians stay out of politics, they remove the light of the gospel from the political arena and abdicate their responsibility to be the salt of the earth that savors and preserves society. As Senator Mark Hatfield put it,

> For the Christian man to reason that God does not want him in politics because there are too many evil men in government is as insensitive as for a Christian doctor to turn his back on an epidemic because there are too many germs there. For the Christian to say that he will not enter politics because he might lose his faith is the same as for the physician to say that he will not heal men because he might catch their diseases.[2]

The Christian who refuses to become involved in politics consigns the realm of politics to the secular and the unregenerate. Edmund Burke said it well: "The fate of good men who refuse to become involved in politics, is to be ruled by evil men."

"Why bother to clean up the world? Christ is coming!" The constant tension between grace and works often causes confusion about the Christian role in politics. Grace means God working on our behalf, whereas a basic premise of political activity is that man can work to improve society. The tension is for the most part resolved when we recognize that God works in and through us; we don't do it on our own. God can work through us to transform political institutions just as he can work through us to preach the gospel and win souls for Jesus Christ.

But the tension is even greater for those evangelicals who believe in the premillennial return of Christ. Many passages in Scripture speak of a day in which Jesus Christ will himself rule the world. Revelation 20:4-7 tells us that this reign will last 1,000 years—hence the term Millennium. Bible-believing Christians disagree as to how and when this will take place, but they generally fall into three camps: premillennialists, postmillennialists, and amillennialists.

Premillennialists believe that before the Millennium there will be a seven-year period of great turbulence, referred to in Scripture as the Tribulation. The Tribulation will end when Jesus Christ returns to the earth at Armageddon, defeats the kings of the earth and the beast and false prophet, and establishes his rule on earth.

Postmillennialists, on the other hand, believe that Christ will return after, not before, the Millennium. Amillennialists believe there will be no literal thousand-year reign on earth, and they interpret the various passages which speak of a Millennium figuratively as referring either to the church age or to heaven.

If one is postmillennial or amillennial, his rationale for political action is obvious: he is working, with God's help, to build or prepare the way for God's kingdom on earth. While he may face occasional defeats and setbacks, he knows that his efforts will bear fruit in the end.

But for the premillennialist it's a different story. Instead of getting better and better as the kingdom of God dawns on the earth, the premillennialist knows things are going to keep getting worse and worse as the world moves closer to the Tribulation. What's the point of fighting a losing battle? Sin and evil are inevitably going to triumph, and they won't be defeated until the Tribulation is finished and Christ himself defeats them at Armageddon. Why bother reforming a world that's inevitably on its way to destruction?

Even if one holds the premillennial, pretribulation position (as I do), there is still good reason to be involved in government. While I believe the general trend of history is downward as the cancer of sin spreads across the world, this is not a steady downhill slide. History has its ups and downs, bright periods as well as dark times. The Pax Romana, during which the world was at peace under the rule of the Roman Empire, was such a bright period. Another was the ninth century under the rule of men like Charlemagne. Still another was the sixteenth and seventeenth centuries when the world was illuminated by the Reformation. The nineteenth century, during which the world enjoyed a large measure of order and culture thanks to America and the British Empire, was still another. Presently we appear to be living in the dark age of humanism, but there are signs that this age may be ending and a new one may be dawning. And even when the world is in a dark period, there can be bright periods in individual nations, states, or communities. God uses individual believers to bring such golden ages into being.

Furthermore, even if we are assured of defeat that does not mean we ought to give up fighting. I think of Whittaker Chambers, once a leading Communist, who left Communism to embrace Christianity and anti-Communism. As he broke with Communism, he wrote that he was leaving the side of probable victory to join the side of probable defeat (in this world). But he did so because he knew it was right.

We battle against evil in the political realm, not because we are assured of winning, but because God has commanded us to do so. Believers, we are told, are the "salt of the earth" (Matthew 5:13). Salt serves two purposes: to flavor, and to preserve. That is the role of believers: to give the world a Christian flavoring, and thereby to preserve the world from destruction. Believers are also the "light of the world" (Matthew 5:14-16); they are to shed the light of God's Word on the world, including its political institutions.⟩

⌈God has not called us to be successful; he has called us to be faithful. As the nobleman in Jesus' parable told his servants to "Occupy till I come" (Luke 19:13), so we are to do the Lord's work faithfully, ever anticipating his return.⟩

America has a wonderful biblical heritage, and a Constitution and governmental system based on sound biblical principles. Even as conditions deteriorate, we are to "Be watchful, and strengthen the things which remain, that are ready to die" (Revelation 3:2).

If all of this sounds unduly pessimistic, it does not mean everything is hopeless. Victories do take place from time to time, and even defeats can by our action be made less severe than they would have been otherwise. It is reassuring and relaxing to trust in the grace of God, to know that while he has given us responsibility he has not made everything depend on us. General Thomas G. "Stonewall" Jackson used to say, "Duty is ours; consequences are God's." He is in firm control of history, and he takes our defeats and converts them into his victories. He—and through him, we—will be victorious in the end!

"But I'm a preacher. I shouldn't mix my ministry with politics." As a preacher, you have a special political responsibility. Have you fulfilled it?

It is your duty to proclaim "the whole counsel of God" to your congregation. Have you educated your congregation as to what God's Word says about government? Have you presented the biblical view of abortion, or capital punishment, or national defense? If not, you have work to do! Your people are citizens and you need to educate them on their civic responsibilities. Some of those in your congregation could be future congressmen, legislators, county commissioners, mayors, or school board members. A future President of the United States may be in your Sunday school! They need to know the biblical principles of government, and it is your job to teach them.

I don't necessarily mean churches should be involved in voter registration and overt political action, or that a pastor should openly endorse a political candidate from the pulpit. The church's role is to teach the principles of the Word of God as they apply to politics and every other field of life. It is then the responsibility of individual Christians within the church to take those principles and apply them to concrete situations in society.

However, a minister is also an individual and has civic responsibilities independent of his office as pastor. At the very least, it is his duty to be informed and to vote intelligently. Whether he should do more is between him and God. I have known of pastors who have served as city councilmen; some have even been members of Congress. I see nothing unbiblical about this. After all, Moses and Samuel held the offices of priest and judge and exercised the gift of prophesy. However, one must be careful to keep the offices distinct, and must carefully consider whether he is capable of doing justice to both roles.

"I'm only one person. I can't do anything." That's true. By yourself you can do nothing. But with God's help you can do anything he wants you to do.

Throughout history God has used single, ordinary people to accomplish great things. To save Israel from the Midianites, God chose Gideon, a simple man from a poor family of one of the lesser tribes. Gideon protested to God, "I am least in my father's house." But God answered simply, "Surely I will be with thee" (Judges 6:15, 16). Or consider David, thought by his father to be least likely among all his sons to be chosen king of Israel; yet it was David whom God chose (1 Samuel 16).

Great political movements triumph not because of the groundswell of the majority, but because of the dedicated effort of a committed minority. Lenin's Bolsheviks (the term literally means "majority") started in 1903 with only Lenin and seven followers. By 1907 they were only seventeen. By 1917 they were still only forty thousand. Yet these forty thousand were able to seize and control Russia, geographically the largest nation on earth. A dedicated and committed few can wield an influence far in excess of their numbers.

God has used single individuals here in this country, too. Ten years ago the Equal Rights Amendment seemed to be steamrollering its way to a speedy ratification. Then one woman, Phyllis Schlafly, entered the arena to fight ERA. Its defeat can be largely attributed to her efforts.

In Texas a few years ago an ordinary couple named Mel and Norma Gabler became concerned about the textbooks their children were reading in the public schools. What began for them as a small-scale, timid protest in a local school district has now become a nationwide ministry as the Gablers analyze and critique textbooks and expose humanist, anti-Christian, immoral, or anti-American content. I'm sure the Gablers never dreamed God would use them like that.

God may not use you in such a dramatic way. To be successful, leaders have to have followers. But God will use you, if you are committed and faithful to him. The important thing is to faithfully do your part, however large or small it may be. It has been said,

I may be only one, but still I am one. I cannot do everything, but I can do something. I will not fail to do that which I can do.

In the next section I will show you some things you can do.

What Can You Do?

"*Search the Scriptures.*" To begin with, get into the Word of God and see what he has to say about the political events of the day. My discussion of these issues in Part Three will, I hope, be helpful in this regard, but it is only a starting-point. Dig deeper!

Read widely. Know what's going on in the world around you. Read about political events. And don't rely on any single source.

Read a variety of sources. When you rely upon only one source of news, you know only what that source chooses to tell you. Its information may be incomplete, or its perspective may be biased. To mislead an audience, it is not necessary to lie; one can also mislead by selective reporting of the truth.

The danger of bias in television is even greater than with other media. A newscaster can convey a positive or negative impression of a candidate or idea not only by what he says, but by how he says it. A tone of voice, a smile, a curl of the lip, a roll of the eyes conveys an unspoken message that the viewer picks up whether he realizes it or not.

And the perspective of media personnel in general tends to be considerably more liberal than that of the general public. Syndicated columnist Patrick J. Buchanan recently related the results of a study by S. Robert Lichter and Stanley Rothman of two hundred and forty influential news media personnel—reporters, editors, columnists, bureau chiefs, news executives, television correspondents, anchormen, producers, film editors. Of these, 54 percent claimed to be left of center, while only 19 percent said they are right of center. Polls of the American people as a whole show the opposite.

In recent elections this group of media leaders showed a much more liberal voting pattern than does the general public. Ninety-three percent of them voted for Lyndon Johnson over Barry Goldwater in 1964, compared with 62 percent of the general public. Eighty-seven percent supported Humphrey over Nixon in 1968, while among the general public there was a slight plurality for Nixon. The media split 81 to 19 percent in favor of McGovern over Nixon in 1972, while the populace split 39 to 61 percent the other way. And in 1976 80 percent of these media leaders supported Carter over Ford, while among the public Carter won by only a very small plurality.

While about half the American public regularly attends church or synagogue, only 8 pecent of these leaders attend regularly and 86 percent "seldom or never" attend. Ninety percent of them endorse the right of a woman to an abortion, 85 percent support the right of homosexuals to teach in public schools, and 54 percent see nothing wrong with adultery.[3]

Are you willing to rely implicitly on these people for your news? I'm not; I prefer to get my news from a wide variety of sources. One of my favorite news magazines is *U.S. News & World Report,* a fact-filled weekly magazine of moderately conservative persuasion. *Time* and *Newsweek* present a somewhat more liberal perspective. *National Review* and *Human Events* are excellent conservative publications. *Moral Majority Report* (499 South Capitol St., Suite 101, Washington, D.C. 20003) gives a good perspective on news of special interest to Christians, as do *Christian Life, Good News Broadcaster, Moody Monthly, Christianity Today, Christian News, Christian Inquirer,* and several other evangelical magazines. Forrest Boyd's radio broadcast, "God's News Behind the News," heard on many Christian radio stations, is also helpful.

As you begin learning, you'll be amazed at how soon others will start coming to you for information.

Integrate God's Word with other information. The believer who ignores the Word of God when making political decisions, as many do, omits using the most potent weapon he has, and fails to apply to modern society the light it so badly needs and which he alone can supply. He becomes as salt that has lost its savor. But God's Word must be integrated with information to formulate a sound political position.

At the time of this writing Central America, and particularly El Salvador, is seething with conflict. What should the United States do? What should be the Christian position? You can search the Scriptures with a fine-tooth comb, and you won't find El Salvador mentioned!

We can formulate principles, however. We know from the Bible that it is wrong for a leader to oppress his people. We also can compare God's Word to the godless philosophy of Karl Marx and see how evil and unscriptural Communism is. We know what God's Word says about revolution, and we know that Scripture justifies warfare at least on some occasions.

But to apply these principles to El Salvador, we have to know what is going on there. Who is causing all the trouble? Is it peasants seeking social justice, or is it foreign Communist aggression? Is the present government oppressive, or is it truly bent on moderate reform? Were the recent elections a farce, or were they fair and representative? Is there a feasible, peaceful solution?

To answer questions like these, we need facts. And the "facts" are often in conflict, because the sources are often biased. That's why it is wise to read widely and get different sides of the issue.

As we get the facts, we can apply the Scriptures to concrete situations and formulate a political position.

Look at the candidates. America is run largely by its elected leaders. To put your political ideas into effect, it is therefore necessary to

(1) persuade your elected representatives that your ideas are correct; or (2) elect representatives who already share your ideas. The latter is usually easier, so let's concentrate on that for now.

In deciding whom to vote for, what should you look for in a candidate? Too many people vote for a candidate because he seems "nice," or is good-looking, wears nice clothes, has a nice family, etc. What are the right things to look for?

(1) His qualifications. What are the demands of the office? Does this candidate have the intelligence, education, work experience, or other background necessary to do the job well?

(2) His character. So far as you know, is there scandal in his background? Does he espouse and exemplify high moral standards, and does he choose good people for his associates? Do his words ring true?

(3) His party affiliation. Even if you are active in a political party, you shouldn't just vote the straight ticket without even considering who's running on the other side. Generally, in most parts of the country, Republicans tend to be more conservative than Democrats; but there are conservatives and liberals, good people and bad people, in both parties. Party affiliation is one relevant consideration, but certainly not the only one.

(4) His spiritual status. Would I vote for a candidate just because he claims to be born again? Not necessarily. I'd consider that as a very positive factor, but I certainly wouldn't make it my only consideration.

Just being born again does not necessariy mean one is qualified to hold public office, nor does it mean it is God's will that he be elected. Nor does it necessarily mean he has more of God's wisdom to share than does the unsaved candidate. The fact that one is born again means that he has trusted Jesus Christ as his Savior and is therefore on the way to heaven. Other than that, it does not mean that he is necessarily any wiser than anyone else concerning what God's Word has to say about government. To put it bluntly, if a fool gets born again, he may simply become a born-again fool! It is only when he begins to study God's Word and apply the wisdom of God to the political affairs of the day that his salt really develops a savor and he becomes the Christian influence that he should be.

God has written the effect of his law upon the hearts of men (Romans 2:14, 15). Unregenerate men therefore are capable of human good (often called civil righteousness). This will not get them into heaven, but it does enable them, through common grace, to be good parents, good citizens, and at times good public officials. God used Cyrus the Great of Persia to free Judah from its captivity in Babylon, and the Bible refers to Cyrus as God's "anointed" (Isaiah 45:1) and calls him a "righteous man" (Isaiah 41:2). This does not necessarily mean that Cyrus was a believer although that is possible. Rather, it means that Cyrus, since he believed that the Jews and other people who had been captured and deported by the Assyrians and Babylonians should be free to return to their homeland and practice their religion, understood and practiced civil righteousness, and therefore God used him to accomplish his purpose.

It is entirely possible that an unsaved man, through the civil righteousness of God's law written upon men's hearts, may have a better understanding of God's design for human government than does a believer. Given such a choice, I would not hesitate to vote for the unsaved candidate.

Still, the unregenerate man is limited in his ability and desire to understand and apply God's Word. Civil righteousness is desirable and necessary for society to function effectively, but it is far inferior to divine righteousness. The believer has the indwelling ministry of Christ and the indwelling ministry of the Holy Spirit to guide him, and he is therefore able to understand and apply God's Word in ways the unbeliever never could.

For that reason I believe the candidate's spiritual status is an important factor, though not the only factor, to consider in voting.

(5) His stand on the issues. I cannot overemphasize the importance of the candidate's political position.

How much sense does it make to study the issues and take a position which you believe to be God's position, and then send a representative to the capitol who votes directly opposite to your beliefs? Yet that is exactly what many voters do!

I remember watching the returns from the Nebraska Democratic primary in 1972. Reporters stopped several voters to interview them. One man was asked what he considered to be the most important issue of the election, and he replied, "Vietnam." Asked what he thought should be done about Vietnam, he said he favored decisive military action to win a quick victory. He was then asked whom he voted for, and he answered, "Humphrey." Without meaning any slight against Hubert Humphrey, it should be noted that Humphrey favored a negotiated peace in Vietnam. This man had just voted for a candidate whose stand was diametrically opposed to his on what he said was the most important issue of the election!

Another person was asked for whom she voted, and she said she was for Wallace. When asked who her second choice would be if Wallace couldn't make it, she replied, "McGovern." Now, meaning no offense to either Governor Wallace or Senator McGovern, those two candidates were as different as night and day. Wallace was the most conservative candidate in the primary, and McGovern was the most liberal. The only thing they had in common was the first name George!

Obviously these voters weren't paying much attention to the candidates' stand on the issues. Do you? Do you know how your elected officials stand? Did you know at the time you voted for them, or against them? Perhaps you are strongly opposed to abortion. Are you sending people to the statehouse who vote for public funding of abortion, contrary to your convictions? Before you vote, find out where the candidate stands on the issues.

How do you find out? Listen to the candidate's speeches. Read his literature. Read what he says in the newspaper. If this doesn't tell you, call him or his headquarters and ask directly.

One problem, of course, is that political promises often have a tendency to evaporate into thin air after the election is over. Party platforms, it is said, are written with disappearing ink. It is easy to tell the voters you're for cuts in federal spending, and then go to Washington and vote for every big spending scheme that is proposed. It helps to know whether the candidate has recently taken this position at the time of this election, or whether he has espoused this position consistently over the years. If he has previously held office, it is helpful to find out how he has voted in the past. Don't be completely cynical though; people do change.

Vote intelligently. After you have studied God's Word, become informed on the issues, taken a position, and studied the candidates, then you are ready to vote intelligently. Do so! (By the way, don't forget—in most states you will not be allowed to vote if you haven't registered.)

Speak up. Once a candidate is elected, though, don't just forget about him. He continues to need your prayers, and also your encouragement.

Let us suppose you consider abortion to be the most important issue of the day, and you decided to vote for a particular candidate because he said he was against abortion. When an abortion issue comes up, write to the candidate (now officeholder). Remind him of his promise, tell him you voted for him because of that promise, and tell him you're counting on him to keep his promise. If he is wavering, that may influence him to stay firm. If he is standing firm, he'll appreciate your letter, because he's under a barrage of pressure from the other side.

Try to remember, though, that a politician must deal with political realities. Politics is the art of the possible, it is said, and sometimes this requires compromise. It is much easier to be dogmatic and ideologically rigid in a pulpit, in a classroom, or in an armchair at home than in a position of public trust where you are responsible for the lives and interests of many people.

Let us suppose that Senator Hanson is elected as a strong opponent of abortion. Senator Hanson, let us say, believes that abortion should be outlawed except where necessary to save the life of the mother. He has sponsored a bill to that effect.

Now, in State X there are one hundred state senators. The plain political reality is, only about thirty of them would support Senator Hanson's bill. On the other hand, if Senator Hanson would amend his bill to allow abortion for rape and incest, an additional twenty-five senators would back it, making a majority.

What should Senator Hanson do? Stand firm with the bill he really wants, even though it is certain to be defeated? Or compromise a little and support the bill that woudn't save every unborn child but would save the vast majority of them? It's a difficult choice to make, but it's the type of choice that faces politicians daily. And many of them are far less clear-cut, for they do not involve the certainty of passage or defeat that this involves. Do you see now why Paul exhorted Timothy to pray for those in authority?

So be understanding and patient, but don't hesitate to speak up. And don't limit yourself to writing to officeholders. One of the best ways of sharing your ideas with others is the "letters to the editor" column in your newspapers and magazines. This is one of the most widely read sections, and it is free. One thing to remember: keep it short! (If you don't, the editor will!) And make sure of your facts!

Work in the political process. Campaigns don't just happen. They succeed because lots of people work to make them succeed. And most of these are volunteers just like you.

When you select a candidate you want to work for, or when you select the political party that best suits your convictions, call his campaign manager or the party headquarters and ask what you can do to help. Many things need doing that aren't particularly glamorous, like stuffing envelopes, conducting voter surveys, going door to door with literature, etc., but these are necessary to a successful campaign. You can do special things like making your home available to the candidate for coffee and providing a question-and-answer session with your neighbors. And don't be afraid to suggest ideas. I am convinced that some of the best campaign strategies of all time have never been implemented because the person who thought of them didn't consider himself important enough to be listened to.

Have you ever gone to the voting booth and found yourself faced with a choice between two losers? Have you ever felt that you had to pick the lesser of the two evils? Did you wonder how such "turkeys" got on the ballot in the first place, and protest in your mind that you deserve a better choice than that?

They got on the ballot because they and their supporters put them there. Or more precisely, because better men and their supporters didn't throw them off.

Candidates are chosen either in primaries or in conventions. You can influence the choice of candidates by being active in the selection process.

Precinct caucuses take place once every two years in most states. In some states any registered voter can attend the caucus in his precinct; in some you have to be registered with that political party or declare an intention to vote for that party's candidate for President. At the precinct caucus, delegates are elected to county, district, or state conventions, candidates are sometimes endorsed, and resolutions concerning political issues are discussed. Resolutions that are adopted are usually forwarded for consideration in the county platform, and from there to the district, state, and national conventions. This is your opportunity to have an input in the party's candidates and philosophy. Most of those who attend these caucuses are ordinary citizens just like yourself, and one or two well-informed persons can often control a precinct.

Be careful though: if you say too much, you may find yourself elected precinct committeeman!

Contribute to campaigns. Campaigns cost money, and candidates rely upon contributions of ordinary citizens for their support. Contrary to popular opinion, the "big-money interests" (whoever they are) do *not* have a stranglehold on campaign financing. I consider it my Christian duty to give of my substance to support candidates in whom I believe. In fact, when I give to a political campaign, I regard that money as having been given to the Lord's work just as if I'd given it to my church. But that means I have a duty to exercise this stewardship wisely and prayerfully.

Run for office yourself. This obviously isn't for everybody, and I'll bet you're saying it definitely isn't for you. But if you can't imagine yourself running for public office, I can only suggest that you take a close look at some of the characters who do run—and win!

Don't misunderstand me. I'm not saying that everyone who reads this book should immediately call a press conference and declare his candidacy for President—at least not yet!

But look how many elective or appointive offices exist on the local level. Consider your own background and ability. Perhaps you know as much about education as some of the present school board members, or as much about road construction as the city street commissioner. How did they get started in politics? They're ordinary people just like you.

Chances are you're not convinced. And maybe this isn't God's plan for you. But don't completely rule it out. God may have plans for you that you've never dreamed of.

A Call to Arms
General Douglas MacArthur warned Americans,

History fails to record a single precedent in which nations subject to moral decay have not passed into political and economic decline. There has been either a spiritual awakening to overcome the moral lapse, or a progressive deterioration leading to ultimate national disaster.[4]

We should add that this political and economic decline is a natural and logical consequence, but it is also a supernatural consequence. It is the result of God's judgment (Leviticus 26:14-39).

I believe the political and economic decline that grips America today is the result of moral decay. I believe God is calling upon believers today to lead the spiritual awakening that can overcome that moral lapse. That's how believers can truly be the salt of the earth, preserving their nation from divine judgment.

After decrying the sin of Judah, their oppression and robbery, their vexation of the poor and needy and the sojourner, God declared in Ezekiel 22:30,

And I sought for a man among them, that should make up the hedge, and stand in the gap before me for the land, that I should not destroy it.

God is looking for believers today to "stand in the gap," to assert themselves in the political arena and transform America's political institutions.

But I omitted the last four words of that verse: ". . . but I found none." The Lord continued in the next verse,

Therefore have I poured out mine indignation upon them; I have consumed them with the fire of my wrath: their own way have I recompensed upon their heads, saith the Lord God.

God's judgment indeed came upon Judah: seventy years of exile in Babylon.

That was true of Judah. I pray it won't be true of America. Will you do your part, as others have done theirs?

When the Jews in Persia were in danger of extermination due to the treachery of Haman, it fell upon Esther to save them. But Esther was hesitant to act, for she knew it could cost her own life. Whereupon Mordecai exhorted her,

For if thou altogether holdest thy peace at this time, then shall there relief and deliverance arise to the Jews from another place; but thou and thy father's house shall be destroyed: and who knoweth whether thou art come to the kingdom for such a time as this? (Esther 4:14)

Believing Christian: who knoweth whether thou art come to the kingdom for such a time as this?

Part III *The Biblical View of the Issues of Government*

11   Left and Right

"All right," you say, "I understand why God instituted government. I understand that I have responsibilities to my government. And I understand that I am to participate in the political process.

"But what position do I take? Should I be a Christian right-winger or a Christian left-winger? Should I be a liberal or a conservative? Should I be a Democrat or a Republican? Or doesn't it matter?"

Or you may be asking, Is there a biblical position on abortion? Is there a biblical approach to capital punishment? Is there a biblical way to deal with Communism?

I believe there is. Many of these subjects are not specifically mentioned in Scripture, though some are. But there are biblical principles that apply to all of them, and from these we can formulate a scriptural position.

Lots of people become very sensitive when we speak of a biblical position on political issues. If I describe a certain position as the biblical view, some people think I am saying that those who do not hold this view are not good Christians. A few qualifications are therefore necessary.

By describing a political viewpoint as biblical, I am *not* implying that those who believe otherwise are any less Christian, any more than I would call someone less Christian simply because he does not share my view of baptism, eternal security, or the proper interpretation of the sons of God of Genesis 6:2-4. All I am saying is that on that particular issue his position is contrary to that of the Word of God as I understand it.

Nor do I deny that God uses Christians in the political arena even though (or perhaps because) their views differ from mine. One of the great strengths of Christianity is that it can flourish under any conditions, and the wisdom of the sovereign plan of God is that he can and does use believers whose political views and affiliations differ radically from those of other Christians.

Should the fact that Bible-believing Christians disagree on baptism, or eternal security, or eschatology prevent us from looking to God's Word and formulating a position on these theological questions? Of course not! And the mere fact that Bible-believing Christians don't always agree on politics does not mean we shouldn't look to the Bible for basic principles to formulate positions on political issues.

Nevertheless, this probably should cause us to assert our views with less dogmatism. While God's Word is perfect and infallible, our interpretations of God's Word are not, and our applications of his Word are even more subject to error. We should therefore be open to the possibility that we have not rightly divided the Word of God and have not correctly apprehended the whole counsel of God. If you find yourself at odds with a fellow-Christian over a political issue, don't make a holy war out of it. Rather, offer to sit down with him and study together what God's Word has to say about the issue, and see if you can come to a common position. If not, simply agree to disagree.

Liberals and Conservatives

You can't read much about politics without running across the terms *liberal* and *conservative*. These labels are used to describe the ideological stance of politicians.

Many dislike these labels, saying they are misleading and poorly defined or tend to stereotype. (Often those who object most strongly are congressmen with liberal voting records who are up for reelection in conservative districts!)

These labels are of limited value. For one thing, the terms mean different things at different times. A century ago those who called themselves liberal favored an unbridled free enterprise system with a minimum of government interference. Today conservatives are the defenders of free enterprise, whereas liberals seek more government regulation of the economy.

Nor do these labels have the same meaning from country to country. In Canada the Liberal Party and the Conservative Party stand for liberalism and conservatism much as the terms are understood in the United States. But in many countries, especially in northern Europe, the Conservative Party stands for a rather watered-down version of the welfare state. And the policies we associate with conservatism are represented by the Liberal Party in Denmark, Italy, and Switzerland, the Liberal-Democratic Party in Japan, and the Liberal Socialist Party in Egypt.

We should also remember that *liberal* and *conservative* are relative terms. For example, compared to many Republicans like President Reagan, Senator Mark Hatfield is a liberal. But compared to leading liberal Democrats like former Vice-President Walter Mondale or Senator Edward Kennedy, Hatfield is a conservative.

Also, the fact that one is a liberal on one issue does not necessarily mean he is a liberal on every issue. The late Senator Henry Jackson, for example, was quite liberal on most domestic issues, but since he favored a strong national defense he was usually allied with conservatives on defense issues. On defense matters Jackson was much more conservative than Hatfield, but on most other issues Hatfield was more conservative than Jackson.

With these qualifications in mind, the terms do have value in describing the political positions of our leaders. And while there are many exceptions, those who take the liberal position on some issues generally take the liberal position on other issues, as do conservatives, for there is a certain ideological consistency in each viewpoint. Liberals usually share certain premises which lead to certain conclusions, and since conservatives usually share opposite premises, they come to opposite conclusions.

Unfortunately the terms are too often used without careful definition. Some have said that liberals favor change, while conservatives want to stand still. That is only partially true. Conservatives usually oppose radical change because it tends to destabilize society. One reason Latin America has failed to develop as rapidly as North America has undoubtedly been the lack of stable governments in that area. But there are many proposed changes that conservatives support and liberals oppose. For example, President Reagan proposed a "New Federalism" under which many federal programs are to be turned over to the states or eliminated entirely. Conservatives generally support these changes, while liberals are fighting to keep the status quo.

Others say that conservatives favor individual freedom, while liberals want more government control. Again that is only partially true. Conservatives generally oppose government regulation of business, farming, and other economic spheres, believing necessary regulation of these areas should come mostly at the state and local levels. But in other areas such as law enforcement and national security, conservatives have generally advocated more government authority while liberals have feared government excesses in these areas.

What, then, are the definitive differences between liberalism and conservatism? I believe there are several.

Human nature. Government is inevitably involved with people. Consequently one's view of human nature affects one's theory of government. And here is the most basic difference between liberals and conservatives: liberals generally believe human nature is basically good, while conservatives believe human nature is basically bad. Furthermore, liberals believe human nature can be improved given the right environmental stimuli (which government can supply), while conservatives believe human nature is basically unchanging and unchangeable. Christian conservatives are likely to say that there is little prospect for improving human nature save through the grace of God; secular conservatives are likely to say that there is little prospect for improving human nature, period.

Social programs. Because they believe the nature of man is basically bad, conservatives regard men as mostly self-serving. For this reason, they have more faith than liberals in the ability and desire of men and women to take care of themselves and their families. For the same reason, they have less faith than liberals in the ability of people to run the lives of other people. Conservatives therefore tend to support the family as the basic structure for meeting people's needs, and they tend to be very skeptical of government programs for welfare and economic regulation. Conversely, liberals are more likely to support such programs.

Government power. Again because they have a low view of human nature, conservatives are suspicious of government power. Knowing that political leaders are sinners just like the rest of us, they oppose too much concentration of power in the hands of any individual or group. Rather, they favor limiting government power; and the powers that must be given to government should be separated among executive, legislative, and judicial branches and divided among federal, state, and local levels. Furthermore, they fear too much power concentrated in the hands of an intolerant majority as well; therefore they favor a limited constitutional republic rather than a pure democracy.

Law of nature. Conservatives are more likely than liberals to believe that society should be governed according to certain laws of nature. Christian conservatives identify the law of nature with the law of God (as have Burke, Locke, Blackstone, Jefferson, and many others); secular conservatives see the law of nature as inherent in the natural scheme of things but are vague as to its origin or effect. Consequently conservatives think of natural rights and laws as God-given absolutes, while liberals are more likely to think in utilitarian terms of the greatest good for the greatest number.

Role of government. Conservatives believe government should generally confine itself to its traditional functions, defined by Adam Smith as national defense, preservation of law and order, and "those public institutions and those public works, which, though they may be in the highest degree advantageous to a great society, are however of such a nature, that the profit could never repay the expense to any individual, or small number of individuals,"[1] such as national parks, public roads, sewage systems, garbage collection, etc. Liberals are more likely to favor government intervention in other spheres of human endeavor, such as economic regulation, education, welfare, etc. The reason goes deeper: conservatives regard the state as the result of either a divine covenant or a social contract[2] by which government is limited to certain functions, whereas liberals generally follow the view of Auguste Comte that the state is a living, growing, and evolving organism.

One friendly reviewer, after examining the rough draft of this book, suggested that I am fundamentally wrong in limiting the role of government to the protection of human rights and liberties. Rather, he suggested, the role of government should include the promotion of virtue, morality, and community, for no society can function effectively without these qualities.

I agree that these qualities are essential for a well-run society, and probably for national survival. Without a firm foundation of love, virtue, morality, and community, even the best political structures will be distorted and abused. But I question whether the promotion of these qualities is the proper function of government. When government is charged with the *promotion* of such positive qualities as love and morality, it is charged also with the *definition* of these qualities— and in their definition and enforcement the potential for abuse and tyranny is unlimited.

I suggest that it is better and in the long run more effective to delegate the responsibility for developing the qualities of love, morality, virtue, and community to voluntary associations within the society—civic and professional organizations, charities, youth clubs, educational institutions, but most especially the church.

Equity or equality? Though conservatives believe that men are to be considered equal in the sight of God, certain inequalities in the economic sphere are not only inevitable but even just and desirable. Those who work harder or have more ability or contribute more or assume more responsibility should enjoy greater economic rewards than those who do less. Liberals are more likely to favor equality.

Property rights. Conservatives champion the right of persons to own property and use it as they see fit. Liberals argue that human rights are more important than property rights and that property rights should be subordinated to the common good. Conservatives answer that the right to own property is just as much a human right as any other right.

Opposition to Communism. Conservatives find themselves philosophically opposed to Communism on every point: the improvability of human nature, the role of government, the theory of the state, government power, economic equality, individual freedom, property rights, radical change. Liberals likewise oppose Communism on many points, especially in its excesses; but because they identify with many of the professed goals of Communism, such as economic equality and relief of suffering, they are more likely to apologize for its failures. Always wanting to believe the best about people, liberals want to believe Communist leaders when they claim they want detente or are merely "agrarian reformers," while conservatives are much more skeptical about such claims. Consequently conservatives are generally more concerned than liberals about the Communist threat to America and are more willing than liberals to support a strong national defense and other national security measures to protect our nation against the Communists.

So what position should the Christian take? We will analyze that on an issue-by-issue basis in the following chapters. Speaking in general terms though, I find that the conservative view of human nature—that man is basically self-serving—is consistent with the biblical view of original sin (Romans 3:10, 23), whereas the liberal view that men are good or at least capable of improvement is not. The conservative view of the law of nature is consistent with the biblical view of the law of God, and Augustine, Aquinas, Luther, Calvin, Locke, Blackstone, Jefferson, and many others have linked the two. The conservative view of the limited purpose and authority of the state is consistent with the biblical view of government, whereas the liberal view of the organic state has no support in Scripture. Since I share the basic premises of conservatism, I personally find myself taking the conservative position on most issues.

Left and Right

Closely related to liberalism and conservatism—and used with even less precision—are the terms *left* and *right*. The terms originated in the Parliament of France where, shortly after the French Revolution, the representatives of the liberal Jacobins sat on the left side of the aisle, and those of the more conservative Girondists sat on the right side. Ever since, left has meant liberal and right has meant conservative.

But left and right go beyond liberalism and conservatism to include extremes on both sides. As the spectrum is commonly perceived today, liberals are slightly to the left of center and conservatives slightly to the right. Somewhat further to the left are the various shades of Socialism and on the extreme left are the Communists. At the opposite extreme, on the far right, are the Nazis and Fascists.

LEFT _____RIGHT

Communism   Socialism   liberalism   conservatism   fascism,
                                                        Nazism

I believe this spectrum is misleading, for Nazism has nothing to do
with traditional conservatism. The term *Nazi* is a contraction of National Socialist. Every principle of Nazism is diametrically opposed to
traditional conservatism—the concentration of power in the hands of
one man or group of men, contempt for the law of nature, violation of
property rights and other natural rights, radical rather than gradual
change. Both in theory and in practice, Nazism is much closer to
Communism than to conservatism, and in practice Nazism and Communism are almost impossible to distinguish. Despite his anti-Communist rhetoric, Hitler did not hesitate to make a pact with Stalin; and
after World War II hundreds of former Nazi officials took important
positions in the Communist government of East Germany.[3]

Many have suggested that the spectrum should be conceptualized as
a circle instead of a straight line, with the two extremes coming
together.

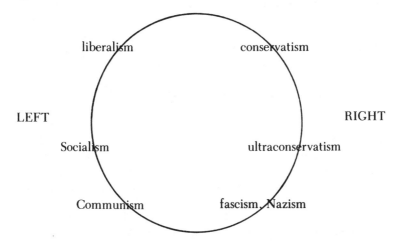

This is better, but there is another means of conceptualizing the
ideological spectrum which makes even more sense. We can chart
each ideology according to the extent to which it advocates the regulation of the lives of individual citizens. On the extreme right is anarchy,
which advocates no government at all. Next is libertarianism (much
different from liberalism), which shares many of the free enterprise
economic principles of conservatism but does not share the conservative emphasis on law and order and national security. Next comes

traditional conservatism, then liberalism and, as we move further left, Socialism. Finally, on the extreme left, we find the totalitarian systems which seek total control over the individual, such as Communism, Nazism, and fascism:

LEFT _____RIGHT
    totalitarianism: Socialism liberalism conservatism libertarianism anarchy
    Communism
    Nazism
    fascism

While this seems the most sensible way to picture the ideological spectrum, the first diagram represents the way it is conceived in most public communication today.

Democrats and Republicans
Throughout American history our country has operated on a two-party system. The Republican Party was founded by antislavery forces shortly before the Civil War and is descended from the Whigs and, before them, the Federalists. The Democratic Party is somewhat older, dating back to the Democratic Republican Party of Thomas Jefferson.

Third parties have had an impact on American history, such as Theodore Roosevelt's Bullmoose Party, Strom Thurmond's States' Rights Party, George Wallace's American Independent Party, and, in the 1980 election, the Libertarian Party of Ed Clark and the independent candidacy of John Anderson. But people have usually found that the best way to have a real impact on national policy is to work through one of the two major parties that run the country, the Democrats or the Republicans.

It is often said that there's not a dime's worth of difference between the two parties. However, I believe there is a considerable difference. In most parts of the country, the Republican Party is considerably more conservative. Certainly there are liberal Republicans and conservative Democrats, and all shades in between. But an analysis of the 1980 platforms of the two major parties shows dramatic differences between the two major parties:[4]

Table 11.1
National Party Platforms In 1980

Issue	Republican Party	Democratic Party
Abortion	Favored constitutional amendment to ban abortion. Favored appointment of antiabortion judges.	Opposed antiabortion amendment. Opposed restrictions on funding abortions.

Equal Rights Amendment	No stand on ratification. Opposed boycott of states that have not ratified ERA.	Favored ratification. Favored boycott.
Strategic Arms Limitation Agreement.	Opposed arms control agreement that would "lock the U.S. into position of military inferiority."	Favored ratification of SALT II.
Health Care	Opposed socialized medicine.	Favored comprehensive national health insurance.
Economy	Stressed reducing inflation, cutting jobs, creating jobs through private sector.	Favored $12 billion federal program to create 80,000 jobs.
Welfare	Opposed federalizing welfare system. Favored restrictions on food stamp eligibility. Opposed guaranteed annual income.	Favored federalizing welfare system. Favored income floor for working poor.
Gun Control	No position.	Favored gun control.
School Prayer	Favored voluntary school prayer.	No position.
Child Care	No position.	Favored national child care system.
Homosexuals	No position.	Favored laws protecting homosexuals from discrimination.
Capital Punishment	Supported capital punishment for some crimes.	No position.
Regulation	Condemned overregulation by federal government.	No position.
Drugs	Advocated crackdown on drugs.	No position.

Granted, these platforms contain much air and lots of politicians disregard them as soon as they take office. Sometimes this is necessary; changed conditions sometimes require change in the game plan. In general however, Republican officeholders tend to vote more conservatively than Democratic officeholders.

Several national organizations rate congressmen according to their voting records. The American Conservative Union, for example, selects certain key issues and rates each congressman as to what percentage of the time he votes the "conservative" position. A "perfect" conservative score, as the ACU sees it, is 100 percent; a perfect liberal voting record would rate a 0 percent.

Conversely, several liberal groups such as the Americans for Democratic Action, the AFL-CIO's Committee on Political Education (COPE), and the League of Women Voters also rate the voting records of congressmen, and their ratings reflect the extent to which the congressman conforms to the liberal position. A congressman who receives a 100 percent from the American Conservative Union is likely to receive a 0 percent rating from the Americans for Democratic Action, and vice versa. However, this does not always follow with mathematical precision because the organizations don't always select the same issues by which to rate the congressmen.

These ratings clearly show a sharp difference between Republican and Democratic officeholders. In 1980, for example, the American Conservative Union's ratings of the United States Senate showed Republican Senators averaging 65 percent and Democratic Senators averaging 22 percent. There were many exceptions, however; Democratic Senators Ed Zorinsky of Nebraska scored 70 percent and David Boren of Oklahoma scored 67 percent, while Republican Senators Lowell Weiker of Connecticut scored only 20 percent, Charles Mathias of Maryland only 7 percent, and Jacob Javits of New York received a 0 percent.[5] On the average, though, Republicans are more conservative than Democrats.

It is unwise to blindly vote for a candidate simply because of his party affiliation, as both parties contain good and bad people. But your political effectiveness will be severely limited if you do not select a party.

So which party should you join? The truth is, everyone has to make this decision for himself. I personally feel that, in the places where I have lived, the Republican Party is more compatible with the biblical principles of government as I perceive them than is the Democratic Party. This is my decision—I am not saying all Christians must come to the same view.

I did *not* say God is a registered Republican, or that the Antichrist will be a Democrat. I didn't say Republicans are God's elect, or that Democrats won't go to heaven unless they repent. I have simply expressed my own commitment politically. You will have to decide for yourself.

In some parts of the country, particularly in the South and Southwest, the Democratic Party is much more conservative than in the North and Northeast, and even in these areas there is much local variation. Also, studies have indicated that the Democratic rank and file is considerably more conservative than the Democratic leadership.

Perhaps you have family, business, or social connections that make it easier for you to work effectively in one party than in another. Possibly you feel that one party has greater need of your influence than the other—though this is often wishful thinking that leads to wasted efforts on a fruitless cause.

At any rate, it is up to you to decide for yourself, after careful study and prayer.

12   *Liberty and Power*

In Independence Hall in Philadelphia stands the Liberty Bell, symbol of American freedom. Emblazoned across the Liberty Bell is a quotation from Scripture: "Proclaim liberty throughout all the land unto all the inhabitants thereof" (Leviticus 25:10). Together the bell and the Scripture symbolize our nation's commitment to freedom and the divine source of that freedom.

Liberty is presented in Scripture as a gift from God. "Where the Spirit of the Lord is, there is liberty" (2 Corinthians 3:17). The term normally means freedom from bondage or servitude. In the spiritual sense this means freedom from bondage to sin and Satan (John 8:34; Romans 8:21). In the political sense it means freedom from slavery or servanthood (Leviticus 25:10) or national freedom from a foreign power (Jeremiah 34:13, 17). In the biblical sense freedom does not mean the right to do whatever one pleases without any restraint whatever; rather, it means the liberty to make one's own decisions before God without restraint by government.

Political freedom has been and is unknown in many parts of the world at most times in history. Periods of freedom are rare, and usually they are short-lived. They usually accompany Christianity.

This is no accident. The biblical view of man and the state provides a basis for political freedom, whereas most world views do not. As we have already seen, the biblical view of government is that the state has only limited authority; there are many areas of human activity that are beyond the state's jurisdiction.

Also, the Bible views man as possessing certain basic human rights, bestowed upon him by the God who created him and gave him human dignity. The negative commands of the Bible are based upon positive rights. When the Bible forbids murder, it protects the right to life.

When the Bible forbids man-stealing, it protects the right to liberty. When the Bible forbids stealing, it protects the right to property. These rights are absolute and cannot be abridged by government. Jefferson put it well in the Declaration of Independence when he referred to the "Laws of Nature and of Nature's God." He went on to say that "all men are created [note he didn't say "evolved"] equal," that "they are endowed by their Creator with certain unalienable Rights," that "among these are Life, Liberty and the pursuit of Happiness." Note the source of human rights according to Jefferson—the Creator!

Furthermore, physical or political liberty is meaningless without spiritual liberty. If man is not a spiritual creature, no real liberty is possible. If man is purely physical, then he is entirely subject to the physical laws of cause and effect, his heredity, and his environment, and he is no more capable of freedom or meaningful choices than an ape or a computer. As Whittaker Chambers said so eloquently,

> Freedom is a need of the soul, and nothing else. It is in striving toward God that the soul strives continually after a condition of freedom. God alone is the inciter and guarantor of freedom. He is the only guarantor. External freedom is only an aspect of interior freedom. Political freedom, as the Western world has known it, is only a political reading of the Bible. Religion and freedom are indivisible. Without freedom the soul dies. Without the soul there is no justification for freedom.[1]

Humanism, for all its talk about freedom, can present no philosophical framework to justify freedom. On what basis do we say that the state is limited if God himself has not limited it? How can we say that men have human rights if they are not bestowed upon him by his Creator? Do amphibians have rights? Apes? Neanderthals? Zinjanthropus or Ramapithecus? And how can political freedom be meaningful if man is merely programmed by his environment and lacks the capacity to enjoy and appreciate freedom? When—in the name of freedom!—the humanists tear away the Christian foundations of this country, they actually destroy the only philosophical foundation upon which true freedom can be sustained.

And yet, desirable though it may be, liberty needs restraint. One might think that anarchy involves total freedom, but in reality it involves the total destruction of freedom. For without restraint men will destroy one another's freedom by killing each other, stealing from one another, enslaving one another, and exploiting one another. The reason, quite obviously, is the basic human condition: sin.

To restrain men's sin natures and safeguard human freedom, governments are established. To be effective, governments have to have power. But governmental power has to be restrained, for the same reason that individual liberty has to be restrained—the fact of sin. For rulers are just as sinful as their subjects. Given absolute and unrestrained power, they will use that power in corrupt and despotic ways. As Lord Acton put it, power tends to corrupt, and absolute power corrupts absolutely. Jefferson recognized this in his first inaugural address:

> Sometimes it is said that man cannot be trusted with the government of himself. Can he, then, be trusted with the government of others? Or have we found angels in the forms of kings to govern him? Let history answer this question.[2]

James Madison, who probably inspired the Constitution more than any other single person, echoed a similar theme:

> But what is government itself but the greatest of all reflections on human nature? If men were angels, no government would be necessary. If angels were to govern men, neither external nor internal controls on government would be necessary. In framing a government which is to be administered by men over men, the great difficulty lies in this: You must first enable the government to control the governed; and in the next place, oblige it to control itself.[3]

Our Puritan forefathers were well aware of the need to limit government power. They came from a Calvinist tradition; the oldest who crossed the Atlantic on the Mayflower was born about 1565, the year after Calvin died. As Calvinists, they believed very strongly in total depravity and original sin. And the doctrine of total depravity is a great leveler, for it means rulers are just as depraved as common people. The Puritan clergyman John Cotton articulated this fear of power when he said,

> It's necessary, therefore, that all power that is on earth be limited, church-power or other. . . . It's counted a matter of danger to the state to limit prerogatives; but it is a further danger not to have them limited; they will be like a tempest if they be not limited. . . . It is therefore fit for every man to be studious of the bounds which the Lord hath set; and for the people, in whom fundamentally all power lies, to give as much power as God in His word gives to men. . . . All intrenchment upon the bounds which God hath not given, they are not enlargements, but burdens and snares.[4]

The brilliant men who gathered at Independence Hall in Philadelphia in 1787 and drafted the Constitution faced a difficult dilemma. On one hand, they knew all too well the dangers of unrestrained government power. Their bitter experience with the King of England has shown them that!

But on the other hand, the chaos of America's first few years of independence under the Articles of Confederation had shown them the problem of too little government power. The states were quarreling with one another over boundaries and fishing rights and were charging one another customs and tariffs on imports and exports. The fledgling nation faced depression and inflation which caused rioting in some places. There was danger from Spain on the west and England to the north, and New England was threatening to secede from the Union. Clearly some form of stronger central government was needed. But how could the government be made strong enough to accomplish its necessary purposes, yet sufficiently restrained so as not to endanger individual freedom?

Lord Acton has noted that the framers of our Constitution solved this dilemma, the greatest dilemma facing political theorists for centuries, with greater ease than anyone else in history. They did so—and this is the key to understanding the real genius of the American Constitution—by *separating and dividing the powers of government among various individuals and groups, so that no one individual or group had too much power.*

First, they employed a separation of powers among the various branches of government: legislative, executive, and judicial. To safeguard this separation of powers, they inserted various checks and balances, by which each branch would limit the power of other branches. The President, for example, can veto acts of Congress, subject to being overridden by a two-thirds vote of both houses of Congress. Congress must advise and consent to the appointment of the President's chief officers. The Supreme Court can declare acts of Congress and actions of the President unconstitutional, but Supreme Court justices are appointed by the President, subject to confirmation by the Senate.

Do you see the biblical view of man's sin nature at work here? Each branch, jealous of its own power, battles against encroachments of power by the other branches. That's the way the framers intended it.

The framers also worked into the Constitution a vertical division of powers. Certain powers were delegated to the federal government; others were reserved to the states. They intended that the states would resist encroachments of power by Washington. They made it clear that the federal government had only such limited powers as were delegated to it by the Constitution, and that any powers not delegated to the federal government were reserved to the states. Lest any doubt exist that that was their intent, they made it clear for all time by passing the Tenth Amendment:

> The powers not delegated to the United States by the Constitution, nor prohibited by it to the States, are reserved to the States respectively, or to the people.

This Tenth Amendment is not a "dead letter" or "redundancy," as many liberal constitutional scholars suggest today; rather, it is the key to understanding and interpreting the Constitution. It means that unless a certain power is expressly or impliedly delegated to the federal government by the Constitution, the federal government does not have that power.

Also, the framers recognized in the Constitution that citizens possess certain individual rights, be they in the majority or in the minority, rights which no government can abridge or take away (rights to freedom of religion and freedom of speech, right to privacy from illegal search and seizure, right to trial by jury, and many others). These rights apply to all citizens, whether they are popular or unpopular, many or few. Government cannot abridge these rights, even if every member of Congress voted to do so and Gallup Polls showed that 99 percent of the public supported that action. The Supreme Court, if it is doing its job properly, would strike that action down as unconstitutional.

In other words, the framers were careful that no individual or group received too much power—even the people as a whole! They never intended that the United States should be a pure, direct democracy in which the majority can do anything it pleases. Rather, they intended a constitutional republic in which the rights of the majority are protected from the tyranny of the majority, and the rights of the minority are protected from the tyranny of the majority. They placed the Constitution, not the people, as the supreme law of the land.

As the Constitutional Convention adjourned, a woman asked Benjamin Franklin, "What sort of government have you given us?" "A republic," Franklin replied, "if you can keep it." The framers were realists; they recognized that the best constitution in the world could be distorted and destroyed by men determined to do so. They knew that this delicate balance between freedom and power had to be carefully maintained, lest it be lost.

I sincerely believe that this basic concept of ordered liberty is in grave danger today. Let me mention a few of the forces that threaten it.

Denial of God-given rights. As we have seen, the framers of our Constitution believed very strongly in the "Laws of Nature and of Nature's God," as Jefferson put it in the Declaration of Independence. They believed that men have rights, not because government has chosen to grant certain rights, but because God has created man with human dignity and has bestowed upon him certain basic rights as part of that human dignity. The purpose of government is to *"secure* these rights" (again quoting the Declaration of Independence), not grant them.

Within the last century, however, a school of thought has arisen that denies the existence of any law of nature or natural rights. Men have rights, if at all, only because society accords them certain rights. Men have only such rights as governments, and particularly judges, choose to accord them. The *rights* of the individual can be sacrificed whenever the *needs* of the majority, as determined by the state, require it. This school of thought, known as legal positivism, dominates legal education today as well as much of the academic and intellectual community. Closely linked with humanism, this school of thought has no basis for believing in individual rights or individual freedom. Obviously freedom cannot last long in such an intellectual climate.

Organic view of the state. Classical political philosophers viewed the state as the result of either a social contract, or a divine delegation of authority, or both. It was static, having certain limited powers that remained constant through the ages.

Under the influence of Jean-Jacques Rousseau, Auguste Comte, Charles Darwin, Herbert Spencer, and others a new view of the state has developed. Instead of a social contract or a divine institution, the state according to this view is an organism, and like all organisms it evolves. It assumes new functions, grows steadily more complex, and gets bigger and bigger.

As it does so, it increasingly intrudes upon individual freedom. The more the government regulates, the less room is left for individual choice. And as government grows, it requires more and more taxes. Taking all taxes together, federal, state and local, the average citizen pays approximately 42 percent of his income in taxes. That means for the first five months of every year, he works not for himself but for the government!

Growing federal power. While all levels of government are mushrooming in size, none is growing as fast as the federal government. In fact, in 1981 the federal government had three million civilian employees. Contrast that with a total of 350 when George Washington took office in 1789!

More and more functions are being transferred to the federal government. All too often liberal judges on the courts justify this federalization by ignoring the Tenth Amendment and giving a distorted meaning to other clauses of the Constitution such as the commerce clause and the general welfare clause. Not only is this unwise; it is downright dangerous in light of the biblical understanding of human sin and the perversion of government power. It is difficult to check abuses of power by the states, but it is not impossible; they are closer to the people, and they are less powerful than the federal government. But let the federal government become supreme and you will unleash a monster that no one can control. Those who share the biblical understanding of man will want to preserve all checks against excessive government power.

Eroding separation of powers. The framers' ingenius system of separation of powers is being eroded today. Each branch of the federal government is usurping powers that rightfully belong to others; and all too often the other branches simply stand by and let it happen.

One example is the growing tendency toward judicial activism. Instead of simply interpreting statutes, judges fashion all sorts of remedies (for example, complicated busing schemes) for current social crises. This is beyond their authority. They should simply interpret the law and pass judgment on its constitutionality.

Courts go beyond "plain meaning" interpretations, giving laws and even constitutional provisions new and innovative meanings that their authors never dreamed of—because the changing needs of society, in the courts' view, require it. Chief Justice Earl Warren spoke of "evolving standards of decency" by which the Eighth Amendment is to be interpreted,[5] and President Woodrow Wilson, seeking "progressive" legislation, asked the court "to interpret the Constitution according to the Darwinian principle."[6] One is reminded of Humpty Dumpty in Lewis Carroll's *Through the Looking Glass:* "When I use a word, it means exactly what I want it to mean, no more and no less."

This is wrong! Courts should interpret the law according to the plain meaning of the authors. If the law is out of date, it should be amended by the legislature; if the Constitution is out of date, it should be amended by the legitimate constitutional process. When the courts change the laws on their own initiative, they are legislating, and the framers of the Constitution never intended them to do that. Christians should ask their elected representatives to appoint judges who appreciate the limits of their power and practice judicial restraint.

Growth of administrative law. Another danger is the proliferation of administrative agencies with their myriad bureaucrats, regulations, etc. Nominally under the executive branch, many of these are in practice beyond the President's control and are unelected czars, answerable to practically no one. And so they go their merry way, issuing order and promulgating regulations ostensibly for the betterment of society.

As a result, within the last few decades a whole new field of law has emerged—administrative law. Many of these agencies have their own tribunals, court systems that hold regular trials and even impose civil penalties. This violates the very concept of separation of powers!

I do not believe the Constitution is divinely inspired or inerrant. But I am convinced that it is the best document yet devised by man for preserving freedom and allocating power. As Christians, let us always honor and defend it.

13 Wealth and Poverty

Remember the Lord thy God: for it is he that giveth thee power to get wealth. (Deuteronomy 8:18)

The typical American Christian is an economic conservative with a guilty conscience.

This is because he hears so much conflicting information about his Christian responsibilities in this area that he doesn't know what to do. He halfheartedly believes in free enterprise because it's the American way and therefore Christian (sort of), and he practices the Puritan work ethic without becoming a workaholic. He earns enough to take care of himself and his family, and mildly resents those who live off the government. But he is reluctant to oppose welfare programs, because he knows he has a Christian duty to help the poor, and he doesn't want to be caught with Cain, saying, "Am I my brother's keeper?" While he abhors Communism, isn't there something in the Bible that says the early Christians practiced Communism? So he goes his confused way, his innate conservatism preventing him from embracing a radical stance, his conscience telling him that maybe he should.

Much confusion could be eliminated if Christians would listen to the Word of God instead of the words of men. I have said many times in this book, but it bears repeating again: *a viewpoint is neither Christian nor moral unless it can be supported, directly or indirectly, by the Word of God properly interpreted and properly applied.*

So what does the Bible say about wealth and poverty? Let's have a look.

The Biblical View of Property

Throughout much of history there has been a persistent, nagging attitude that property and material things in general are evil. This view may have its source in the gnostic heresies of the early centuries of Christendom. Among other things, the gnostics taught that the universe is divided into spirit and matter, spirit being good while matter is bad. Property, wealth, luxury are sinful; therefore the more you disdain material things, the more spiritual you are.

This is not the biblical view. Not everything spiritual is good (Satan and his demons are spirits). Also, material things are not evil in themselves. God created all material things, and he pronounced them good (Genesis 1:4, 10, 12, 18, 21, 25, 31). Material things are not as good as they used to be, for they are increasingly corrupted by the Fall; but God created them good.

Why did God create matter? One obvious reason is that he knew we would need material things for our sustenance and comfort; consequently he gave man dominion over material things (Genesis 1:26-31). Material things, in other words, have utilitarian value.

Another purpose of God in creating matter was to show forth his creative personality. By looking at his handiwork we can learn a great deal about God. Even though creation is not as perfect as it used to be, we still see in creation the beauty, design, purpose, orderliness, and majesty of God. Psalm 19:1-3 tells us, "The heavens declare the glory of God; and the firmament showeth his handiwork," and Romans 1:20 reminds us that everyone can see the eternal power and deity of God through creation. Jesus used the ravens and the lilies of the field as object lessons of God's bountiful provision (Luke 12:22-30).

We value property for the same reasons. Certainly material things have utilitarian value for us. More than that, however, they are expressions of our creative intelligence. Obviously this is true of the work of art I paint, the song I compose, or the book I write. It is just as true of the house I build. And it is not only true of the things we make with our own hands or minds; it is also true of the things we buy. The way we decorate our homes, the cars we drive, the clothes we wear—all of these reflect our creative intelligence; all of these are extensions of our personalities.

I have always preferred my suits with a Western styling, but until recently I couldn't figure out why. I own a small acreage of pastureland which I occasionally rent out for cattle pasture, and I enjoy living in the country, but by no stretch of the imagination could I be called a cowboy. I don't own any cattle, and don't ask me to brand a steer, because I don't know how! But I finally realized that Western suits and cowboy boots are my means of expressing my personality.

I really hadn't felt the need to express myself in that way until I became a lawyer. Then I found myself inwardly rebelling against the image of what a lawyer is supposed to be. Sophisticated, citified, dressed in fancy three-piece suits and ties—that just isn't me! I'm an independent and adventuresome person, one who enjoys backpacking, canoeing, horseback riding, snowshoeing, cross-country skiing, and other such things. And I identify with those things, even if my hectic schedule doesn't always allow me to enjoy them as much as I'd like. My Western suits, I finally realized, are my way of telling the city and the legal profession that they haven't fully gotten control of me yet. And I doubt that they ever will!

Property also represents our feelings about ourselves and other persons. When you give a gift to someone, you give a message to that person. You say something about the way you feel about him or her, both by the fact that you have given him a gift, and by the particular gift you have selected for him.

God's Word forbids treating our property cavalierly, as though it were meaningless junk. Property is from God and is to be valued. Frequently in his parables, such as that of the pearl of great price or the lost sheep or lost coin, Jesus used a principle his listeners would readily accept—the value people place on physical things—to demonstrate the greater value we should place on spiritual things such as the kingdom of God and lost souls. Two parables (the talents and the unjust steward) show that we are to value property and treat it carefully. The very commandment "Thou shalt not steal" was given because property has value. The Old Testament contains many laws concerning trespassing on property, theft and restitution, etc.

Nevertheless, the value of property needs to be kept in perspective. Clothing and other physical things are an expression of one's personality, but should never be a substitute for it. And they must never be deemed more important than spiritual things. My wife recalls an evening when she assisted the victims of an apartment house fire. No one was killed or injured, but many were anguished as they watched their earthly possessions go up in smoke. Some acted as though the world was coming to an end, when they should have rejoiced that they and their loved ones were safe. As she watched them and tried to comfort them, my wife thought of Matthew 6:19-21:

> Lay not up for yourselves treasures upon earth, where moth and rust doth corrupt, and where thieves break through and steal: but lay up for yourselves treasures in heaven, where neither moth nor rust doth corrupt, and where thieves do not break through nor steal: for where your treasure is, there will your heart be also.

Obviously what is needed is a balanced view, one that values property but does not place property above God or above people, one that recognizes the usefulness of property but does not look to property for ultimate security.

Someone will ask, "But doesn't the Bible say money is the root of all evil?" Not exactly. Paul says in 1 Timothy 6:10 that "The *love* of money is the root of all evil." (The literal Greek reading is "a" root, not "the" root.) The problem is not money, but our attitude toward money. The rich young ruler went away sorrowfully, without accepting Christ, not just because he had great possessions, but because he loved those possessions more than he loved God (Matthew 19:16-26; Mark 10:17-27; Luke 18:18-27). Others in the New Testament had great wealth, men such as Nicodemus and Joseph of Arimathea. Their wealth, however, did not prevent them from becoming Christians, because they had the proper attitude toward it.

Property Ownership—Individual or State?

As we have seen, the commandment "Thou shalt not steal" (Exodus 20:15) is based on the assumption that property has value, and that some people have rights to certain property that are superior to the rights of other people toward that same property. The reason I cannot steal someone's else's property is that his right to that property is superior to mine.

But does the commandment really establish private ownership of property? Could it not also prohibit stealing the property of the state or the commune? A literal reading of the commandment does make that possible, but the historical context makes it highly unlikely since state property or communal property did not exist in Israel at that time.

The last of the Ten Commandments, however, clearly establishes private ownership of property:

> Thou shalt not covet thy neighbor's house, thou shalt not covet thy neighbor's wife, nor his manservant, nor his maidservant, nor his ox, nor his ass, nor any thing that is thy neighbor's. (Exodus 20:17)

Old Testament Israel had a unique system of ownership of real estate, owing to the unique relationship to their land based on the Abrahamic, Mosaic, and Davidic covenants. God had promised the land of Palestine to Israel forever; and to preserve it for Israel in perpetuity he gave special commands that the land was not to be sold to foreigners. To ensure that the various tribes kept their allotted areas in the Promised Land, land was given to the tribes and thereafter divided according to clans and families. Land ownership was in the family, not the individual. The individual could not sell the land "for ever" (Leviticus 25:23); he could only sell a right to use the land for a limited period of time, until the next year of Jubilee. Every seventh year was the Sabbath year, and after every seventh Sabbath, or once every fifty years, came the year of Jubilee in which all indentured servants were freed and all real estate reverted to the rightful family of ownership (Leviticus 25:23-28). In this way the land was to be kept in Israelite hands and the covenant of God fulfilled. This, however, is owing to Israel's unique relationship with the land under her covenant with God. It is not normative for other societies.

In almost every respect except real estate, Israel practiced private ownership of property. Much of the Mosaic law sets forth principles for compensation for the loss or damage of someone else's property (see especially Exodus 21 and 22). In fact, private ownership of property predates the Mosaic law by thousands of years; Abraham and Job were men of property (Genesis 13:2; 23:5-20; Job 1:3; 42:12). The Mosaic law simply assumes private ownership of property as the natural order of things, and is structured to safeguard property rights.

Jesus used the principles of private property ownership in his parables, such as that of the vineyard, the unjust steward, the talents, the lost sheep and lost coin, and the pearl of great price. Private property will be the order of the day even during the Millennium:

> And they shall build houses, and inhabit them; and they shall plant vineyards, and eat the fruit of them. They shall not build, and another inhabit; they shall not plant, and another eat: for as the days of a tree are the days of my people, and mine elect shall long enjoy the work of their hands. (Isaiah 65:21, 22)

Private property, then, is the natural order from beginning to end, is sanctioned by the Mosaic law, and is implicitly recognized by Jesus. Ultimately, of course, all property belongs to God. "The earth is the Lord's, and the fulness thereof" (Psalm 24:1). But with few exceptions he has entrusted property to individuals, not to the state.

But didn't the early church change all that? Didn't the early Christians practice Communism? Let's look at Acts 4:32-35:

> And the multitude of them that believed were of one heart and of one soul: neither said any of them that aught of the things which he possessed was his own; but they had all things common. And with great power gave the apostles witness of the resurrection of the Lord Jesus: and great grace was upon them all. Neither was there any among them that lacked: for as many as were possessors of lands or houses sold them, and brought the prices of the things that were sold, and laid them down at the apostles' feet: and distribution was made unto every man according as he had need.

As we consider this passage, we first note that these early Christians did not set up a new economic order, nor did they establish a new government or a new society. Rather, they devised a way of life for themselves, one which would enable them to meet their needs as they lived and worked in the city of Jerusalem. Rather than a Communist economic order, this system of the early Christians could better be compared to the voluntary co-operatives formed by farmers in many parts of the Midwest and other parts of the country, by which farmers voluntarily form a co-op or association or partnership in which certain farm machinery is held by the co-op and subject to use by all the members, grain and seed are bought and sold by the co-op to give better buying power, etc. Many of these new Jewish Christians were in an emergency situation, having been disinherited by their families and perhaps denied employment as well. This voluntary pooling of resources was their way of surviving in an emergency. There is no evidence that the practice ever spread beyond Jerusalem.

Second, while we may laud the dedication and unselfishness of these Christians, nowhere in Scripture are we told that God had commanded them to pool their possessions or even that God approved their doing so. And the judgment of Ananias and Sapphira (Acts 5:1-11) for keeping back part of the price of their possessions does not indicate divine approval of this experiment, for the sin of Ananias and Sapphira was not refusing to share their resources, but lying to the Holy Spirit—pretending that they had given everything when in fact they had not (vv. 3, 4). Peter's words in verse 4 ("While it remained, was it not thine own? and after it was sold, was it not in thine own power?") would certainly indicate that Ananias and Sapphira had full liberty as Christians to decide whether to share all or part of their possessions. But they did not have the right to lie to the Holy Spirit and pretend that they had given everything when they had not.

Third, after the Ananias and Sapphira incident we read nothing at all about this common sharing. This further indicates that it may have been only a temporary experiment, intended to meet an emergency situation and not normative for the church at all times. And nowhere are we told whether or not the venture was successful. The fact that Paul had to take up collections from other churches to aid the saints at Jerusalem (Romans 15:25-31; 1 Corinthians 16:1-3; Galatians 2:10) may indicate that it was not, and that the Jerusalem church as a result became a burden on the other churches. Paul's direction to the Thessalonian Christians would appear to be more normative for the church of today:

> For even when we were with you, this we commanded you, that if any would not work, neither should he eat. For we hear that there are some which walk among you disorderly, working not at all, but are busybodies. Now them that are such we command and exhort by our Lord Jesus Christ, that with quietness they work, and eat their own bread. (2 Thessalonians 3:10-12)

Abundance and Scarcity

We have seen that God created all things and pronounced them good. There is nothing intrinsically evil about property, and there is nothing wrong with being wealthy so long as your wealth was acquired honestly and fairly. When James declared, "Go to now, ye rich men, weep and howl for your miseries that shall come upon you" (James 5:1), he condemned the rich men not because they were wealthy but because they had acquired their wealth by fraud: "Behold, the hire of the laborers who have reaped down your fields, which is of you kept back by fraud, crieth" (5:4).

There is danger in wealth, however. The rich man who has every material comfort is less likely to look heavenward; he has his own "heaven" here on earth. And the man who has been successful in this life is less likely to recognize himself as a sinner in need of God's grace; he's managed to make it on his own in this life, so why not in the next life as well? It is perhaps for this reason that Paul wrote that "not many wise men after the flesh, not many mighty, not many noble, are called" (1 Corinthians 1:26). Significantly, he said "not *many*"; he didn't say "not *any*"! Ironside says that this led a wealthy Canadian lady to say that she was saved by the letter *m*.

If there's nothing wrong with property and wealth, then why didn't God create enough abundance so that everyone could be a millionaire?

He did! At the time of creation, the world was a very productive place. Since the Fall, sin has spread like a cancer across the earth, which has become less and less productive:

> . . . cursed is the ground for thy sake; in sorrow shalt thou eat of it all the days of thy life; thorns also and thistles shall it bring forth to thee; and thou shalt eat the herb of the field: in the sweat of thy face shalt thou eat bread, till thou return unto the ground; for out of it wast thou taken: for dust thou art, and unto dust thou shalt return.

The curse resulting from the Fall is the ultimate case of scarcity and poverty, but there are other more immediate causes. God at times uses poverty as a test for believers, as he did with Job. It may be said that God puts some believers through a "poverty test" and others through a "prosperity test." There are some whom God will never allow to become wealthy, because he knows they could never handle wealth; they'd become proud and self-sufficient and forget about God. There are others whom God will never allow to become poor, because he knows that they could never handle poverty; they'd simply come apart. He may allow some to become wealthy as a sign of his grace; he may allow others to lose their wealth and become poor in order to "break" them and bring them to Christ. God knows our hearts and has a perfect plan designed for the ultimate good of each one of us.

This is not to discount temporal causes of abundance and poverty. Some societies are poor because they have not developed their natural wealth properly, failing to exercise the creation mandate of Genesis 1:26-31. Others are poor because they have failed to organize their economies in accordance with the principles of God's Word. That is true of persons as well as of nations. Some persons are constantly poor because of unwise stewardship, irresponsible management, or a failure to develop and use their God-given abilities. Others are poor simply because other things are more important to them than wealth. Still others may be poor because of some type of injustice at the hands of other men, though God always has a purpose in allowing this.

There is no shame in being poor. Certainly believers should not disparage a person who is poor or curry favor with another for being rich (James 2:1-9). Neither is it a disgrace to be rich. There is a kind of reverse snobbery today that looks down upon wealth and elevates poverty. Part of this may be based on a misunderstanding of God's Word; much of it is just plain jealousy.

Not only is wealth looked down upon today; it is also resented. A generation or so ago the common attitude was, "You have something I don't have; I'm going to work and save so I can get one like it." Today the attitude is, "You have something I don't have; therefore you are to blame for the fact that I don't have it." David Chilton compares this attitude to the plain coed who threw acid in the face of her beautiful roommate—blaming the roommate for her own ugliness, and somehow believing that destroying her roommate's beauty was the way to become beautiful herself.

Responsibility to the Poor

While the Bible imposes no guilt upon those who are wealthy, it does impose an obligation to help those who are in need. Exodus 22:21-25, for example, singles out four categories of persons and commands that they be treated fairly: widows, orphans, travelers or foreigners, and poor people. The reason is quite obvious: these persons are vulnerable. Widows often had few resources and, especially in that day, little knowledge of business affairs, and so were easily subject to exploitation. Orphans were deprived of their natural guardians and had no one to protect them. Travelers were especially vulnerable; if you've ever had car trouble in a strange town and found yourself at the mercy of an auto mechanic there, you know the vulnerability of a stranger. And poor people had few resources with which to defend themselves or provide for themselves.

These people were entitled to honesty, fairness, and equal justice;

however, they were not entitled to special privileges. As Moses cautions in Exodus 23:3, "Neither shalt thou countenance a poor man in his cause." I have seen lawsuits in which certain jurors said in deliberations that they wanted to rule in favor of the defendant even though he was clearly in the wrong, because he was a poor working man and the plaintiff was rich. That's not what the Bible commands!

The Old Testament prophets repeatedly condemned the rulers of Israel and Judah for their corruption and injustice toward these disadvantaged classes of society. As Isaiah says, "Thy princes (judges) are rebellious, and companions of thieves: every one loveth gifts, and followeth after rewards: they judge not the fatherless, neither doth the cause of the widow come unto them" (Isaiah 1:23; cf. Micah 3:11; Amos 8:4-6). The judges, Isaiah says, took bribes for hearing cases and deciding them a certain way. They refused to even hear cases from widows and the fatherless, because those classes wouldn't pay bribes—not necessarily because they were any less sinful, but because they didn't have money.

The prophets exhorted Israel and Judah to show compassion. Judges were to treat all classes fairly, making especially sure that they were fair to disadvantage persons:

> . . . Execute true judgment, and shew mercy and compassions every man to his brother: and oppress not the widow, nor the fatherless, the stranger, nor the poor; and let none of you imagine evil against his brother in your heart. (Zechariah 7:9, 10)

This is not a basis for government redistribution of wealth; rather, it is a call for fairness, honesty, and equal justice under law.

In the New Testament, Christians are exhorted to go beyond the formal requirements of justice and take positive action on behalf of the poor.

> Pure religion and undefiled before God and the Father is this, To visit the fatherless and widows in their affliction, and to keep himself unspotted from the world. (James 1:27)

> If a brother or sister be naked, and destitute of daily food, and one of you say unto them, Depart in peace, be ye warmed and filled; notwithstanding ye give them not those things which are needful to the body; what doth it profit? (James 2:15, 16)

And Matthew 25:31-46 declares that in the last days one test of whether or not a person is a true believer in Christ will be whether or not he showed compassion to the poor. No one is ever saved by helping the poor, but helping the poor is one means of showing the world that you are saved.

How to Help the Poor

We have a clear scriptural mandate to help the poor, but how do we go about it?

Unfortunately many on the liberal wing of the political spectrum seem to equate every government spending scheme on behalf of the poor with Christian compassion. Christians who hesitate to support such schemes are often unfairly labeled as "insensitive" or "lacking in social conscience." The real issue that divides liberal and conservatives is not *whether* to help the poor, but *how* to help them.

It is wrong to think that every welfare proposal deserves our unqualified support. Some welfare programs are corrupt, or are proposed by persons with selfish motives such as greed or political ambition. Judas Iscariot proposed one such welfare program:

> Then took Mary a pound of ointment of spikenard, very costly, and anointed the feet of Jesus, and wiped his feet with her hair: and the house was filled with the odor of the ointment. Then saith one of his disciples, Judas Iscariot, Simon's son, which should betray him, Why was not this ointment sold for three hundred pence, and given to the poor? This he said, not that he cared for the poor; but because he was a thief, and had the bag, and bare what was put therein. Then said Jesus, Let her alone: against the day of my burying hath she kept this. For the poor always ye have with you; but me ye have not always. (John 12:3-8)

Other welfare programs are wasteful, inefficient, or subject to abuse. Joseph A. Califano, Secretary of Health, Education and Welfare under President Carter and usually a liberal defender of welfare programs, acknowledged that as much as 10 percent of funds for welfare and Medicaid are misspent because of fraud, error, and abuse.[1] Many of his conservative critics would say the figure is actually much higher. J. Roger Edgar, chief of the fraud section of the civil division of the U.S. Justice Department under President Carter, says of welfare fraud,

> There isn't a program in the country that isn't affected by fraud. Every time the government spends money, somebody tries to steal it. In the end, it is the taxpayer who pays.[2]

Welfare fraud and abuse could cost the taxpayers as much as $25 billion a year.[3] Some of the chief causes of fraud and abuse seem to be caseworkers accepting welfare applications without proper identification and screening procedures, continuing to send checks after they should have stopped, failure to periodically check the recipient to determine whether he remains eligible, and payment of emergency bills for "lost" or "stolen" welfare checks without investigating for fraud. Some of the more common techniques for abusing the welfare system include a husband moving out of the house so that his family can collect welfare and then sneaking back for "visits," doctors filing false or inflated claims under medicaid, recipients working and not reporting their income, and registering for welfare in multiple places or under various aliases. I certainly do not suggest that this is true of all or most welfare recipients, but it is widespread enough to merit serious concern.

Another problem with current welfare programs is that too many of them do not really help the recipients in the long run. Instead of providing short-term assistance to tide a person over in a genuine emergency, welfare too often becomes a way of life. The welfare bureaucracy—381,000 strong, or one welfare worker for every sixty-one recipients[4]—too easily locks its recipients into a life-style of unemployment and noninitiative. A young mother recently wrote to a national columnist, saying that she had started receiving welfare and intended to do so only temporarily, but now that she was in the system it was hard to get out. If she gets a part-time job, she has to report everything she earns, and her welfare grant is reduced dollar-for-dollar by what she earns. When she considers all the fringe benefits of being on welfare (food stamps, rent subsidies, medical and dental care, psychiatric care, and the like) and all the expenses and inconveniences of working (transportation, day-care, extra clothes, etc.), it just isn't worth it to work. As Wilbur J. Cohen, Secretary of Health, Education and Welfare under President Lyndon Johnson, said, "The law does not encourage the man to stay with the family when he's underemployed. There's no provision for the working poor."[5] The low-income person who wishes to work becomes increasingly frustrated as he sees others living off the government and living better than he does. Consequently he eventually loses his pride and initiative and becomes a welfare recipient himself. That's why Paul commanded that "if any would not work, neither should he eat"; for Paul recognized that some would take advantage of others' charity, "working not at all, but are busybodies." He therefore directed those persons to "work, and eat their own bread" (2 Thessalonians 3:10-12).

Still another problem with many welfare programs is that they become unduly burdensome to others. Predictably, as people have increasingly come to regard welfare as a right rather than a privilege, the number of people on welfare today is three times higher than during the Great Depression of the 1930s. In fact, social welfare is the largest single expense the taxpayers face today. This is unfairly burdensome to many, especially those who pay taxes to support this system and are in many cases unable to live as well as those who live off the system. Writer Kathleen Kroll recalls complaining to a grocer about outlandish lobster prices. The grocer showed her some food stamps and said, "See these? The only lobster sales I've had today were paid for by these. Sad commentary, huh?"[6]

And yet, we *do* have an obligation to help the poor. The problem is, how can we help them in a way that really does help them, in a way that is efficient, and in a way that is fair to all concerned, including the taxpayers?

I don't pretend to have any magic solutions, but I can offer a few guidelines by which Christians may judge programs designed to help the poor.

The First Guideline: Voluntary charity is better than government action. It is amazing how those who promote government welfare programs can be extremely generous with other people's money. The Senator who calls for massive welfare expenditures is often labeled a generous man, a philanthropist, a friend of the poor. Don't forget though, it's not his own money he wants to spend. It's the taxpayers'— yours and mine!

When the frontiersman Davey Crockett was in Congress, someone brought the plight of a widow to the attention of Congress and urged a bill giving relief to her. Congressman Crockett opposed this idea, saying they should contribute to her themselves. He set up a relief fund for her, but he was the only Congressman who contributed. He noted that legislators are much more eager to spend other people's money than to spend their own.

Private charities are preferable to government welfare because they do not involve coercive giving, and consequently the giver and recipient are both blessed. There is little blessing in being taxed to support a welfare system because the vital element of love has been replaced by coercion. "And though I bestow all my goods to feed the poor, and though I give my body to be burned, and have not charity [love], it profiteth me nothing" (1 Corinthians 13:3).

Private charities are also likely to be more efficient, since they do not have an unlimited supply of funds and must therefore be more cost-conscious. Furthermore, private charities are more flexible. Since they are unburdened by massive government regulations, they can tailor their programs more specifically to meet their recipients' needs.

There are many kinds of private charities, but one of the foremost should be the church itself. Throughout history the church has been the greatest benevolent institution the world has ever known; but it could and should do more. In fact, our nation might not have the welfare mess it has today if the church had been faithful to its calling. What is your church doing to help the poor?

One of the most encouraging actions I have heard of recently is the formation of a Community Involvement Task Force by eleven Lutheran churches in the Tulsa, Oklahoma area. The Task Force was formed because of proposed budget cuts by the Reagan administration. Representatives of the eleven churches are to meet once a week for six to eight weeks to investigate the actual effect the economic policy has had and will have on local social service agencies; determine what needs the agencies may realize while operating in the new economic environment; recommend appropriate actions the churches should pursue to respond to those needs.[7]

This group of churches is seeking ways to fill the gap as social programs are cut and eliminated. That's great, and President Reagan would heartily approve. He is quoted as saying, "If every church would care for its own, we'd have no indigent problem in the United States."[8] In this respect traditional Christians could learn a great deal from the Mormons, the Amish, and other religious groups that truly take care of their own.

The Second Guideline: It is better to provide jobs and job training than to provide handouts. There's an old proverb: If you give a man a fish, you feed him for a day. But if you teach him how to fish, you feed him for a lifetime.

Merely giving people money does not solve their problems, at least not on any long-term basis. They need to develop the ability to take care of themselves.

That's one reason welfare programs are often counterproductive and self-defeating. Instead of creating independence, they create dependence. They turn people into parasites.

Let us suppose that you have a million dollars that you want to devote to poverty relief. How should you go about it?

You could go to the poorest district of town and give a $1000 bill to each of the first one thousand persons you see. A lot of people would be happy—but for how long? How much of that money would be of any lasting benefit to the community? If you were to visit that neighborhood again a year later, it is doubtful that very much, if any, of that money would have caused any visible improvement in the lives of those people.

Let us suppose, instead, that you decide to use that million dollars on pure selfish luxury. So you go out and buy yourself one hundred Cadillacs at a cost of $10,000 apiece. What a waste, right? And yet, someone has to make those Cadillacs. Someone has to mine the steel, tap the rubber, form the plastic, and produce all the other materials that went into the making of those Cadillacs. Someone has to work the assembly line to produce those Cadillacs, someone has to transport them to the local dealership, and a dealer has to sell them to you. Your act of self-indulgence has produced jobs and income for lots of people, and in the long run it may have done more lasting good than if you had given the money away.

But there's a much better way. You go into that poor neighborhood and use your million dollars to set up a factory that will meet the needs of many consumers in the area and will at the same time employ local residents. You have not only met consumer needs; you have also provided jobs, stability, and a whole new way of life for lots of people. And in the process, you just may have made yourself a tidy profit!

The Third Guideline: Welfare programs should provide incentive to work. There should never be a situation in which it is economically better to be idle than to work. Incentives should be built into the system that encourage welfare recipients to work at even the lowest-paying jobs, and the system should make sure they are financially ahead by doing so. For example, instead of reducing a person's welfare grant dollar-for-dollar because of his earned income, why not reduce it fifty cents for each earned dollar? If a person's welfare grant is $500 per month and he finds a part-time job that pays $300, reduce his welfare grant by $150 instead of by $300. That may cost the government more in the short run, but in the long run I believe it would get people off welfare and save money.

"Workfare" programs such as President Reagan initiated when he was Governor of California deserve serious consideration. California's Welfare Reform Act of 1971 required able-bodied welfare recipients to spend twenty hours per week in public service jobs and twenty hours per week looking for private employment. If a person refuses, 2 Thessalonians 3:10 comes into play: "If any would not work, neither should he eat."

The Fourth Guideline: Welfare programs should be structured to minimize fraud. Human nature being what the Bible says it is, we have to assume that some people will take advantage of every possible opportunity to defraud and abuse welfare programs. Probably fraud can never be totally eliminated, but such programs should be carefully scrutinized for loopholes that would allow fraud.

Some things can be done. New York City had considerable success in eliminating ineligible recipients by using a computer to compare the welfare rolls with Social Security rolls, public employee rolls, etc., and eliminate duplication. They also employed stricter screening procedures for applicants and periodically rechecked applicants for eligibility.[9] Under Governor Reagan California tightened its procedures to verify income of welfare recipients and strengthened efforts to find absentee fathers and compel them to support their children. As a result, California's welfare rolls dropped from 1.5 million in 1972 to 1.3 million in 1974, though since Reagan left office they have started rising again.[10]

Welfare offices could periodically require that nondisabled recipients come to the office personally and pick up their checks; this would help to eliminate those who move to other localities and have their checks forwarded while also collecting welfare elsewhere. Photo identification cards could be required; this could help eliminate fraud and duplication. Stiffer criminal penalties could be enacted and enforced against welfare abusers. Welfare officials could more actively encourage citizens to report suspected fraud. (I am told of a lady in my home town who called the Social Services to report a neighbor for fraud and was told by the welfare worker to mind her own business!)

The Fifth Guideline: Distinguish deserving poor from underserving poor. We must distinguish between those who *cannot* work and those who *will not* work. Certainly no one would condemn those who are on welfare because they are disabled (though many disabled people are able to be self-supporting and even wealthy if they have enough determination. Take the example of Joni Eareckson who, though a quadriplegic, has developed a thriving business designing greeting cards—holding a paintbrush with her teeth). But what of those who could work but are just plain lazy?

The Bible commands compassion for those who are poor through no fault of their own, but it has harsh words for those who are lazy. Consider these words from the Book of Proverbs:

> Go to the ant, thou sluggard; consider her ways, and be wise: which having no guide, overseer, or ruler, provideth her meat in the summer, and gathereth her food in the harvest. How long wilt thou sleep, O sluggard? When wilt thou arise out of thy sleep? (6:6-9) The hand of the diligent shall bear rule: but the slothful shall be under tribute. (12:24) The soul of the sluggard desireth, and hath nothing: but the soul of the diligent shall be made fat. (13:4)

Solomon was a very wise man and had a keen understanding of human nature. He recognized some of the excuses men might give for not working:

> The slothful man saith, There is a lion in the way; a lion is in the streets. As the door turneth upon his hinges, so doth the slothful upon his bed. (26:13, 14)

But Solomon didn't sympathize with those excuses:

> The sluggard will not plow by reason of the cold; therefore shall he beg in harvest, and have nothing. (20:4)

Paul's advice is right in line with this principle: "If any would not work, neither should he eat" (2 Thessalonians 3:10). Note that Paul did not say "If any *could* not work," but "if any *would* not work." Paul distinguishes between the deserving poor and the undeserving poor.

The Sixth Guideline: Welfare programs should encourage families to take care of their own. God's Word has very harsh words for those who refuse to support their own families:

> But if any provide not for his own, and specially for those of his own house, he hath denied the faith, and is worse than an infidel. (1 Timothy 5:8)

In context Paul's words refer to support for elderly widows—mothers, grandmothers, aunts. What would Paul say about our modern tendency to pass this responsibility off to the government with Social Security and old-age assistance?

If Paul said this about our duty to support our elderly relatives, think how much more the principle applies to our obligation to support our spouses and children. What would Paul say about absentee fathers who don't support their children? There is no reason why the taxpayers should have to support a child if the child has a healthy father who is able to do so. Laws that require such support and that enable authorities to track down absentee fathers and enforce child support obligations should be supported and vigorously enforced. More than that, laws that make it easier for families to collect welfare if the husband doesn't live at home should be carefully scrutinized. It should never be financially advantageous to break up a family.

Free Enterprise or Socialism?

Most American Christians support free enterprise, if for no other reason than that is the "American way." In some countries though, many Christians are socialists. What is the "Christian" economic system? Is it free enterprise, in which persons are free to buy, sell, and own property, go into business for themselves or in association with others, let the consumers determine the market by the law of supply and demand, and reap the benefits of their success or bear the costs of their failure? Or is it socialism, in which the government owns the means of production and in which private business and private ownership of property are nonexistent or severely curtailed? Or is the "Christian" system something in between, since very few economic systems are pure free enterprise or pure socialism?

I certainly would never say that a person is not a Christian simply because he holds a different view of economics. Christians can differ about a lot of things and still be brothers in Christ.

Still, the Bible does have much to say about economics. And since all true Christians believe the same Bible, we should all be interested in what the Bible has to say about this subject. When our viewpoints differ as widely as socialism and free enterprise, it seems unlikely that both sides could be applying the Scriptures correctly.

Stated simply, I believe free enterprise is more consistent with the principles of Scripture than is socialism. Here's why.

Free enterprise is practiced in the Bible. The Bible does not contain precise commands concerning an economic system, but assumes free enterprise to be the natural order. Men buy and sell vineyards, raise and sell livestock and grain, enter into business arrangements by themselves or with others, and prosper if they're successful and don't prosper if they fail. We see Lydia as a seller of purple cloth, Peter as a commercial fisherman, and others engaged in free enterprise activities. As a youth Jesus probably worked as an apprentice in his father's carpentry shop.

Free enterprise is consistent with the biblical view of human nature. Because of man's sin nature, he is basically selfish and interested in that which directly benefits him or those close to him. He is incapable of sustained activity motivated solely by altruism or the benefit of others.

Socialism and Communism tend to be economic failures because they are based upon a false understanding of human nature, the view that man is basically good or improvable. Such systems would have men work and produce at their jobs, not for any direct benefit to themselves, but for the benefit of the commune, or for the benefit of society as a whole. The individual quickly realizes that how hard or how well he works has little to do with any benefits he enjoys, and that if he slacks off a little in his work he takes home the same paycheck as before.

By contrast, under the free enterprise system the worker knows that he benefits in proportion to the quality or quantity of his work. As a farmer, if he works very hard at producing a good crop, he will receive much more income than he will if he sleeps all day, lets his field grow up in weeds, etc. If he works for someone else, he knows that his job is secure only so long as he is sufficiently productive to make it profitable for his employer to keep him. If he does well, he will be retained, rewarded, and promoted; if he does not, he will be dismissed. Admittedly this does not always work out perfectly in practice, for other factors enter in and human beings are almost impossible to predict with certainty. But in a very real sense every worker in the free enterprise system is in business for himself. Even an employee is in some sense an independent businessman who has contracted with an employer to perform certain services in return for payment.

In short, the difference is that under free enterprise the individual has a natural incentive to produce; under socialism and Communism he does not. Socialist and Communist leaders therefore have to choose between two options. First, they can allow their economies to stagnate, as have the socialist economies of many nations of Europe. Or second, they can supply an artificial incentive by governmental force—work or be shot! Consider the Soviet Union and Cambodia, where workers are routinely liquidated for being "unproductive." Not only is such compulsion unpleasant and inimical to human freedom; it also doesn't work nearly as well as the profit incentive of the free enterprise system. Free enterprise provides an incentive while Communism and socialism do not. With that incentive, the individual citizen works and produces; without it, he becomes lazy and sluggish.

And yet, while ostensibly working for himself and motivated by self-interest, the worker in the free enterprise system benefits all of society. The farmer who works hard and produces a good crop feeds an entire community. The worker on the assembly line produces an automobile that will be of value to other citizens. The entrepreneur who develops a new product and manufactures and sells it, gets rich— because other people find his product desirable, and they buy it. Adam Smith, the famous eighteenth-century economist whose book *The Wealth of Nations* greatly influenced the American founding fathers, described this process as an "invisible hand" by which each man, while working for himself, also works for the benefits of others. It is well said, "The quickest way to become rich in every way is to contribute something of value to the world."[11]

The strength of the free enterprise system, then, is that it is based on a realistic, biblical view of the nature of man. It recognizes that for the most part fallen men will not produce, over a long period of time, unless they and their loved ones profit thereby.

This does not mean, however, that free enterprise glorifies or approves sin. Seeking material gain is not sinful. So long as it is done honorably, seeking prosperity for oneself and one's loved ones is a positive good. The free enterprise system simply accommodates the limits of man's nature, for it recognizes that man is incapable of sustained productive effort for loftier motives than this.

Having said that, it should be added that free enterprise works best in a society which is influenced by the biblical ethic. Where a legitimate desire for self-gain gives way to unbridled self-lust and unprincipled, cutthroat competition, you have capitalism at its worst—and such capitalists frequently lay the groundwork for their own destruction by exploitation which fans the fires of revolt against the system. Unfortunately that was true to a large extent in the capitalist society of late nineteenth-century and early twentieth-century America, during which time the industrial leaders of America were influenced by the tooth-and-claw, survival-of-the-fittest, Social Darwinist capitalism of Herbert Spencer rather than biblical capitalism.

Free enterprise works best when capitalists pursue their legitimate self-interest in the hope of making a profit—with a sense of self-discipline, honor, honesty, fairness, and charity for others. When men fail to discipline themselves, government must discipline them. Thus begins the destruction of freedom.

Free enterprise maximizes human freedom. As we have seen, the Bible treats human freedom as a desirable condition. Free enterprise maximizes the right of the individual to make his own choices in economic matters. He is free to choose whom to work for or whom to hire, what type of job to take, what type of training he wishes to undergo. He is free to form his own business and succeed or fail with it; he is free to associate with others in joint enterprises such as partnerships or corporations; he is even free to join with others in communes or co-ops if he so desires. The free enterprise system is broad enough to accommodate all of these choices and many more.

God never intended man to be a mere automaton, a robot taking directions from the state. God gave man a substantial measure of freedom. The free enterprise system is consistent with human freedom.

Free enterprise recognizes private property rights. We have previously seen that the Bible recognizes the individual's right to own property. The free enterprise system, in which the means of production are owned by private individuals either by themselves or in association with others, is consistent with property rights. Socialism, under which government owns the means of production, and Communism, under which private property is abolished, are not.

Free enterprise most closely approximates economic justice for all. Under free enterprise, each man profits as he benefits society. The individual who produces more, profits more. And each man profits from the fruit of his own labor.

The Bible recognizes the injustice of one man profiting from another man's labors, and promises that in the Millennium it shall not be so: "They shall not plant, and another eat" (Isaiah 65:22). That's why Paul commanded, "If any would not work, neither should he eat" (2 Thessalonians 3:10).

Two of Jesus' parables contain interesting economic principles. In the parable of the talents (Matthew 25:14-30) the servants who had been given five and ten talents were rewarded because they had used them profitably, while the servant who had been given only one talent was deprived of it because he hid it rather than putting it to good use. The rich got richer, and the poor got poorer!

Yet in the parable of the laborers in the vineyard, the owner paid the same wage to all his laborers—those who were hired early in the morning, those hired in midmorning, those hired at noon and midafternoon, and those hired only an hour before closing. Those who worked all day received no more than those who worked only an hour. Norman Thomas, former national chairman of the Socialist Party, has used this parable to justify Socialism!

Actually neither of these parables was primarily intended to convey economic principles. The first parable illustrates the distribution and use of spiritual gifts; the second illustrates salvation by grace. But they have economic significance because of the assumptions implicit within them. Jesus told these parables because everyone who heard them would recognize the basic economic realities of the situations—that the owner of the vineyard and the man who traveled to a far country each had the right to contract with his employees as he saw fit. Those who were asked to work the whole day for a denarius were free to accept the offer of employment or reject it. They accepted it because they thought it was fair. If it was fair when they accepted it, they had no cause to grumble simply because the owner decided to be more generous with other employees. The assumed principle is that the owner of the vineyard—or factory, or store, or whatever—has the right to run his business as he sees fit.

Still, an employer should be fair with his employees. Obviously he may not defraud them (James 5:1-4). The law of the land should reflect this moral principle. Paul says in Colossians 4:1, "Masters, give unto your servants that which is just and equal." But the Greek word *isotes* actually means equitable, not equal. Paul is not saying that every employee deserves the same wage, but that every employee should be paid justly and fairly. Certainly those who have more skill, training, responsibility, diligence, or initiative deserve more compensation than others. It is as much an injustice to pay unequals equally, as to pay equals unequally.

Alexander Hamilton said it well: "Inequality will exist as long as liberty exists. It unavoidably results from that very liberty itself."[12]

Under the free enterprise system, your economic worth is determined by your value on the marketplace. You contract with your employer, individually or collectively through your union, to work for him in return for the highest wage he is willing to pay; and he determines how much he is willing to pay, based on how much your work is worth to him. If you have special skills or special training or an advanced degree that others don't have, your services are a scarce commodity on the labor market, and as a result they are worth more. If you feel your work is worth more than your employer is willing to pay, you are free to quit working for him and work instead for someone who is willing to pay you what you're worth. If you can't find anyone who's willing to pay the wage you demand, it may be that you're not worth as much economically as you think you are.

Free men are not equal, and equal men are not free! If the government determined everybody's wages, that would be economic bond-age, for it would restrict those who want to earn more as much as it would help those who would otherwise have less. The free enterprise system, by which every man's economic worth is determined by its value in the marketplace, is the best means of insuring economic justice for all.

The free enterprise system provides the best opportunity for giving. The free enterprise system, which enables people to work and earn a profit, also frees people to voluntarily share their profits with others. As Dr. Warren C. Hultgren of First Baptist Church of Tulsa has noted,

> It continues to amaze me . . . the large number of busy executives who spend so many countless hours on community projects and humanitarian causes that have no direct bearing on their business interests.[13]

This should be especially true of Christians. As Paul describes the exercise of spiritual gifts in Romans 12, he says in verse 8:

> He that giveth, let him do it with simplicity [better translation: liberality].

This is God's poverty program—Christians working to earn an abundance for themselves, and then sharing that abundance with others.

> Let him that stole steal no more: but rather let him labor, working with his hands the thing which is good, that he may have to give to him that needeth. (Ephesians 4:28)

I believe God has given some Christians a special gift for making money and sharing it for the glory of God. One believer may be a tremendous organizer who can put together a profitable business; another may have a "Midas touch" with the stock market whereby every stock he touches turns to gold. An example is Dr. Raymond LeTourneau, the wealthy Texas businessman who founded LeTour-neau College. LeTourneau resolved to turn over 90 percent of his assets to the Lord's work, keeping only 10 percent for himself. He further resolved that he would give 90 percent of the annual income off that remaining 10 percent to the Lord's work as well. He did so, and still remained a wealthy man! That could happen only in a free enterprise economy.

Free enterprise limits government power. As we saw in Chapter 12 the sinful nature of man requires that government power be limited, lest absolute power be used for tyrannical purposes. Under Socialism, government controls the economy. Such power can be the basis for tyranny and totalitarianism.

Political scientists often divide liberty into two classes, political liberty and economic liberty, and they argue about whether it is possible to have one without the other. It may be possible; many Socialist nations in Europe retain the freedom to elect government officials, criticize government policy, etc. But I believe it is difficult in the long run to maintain political liberty without economic liberty. The society that compromises economic liberty is likely to regard liberty in general as relative rather than absolute, and it is therefore likely to tolerate more restraints on liberty. Furthermore, the danger exists that politicians will use economic power to gain or keep political power. For example, a socialist politician may promise to build a government factory in a locality in return for that locality's votes in the next election. A socialist president may "punish" a state that voted for his opponent by locating a hydroelectric plant in a neighboring state instead, or he may promise government contracts to a large company in return for a campaign contribution from that company. This is increasingly a problem as government becomes more and more involved with the economy.

Under free enterprise, the role of government in the economic life of the nation is sharply limited. The independent power wielded by businesses and by labor unions constitutes a further check on government power. Such a check is necessary in light of the biblical view of the nature of man.

In Revelation 13 we are told that in the last days the Antichrist will establish a dictatorship over much of the earth. Not only will he have absolute political power; he will have absolute economic power as well: "that no man might buy or sell, save he that had the mark, or the name of the beast, or the number of his name" (Revelation 13:17). Socialism is much more consistent with the bondage offered by Satan than with the liberty offered by Jesus Christ.

It is the free enterprise system—people producing for profit—that has made America the prosperous nation it is today. It is the free enterprise system—people looking for a better way to do things for profit—that has produced the marvelous technology of American society. It is the free enterprise system—each man working for himself— that has enabled Americans of all classes to enjoy luxuries unknown to kings a century ago. And the reason free enterprise works so well is that it is based on solid biblical principles. Let us think twice before abandoning it.

A Word About Liberation Theology
Any discussion of wealth or property today would be incomplete without some mention of "liberation theology." The term has reared its

head in recent years and has attracted considerable attention, if not from the worshipers in the pews, at least from the religious and secular media.

Liberation theology is difficult to define because, like the social gospel of a few generations ago, it has so many variations. Really, it is more a movement than a theology. It crosses many denominations— Protestant and Catholic, liberal and evangelical. To a large extent it seems associated with Latin America; yet it exists throughout the underdeveloped nations of the world and has its adherents in the developed nations as well.

Its central distinguishing characteristic would probably be the conviction that Jesus and his gospel require a close identification with the poor, the downtroden, and the oppressed of this world. And identification is not enough. According to liberation theologians, Christians must work to liberate the poor from their oppression; and in order to do this, they must work to revamp the socioeconomic structures of the nation and the world.

I have more in common with liberation theologians than many might suspect. I admire their concern for the poor, and I share that concern. Like the liberation theologians, I strongly believe that biblical faith requires social commitment and social action. Like them, I strongly believe that Christians should work through the political process to bring about change in this world. That is my reason for writing this book.

But I see some problems in liberation theology:

First, some liberation theologians have a tendency to confuse salvation with social action. Like many of those who espoused the social gospel a few generations ago, some liberation theologians leave the impression that personal salvation comes about through social action, or that one is saved by means of social action. Nothing could be further from the truth. Salvation is first and foundational. Social action results from it.

Also, I note a tendency among some liberation theologians to ignore the Word of God. Too often they speak vaguely of "Christian principles" without solid biblical exegesis. I hasten to add, however, that this is not true of all of them.

Then too, some liberation theologians seem to think that, by changing social structures, they can change people. I disagree, for I find nothing in Scripture or experience to support that viewpoint. An effective social structure, such as our constitutional system, can help to restrain man's sinful nature, but it cannot change it.

Also, liberation theologians tend to equate inequality with injustice and oppression. Because *A* is rich and *B* is poor, they assume *A* must have exploited and oppressed *B*.

But that is not necessarily true. Let us suppose *A* and *B* live next door to each other. *A* works hard at a middle-class job and earns $20,000 per year. *B* does not work, even though he is able to do so, collects welfare, and receives $10,000 per year. Each payday a substantial portion of *A's* paycheck is withheld for payroll taxes, a substantial portion of which goes to provide welfare for *B* and others similarly situated.

Now in the situation described above, who is exploiting whom? Is *A* exploiting *B*, or is *B* exploiting *A*? Inequality is not always the result of oppression.

Furthermore, liberation theologians often rather naively make the United States and/or the capitalist system the scapegoats for all of the world's problems. They forget that American investment has brought much industry, productivity, income, and employment to underdeveloped nations, and possibly could bring more if not fettered by government regulation. They forget also that Socialism has generally failed to bring about prosperity for the poor. The result of Socialism is that rich and poor both become equally poorer!

Last, liberation theologians tend to be very naive about the nature of Communism. They emphatically denounce U.S. aggression in Vietnam or Grenada or Nicaragua, but they blindly ignore Soviet aggression in Afghanistan, Czechoslovakia, or El Salvador.

If applied with sound biblical exegesis and good economic and political common sense, liberation theology has the potential to become a major force for Christian revival in the underdeveloped world. In the absence of such redeeming virtues, it carries the risk of being irresponsible and dangerous.

14 The Family

We have previously discussed the two kingdoms—the church and the state. Both of these kingdoms were instituted by God for the ordering and preservation of society.

There is a third divine institution which, while perhaps not a kingdom, is nevertheless just as important. I speak of the basic unit of society, the family.

Long before the first state or the first church dawned upon the world, God formed the first family. Very shortly after God created Adam he said, "It is not good that the man should be alone; I will make him a help meet for him" (Genesis 2:18). He provided Adam with a wife and children, and thereafter he provided families for believers such as Seth and unbelievers such as Cain, indicating that marriage is a civil institution which binds believers and unbelievers alike. When God sent the great flood to destroy the sinful world, he preserved Noah and his people as a family. Later he gave special commands to fortify the family, such as Exodus 20:12: "Honor thy father and thy mother. . . ." And he placed in family members a strong love for each other to cement this family unit and keep it intact.

Reasons for the Family
The institution of the family was not just God's personal whim. In his omniscience he knew that people needed such an institution, and in their fallen state of sin they would need the family even more. Here are some of his reasons:

Leadership. Humans cannot function without leadership, at least not when they must live and work together. And the basic unit of authority in human society is the family. The husband is the head of the wife (1 Corinthians 11:3; Ephesians 5:23), and children are to obey their parents (Exodus 20:12; Ephesians 6:1; Colossians 3:20).

Guidance and instruction. Husbands are to instruct their wives in the things of the Lord (1 Corinthians 14:35), and parents are to instruct their children.

> And, ye fathers, provoke not your children to wrath: but bring them up in the nurture and admonition of the Lord. (Ephesians 6:4)

> Hear, ye children, the instruction of a father, and attend to know understanding. For I give you good doctrine, forsake ye not my law. (Proverbs 4:1, 2)

> Hear, O my son, and receive my sayings; and the years of thy life shall be many. I have taught thee in the way of wisdom; I have led thee in right paths. (Proverbs 4:10, 11)

> And thou shalt love the Lord thy God with all thine heart, and with all thy soul, and with all thy might. And these words, which I command thee this day, shall be in thine heart: and thou shalt teach them diligently unto thy children, and shalt talk of them when thou sittest in thine house, and when thou walkest by the way, and when thou liest down, and when thou risest up. (Deuteronomy 6:5-7; cf. 11:18-21)

While these commands can be applied to both parents, they are most clearly directed toward fathers. Yet fathers today, even Christian fathers, are woefully negligent in training their children. In most Christian homes the primary source of guidance and instruction is an alien school system that usually does not reflect Christian values, counterbalanced (it is hoped) by an hour or less of Sunday school per week. What little home instruction most children get, comes largely from the mothers.

Provision. God has placed children in the care of their parents, not in the care of the state. It is the privilege and duty of parents to guide their children and make decisions for them, and it is the privilege and duty of parents to provide for their children. Paul says in 1 Timothy 5:8, "But if any provide not for his own, and specially for those of his own house, he hath denied the faith, and is worse than an infidel." He is speaking particularly of the need to provide for widowed relatives; how much more does his exhortation apply to the provision for one's own children!

Note that Paul says the man who refuses to provide for his own household is worse than an infidel. Why worse? Because even the infidel, in his sinful and unregenerate state, has within his heart a God-given love for his children. It is abnormal even for infidels to fail to take care of their own children. Because of common grace, infidels can be loving husbands and loving parents; sometimes they even put

Christians to shame in this regard. Jesus recognized the ability of the unregenerate to care for his children when he said,

> Or what man is there of you, whom if his son ask bread, will he give him a stone? Or if he ask a fish, will he give him a serpent? If ye then, being evil, know how to give good gifts unto your children, how much more shall your Father which is in heaven give good things to them that ask him? (Matthew 7:9-11)

Can you imagine what a tax burden it would be if the state provided for all the children in America, instead of parents doing so? Can you imagine what an inefficient system that would be?

Fortunately God has a better institution to provide for children—the family.

Security. The family provides its members with stability. It provides a set of loved ones, a group of companions, and a haven of refuge. It gives a sense of identity and a sense of belonging.

I am convinced that the current instability, insecurity, and loneliness that seem so prevalent among people today are due in large part to the breakdown of the family.

Individualism. Can you imagine what the world would be like if every child were raised by the state? We would all be rubber stamps of one another!

Fortunately most of us were raised by our parents, not by the state. We learned our parents' unique ideas, though we may not have followed all of them. We copied their idiosyncracies; we adopted their special habits and traditions. In this way the family unit acts as a check on state power, as a buffer zone between the government and the individual. If the state raised all children, the power of the state to brainwash and to enforce conformity would be staggering.

Channels for sexual desire. God placed within man a sexual desire (Genesis 1:28), and he has established marriage as the institution through which sexual desire may be expressed: ". . . to avoid fornication, let every man have his own wife, and let every woman have her own husband" (1 Corinthians 7:2).

This regulation of sexual energy is necessary to maintain a civilized society. J. D. Unwin conducted an exhaustive study of eighty primitive cultures and sixteen civilized societies, to determine whether there was a relationship between sexual practices and the level of civilization. He concluded that no society can display productive social energy unless sexual energy is restrained, and that the greatest energy is displayed by those societies which require that sexual expression take place only within monogamous marriage.[1] In short, civilization cannot survive unless there is some restraint upon sexual expression. The institution of the family supplies that restraint.

Source of national strength. By providing leadership, guidance, restraint, security, and values, the family unit promotes the greatness of the nation. Should the family fail in these responsibilities, the nation will suffer as a result.

Threats to the Family

Attacks on the family are far from new. State rearing of children was conceptualized as far back as Plato's *Republic* and as recently as Aldous Huxley's *Brave New World*. Karl Marx called for the abolition of the family in *The Communist Manifesto:*

> Abolition of the family! Even the most radical flare up at this infamous proposal of the Communists.
>
> On what foundation is the present family, the bourgeois family, based? On capital, on private gain. In its completely developed form this family exists only among the bourgeoisie. But this state of things finds its complement in the practical absence of the family among the proletarians, and in public prostitution.
>
> The bourgeois family will vanish as a matter of course when its complement vanishes, and both will vanish with the vanishing of capital.
>
> Do you charge us with wanting to stop the exploitation of children by their parents? To this crime we plead guilty.[2]

Christians today are concerned about the survival of the famiy as an institution, because a wide variety of forces now threaten the family. Some of these, such as increased mobility and urbanization, are not directly related to politics. Others, however, are very political, and in many instances they involve government laws or policies that are inimical to the best interests of the family. For this reason, *profamily* has become a common expression in recent years, and the family has entered the political arena as a highly volatile issue.

Let's examine a few of the major political issues that affect the family.

Easy divorce. The Bible takes a dim view of divorce. Jesus said in Luke 16:18, "Whosoever putteth away his wife, and marrieth another, committeth adultery: and whosoever marrieth her that is put away from her husband committeth adultery." "What therefore God hath joined together," he said, "let not man put asunder" (Mark 10:9).

Nevertheless, the civil laws of Israel did allow divorce when one found "uncleanness" in his spouse (Deuteronomy 24:1-4). Jesus said that Moses gave that precept "for the hardness of your heart" (Mark 10:5) and allowed it only when some cause or fault could be shown. Divorce, at best, is a civil accommodation to the sinful nature of man. It is never the perfect will of God.

The legal system's view of divorce used to be much closer to the biblical view than it is today. Marriage used to be regarded as a lifelong contract which could be broken, if at all, only by the misconduct of one of the partners. The various state statutes spelled out the various acts of misconduct which could constitute "grounds" for divorce: generally adultery, desertion, cruel and inhumane treatment, nonsupport, etc. Unless a partner could prove such misconduct or "breach of contract" by the other partner, he could not get a divorce.

Since the late 1960s, a new concept has become popular: no-fault divorce. Instead of having to prove that the other party is at fault, one need only prove that the parties are "incompatible" or have "irreconcilable differences" or simply that they don't want to be married to each other anymore. To avoid stigma on the parties, even the term *divorce* is often changed by statute to "dissolution of marriage."

In the late 1960s and early 1970s, it appeared that no-fault divorce would sweep the country as state after state adopted no-fault laws. By the mid-1970s, however, the momentum toward no-fault divorce seemed to have slowed down quite a bit. As it is, about one-third of the states now have no-fault divorce. An additional one-third retain the traditional grounds for divorce but add another ground called "incompatibility" or "irreconcilable differences," thus making their statutes in effect "no-fault" divorce. Even in the remaining third of the states, where traditional grounds still apply, some judges interpret "cruel and inhumane treatment" as a catch-all that includes practically anything.

The result is that divorce today is easy to obtain, and divorce rates have risen dramatically. It is estimated that between 40 and 50 percent of marriages today will end in divorce.

Proponents of no-fault divorce have argued that no-fault statutes would eliminate bitterness from divorce proceedings. My observation as an attorney who has practiced in both fault and no-fault states is that the bitterness is about the same as ever, especially in cases which involve property or child custody disputes.

It would be wrong to attribute the soaring divorce rate solely to no-fault statutes. But no-fault laws have probably contributed to the social acceptability of divorce, and that in return has probably caused many to seek divorce rather than work to preserve and improve their marriages.

My basic objection to no-fault divorce, besides the fact that it is unscriptural, is that it constitutes a further retreat from the concept of personal responsibility. People used to think that if a marriage failed it was because one or both parties refused to make the necessary sacrifices to make the marriage work. Under the no-fault view, the marriage failure is nobody's fault—it was simply a bad situation, they were incompatible.

No-fault divorce can injure innocent persons. I have often counseled a person in a divorce situation who (from his own testimony at least, and in some cases by the other party's admission) was an excellent spouse, but the other party wants a divorce simply because he is tired of being married or is interested in someone else. The spouse who has wanted nothing but a marriage, home, and family can lose everything through no fault of his own. If no-fault statutes are to exist at all, they should apply only if both parties consent to proceed under the no-fault provisions (this is the case in Alaska, Maine, Massachusetts, Mississippi, and West Virginia).

Someone may say, "My marriage is my own business! It's my life, and I can do what I want with it!"

The problem is, your marriage affects other people besides yourself. It affects your spouse, your children, other loved ones, and society as a whole. It strikes at the institution God created for the ordering of society, the human family. In many countries the breakdown of the family has led to the breakdown of the nation as a whole. Rome was once a powerful empire, but when morals and family life declined, the empire declined as well. Divorce became easily obtainable, and wife-swapping became a common practice. Seneca said of Rome in his day,

> Does any woman now blush on account of a divorce, since the time when certain distinguished women of noble family reckoned their years not by the number of the (annual) consuls, but by that of their husbands and go forth (from their husbands) for the sake of being married, and married for the sake of being divorced? . . . Modesty is a demonstration of deformity.[3]

Another Roman, Juvenal, echoed a similar theme:

> So the number (of husbands) increases; so eight husbands have become hers in five autumns, a worthy fact for the inscription on her tomb.[4]

Divorce is not simply a religious issue. It is not simply a moral issue. It is not simply a legal issue. It is a political issue as well. No-fault statutes exist because they were passed by legislators and signed by governors as part of the political process and in response to political pressure. They can be changed in the same way.

Tax policies. In some ways current tax policies adversely affect the family. Different tax tables apply for married persons filing jointly, married persons filing separately, and single persons. In some tax brackets, two working people who are married to each other have to pay more tax than if they were single and simply living together. There are reports of instances in which high-income married persons have gone through the formalities of divorce and continued living together, in order to save thousands of dollars in taxes. The deduction for a married couple when both work has partially alleviated this problem, but not entirely.

This is wrong! Under no circumstances should the tax laws encourage immorality. They should be revised to prevent this.

Welfare policies. Welfare laws differ from state to state. In some states a family is not eligible for public assistance if there is an able-bodied father at home. To make their families eligible, many fathers divorce or abandon their wives and children. Some secretly send money to their families, and some sneak back home at night for "visits." Such cheating obviously cannot be condoned, but neither can the system that encourages it. It should never be economically advantageous for families to separate, and welfare laws should be revised accordingly.

Child welfare policies can also destroy the family unit. Unfortunately, it is sometimes necessary for welfare officials to intervene when children aren't receiving proper care. This can lead to temporary foster care, and even to permanent termination of parental rights.

Sometimes there may be no alternative, but I believe children are taken from their parents more often than necessary. The New York City Comptroller's Office studied the problem of foster care in 1978 and concluded that some 11,000 children had been kept in foster care status an average of five and a half years longer than necessary and that many of them had been moved from one foster home to another, causing permanant trauma and psychological damage.

Dr. Vincent DeFrancis, Director of the Children's Division of the American Humane Association, estimates that a good caseworker could salvage a minimum of twenty-five homes a year without placing the children outside the home, and the cost of doing so would be far less than foster care. Unfortunately, he says, many welfare departments do not try very hard to salvage homes because it is easier to obtain government funds for foster care than for programs which try to salvage the family. As a result, many foster children are shifted from one foster home to another for many formative years of their lives. Even though a child's home situation may be less than desirable, the effect of taking him out of that home and placing him elsewhere is very traumatic and damaging. Even the most abused or neglected child does not want to be separated from the only home he has ever known. Even though most foster parents are undoubtedly dedicated and loving, Dr. DeFrancis insists that foster care can in many cases do more harm than good.

God's Word condemns child abuse (Ephesians 6:4; Colossians 3:21), and the willful child abuser can be tried like any other criminal. But God entrusted children to their parents' care, and he created in parents a natural love for their children that far surpasses any love that the state or foster care can give them. Parents should therefore be given wide latitude in determining how their children should be raised.

What may seem like child abuse or neglect to one person may be merely a different philosphy or method of raising children. A social worker who believes children should never be spanked is likely to think that a parent who spanks his children is barbaric and abusive, while the parent is likely to believe the social worker is overly permissive. Proverbs 13:24, 22;15, and 23:13, 14 give me a clue as to who is right, but each parent should be free within reasonable limits to determine what method of parenting works best. I have seen child abuse allegations brought over such issues as feeding schedules and amounts, even though there were experts supporting both the parents' opinion and the social worker's viewpoint.

Except in the rarest of circumstances, government should not stand between parents and their children. When it becomes absolutely necessary that government intervene, that intervention should be as brief as possible, as minimal as possible, and always with the goal of bringing the family back together again.

Erosion of interspousal immunity. In law, certain types of communications are privileged; that is, they may not be revealed. In general, a doctor may not testify as to things his patient has told him, a lawyer may not testify as to things his client has told him, a clergyman may not testify as to things his parishioner has told him. The law's purpose in protecting such privileged communications is to encourage full and free disclosure between these parties—doctors can treat their patients better, lawyers can represent their clients better, clergymen can counsel and intercede for their parishioners better if they know the full story.

Traditionally, communications between a husband and wife were privileged in just the same way. With some exceptions, a husband could not testify against his wife, and a wife could not testify against her husband. There were sound reasons for this rule. The court recognized that the family unit functions better if husbands and wives freely communicate with each other rather than keep secrets from each other, and that spouses could not communicate so freely with each other if they knew the other spouse might have to testify against them in court. Furthermore, the biblical observation that a husband and wife were "one flesh" was taken seriously by the courts; and since a husband and wife were one flesh, the testimony of one against the other was tantamount to self-incrimination.

In recent years, however, the husband-wife privilege has been seriously eroded. More and more, we read of cases in which wives have been required to testify against their husbands, or vice versa. This trend is partly due to insurance, but it also reflects the general breakdown of family relationships and indicates that the marital relationship is not given the sacred respect it once enjoyed.

One can readily understand the frustration of an attorney or prosecutor who needs that bit of evidence that only a spouse can provide.
But the temporary advantage in a few cases is not worth the strain this
places upon the marital relationship. The erosion of this privilege
should be strenuously resisted.

The public schools. As we have seen, Scripture gives parents the
right and duty to educate their children (Deuteronomy 6:5-7; 11:18-
21; Proverbs 4:1, 2, 10, 11; Ephesians 6:4). Traditionally, parents have
fulfilled this duty with help from the church or synagogue. Within the
last century and a half, however, the state has gradually usurped this
function. As long as the public schools taught nominally Christian
values to their children, many Christians did not object to the state
taking over education. Within the past few decades, however, and
particularly within the past few years, more and more parents have
become concerned that the public schools may be teaching values to
their children that place them at odds with their parents.

The problems of education will be more fully discussed in Chapter
16. In this chapter let us concentrate upon the effect of the public
schools upon the family.

The average child spends about seven hours per day at school
during regular school hours. But it doesn't end there. Before and after
school there are extracurricular activities—band, pep club, athletics,
and the like. In the evenings and on weekends there are sports events
and other activities, and, of course, homework. There is little time left
for the family. The school, not the family, has become the center of the
child's existence.

And all the time the child is under public school control, he absorbs
public school ideas and public school values. Some of these may be
compatible with his parents' values. All too often they are not.

The Christian parent who believes in special creation may find his
children brainwashed by evolutionists. The parent may believe that
the source of values is God and his revealed Word, but the child may
learn from his teachers that values are relative and that we must
discover them for ourselves. The parent may believe that sex is to be
confined to marriage, but the school health teacher may teach that
premarital sex is okay "if you really care about each other."

Yes, parents can combat much of this by carefully instructing their
children at home, and they should be careful to do so. But why should
parents have to support a school system that teaches alien values or
compete with the state for their children's allegiance, perhaps for their
children's very souls?

Abortion and birth control. Throughout much of America today, a
minor may obtain birth control information, contraceptives, and even
an abortion without her parents' consent and sometimes even without

her parents' knowledge. All too often this comes through government agencies or agencies that receive government funding.

Such dissemination of birth control devices is necessary, it is argued, to prevent teenage pregnancies. Yet the more widespread sex education and contraceptives become, the more teenage pregnancies increase. So abortion is necessary, they argue, to prevent illegitimate births. Yet today, with one and a half million abortions per year, there are more illegitimate births than ever. When will we learn that we cannot eliminate social evils by accommodating immorality?

Recent court decisions have struck down statutes that require parental consent for a minor's abortion. Others have upheld statutes which require parental notification (but not parental consent). Many believe that even a statute which requires parental consent might be upheld by the courts, if it is properly drawn. Such legislation is desperately needed, not only to save the lives of unborn babies, but to save many teenagers from promiscuity and immorality. The state must not usurp the role of the parents in this regard.

Women's liberation. Many feminists demand the right to break out of the traditional stereotype of housewife and mother, and to compete in the business world on an equal basis with men. But some are not content with that. They ridicule and disparage those women who do want to be housewives and mothers.

Led by Phyllis Schlafly and others, many traditional housewives have fought back. Owing largely to their efforts, the Equal Rights Amendment was defeated, though it has been reintroduced.

Others, however, have become confused. Many had planned all their lives to become housewives and mothers, believing such a calling would bring meaning and fulfillment to their lives. Now they are told by the feminists that it is "demeaning" and "unfulfilling" to be a housewife, and they don't know what to believe. They are frustrated as housewives and feel guilty for not being "more," but don't feel any inclination for anything else. And the husband, who planned all his life to be a traditional husband and father and thought he was marrying a traditional wife, feels threatened, insecure, and resentful about these changes in his wife. If the wife goes to work, he may resent sharing the housework; that wasn't what he bargained for when he entered the marriage.

The confusion affects children as well. Tim LaHaye mentions an order of the California State Board of Education which forbids the inclusion of pictures in school textbooks depicting women with aprons and vacuums. The texts show men performing household chores and women as mechanics and other positions.[5] As a result, children lose their sexual identity. Girls especially become confused as their parents prepare them for one life-style but the schools and the media prepare them for another.

Such disparagement of the wife and mother is utter nonsense. It is hard to imagine a position more challenging than that of a "domestic engineer." A wife and mother has to be a psychologist, doctor, nutritionist, tailor, policewoman, public relations expert, teacher, preacher, interior decorator, chef, electrician, plumber, mechanic, gardener, sanitation engineer, and many other things as well. Why anyone would leave this for the "challenge" and "fulfillment" of pumping gas or working an assembly line is beyond me!

Many feminist leaders are outspoken in their condemnation of family life. Speaking in Houston, Texas, feminist leader Gloria Steinem declared, ". . . for the sake of those who wish to live in equal partnership, we have to abolish and reform the institution of legal marriage." One might wonder how Ms. Steinem proposes to "reform" marriage and "abolish" it at the same time, but her basic attitude toward marriage is clear.[6] Dr. MaryJo Bane, associate director of Wellesley College's Center for Research on Women, says, "The fact that children are raised in families means there's no equality . . . in order to raise children with equality, we must take them away from families and raise them. . . ."[7] The Declaration of Feminism similarly declares,

Marriage has existed for the benefit of men and has been a legally sanctioned method of control over women . . . the end of the institution of marriage is a necessary condition for the liberation of women. Therefore, it is important for us to encourage women to leave their husbands and not to live individually with men . . . we must work to destroy it (marriage).[8]

God's Word gives women respect and respectability which they had never enjoyed in any other culture, and we must do what we can to preserve biblical standards. But it establishes the man as the head of the house:

But I would have you know, that the head of every man is Christ; and the head of the woman is the man; and the head of Christ is God. (1 Corinthians 11:3)

Wives, submit yourselves unto your own husbands, as unto the Lord. For the husband is the head of the wife, even as Christ is the head of the church; and he is the saviour of the body. Therefore, as the church is subject unto Christ, so let the wives be to their own husbands in everything. Husbands, love your wives, even as Christ also loved the church, and gave himself for it. (Ephesians 5:22-26)

Likewise, ye wives, be in subjection to your own husbands; that, if any obey not the word, they also may without the word be won by the behavior of the wives, . . . For after this manner in the old time the holy women also, who trusted in God, adorned themselves, being in subjection unto their own husbands: even as Sarah obeyed Abraham, calling him lord; whose daughters ye are, as long as ye do well, and are not afraid with amazement; Likewise, ye husbands, dwell with them according to knowledge, giving honor unto the wife, as unto the weaker vessel, and as being heirs together of the grace of life; that your prayers be not hindered. (1 Peter 3:1, 5-7)

Let the woman learn in silence with all subjection. But I permit not a woman to teach, nor to usurp authority over the man, but to be in silence. For Adam was first formed, then Eve. And Adam was not deceived, but the woman being deceived was in the transgression. Notwithstanding she shall be saved in childbearing, if they continue in faith and love and holiness with sobriety. (1 Timothy 2:11-15)

Some have tried to explain these passages, claiming that the attitude of Paul and Peter toward women's rights was simply an accommodation to the custom of the times. Women were to be in subjection at that time because that was the contemporary custom, and if they were to violate that custom, they would bring the church into disrepute. Today things are different, so these passages no longer apply.

But that's not the reason given by the authors of Scripture. Nowhere do Peter and Paul explain these commands by reference to local custom. Peter cites as precedent Sarah's obedience to Abraham two thousand years earlier, and Paul goes way back to Adam and Eve and God's order of creation. There is simply no way of getting around the fact that God's Word calls for male leadership in the family.

Obviously there are exceptions. If a husband dies, or deserts his wife, or lacks the strength of character to lead the family, the woman may have no choice but to take charge. I personally believe there would be no women's liberation movement today, were it not for the weakness of men. But that is the exception, not the rule. The normal order of God's institution is the family with the husband and father as its head.

This does not have to mean inequality. "Equal" does not mean "same." There are differences between men and women. There are things men can do that women can't, and there are things women can do that men can't. Leadership in the family and the church is normally the responsibility of men.

Gay liberation. Few sins are denounced in Scripture as strongly as homosexuality:

Thou shalt not lie with mankind, as with womankind: it is abomination. (Leviticus 18:22)

For this cause God gave them up unto vile affections: for even their women did change the natural use into that which is against nature: and likewise also the men, leaving the natural use of the woman, burned in their lust one toward another; men with men working that which is unseemly, and receiving in themselves that recompense of their error which was meet. (Romans 1:26, 27)

Both Old and New Testaments clearly condemn homosexuality. This does not mean Christians are to hate homosexuals. We must love them, reach out to them, and seek to help them in every way possible. We ought to love homosexuals as God loves them, and to hate homosexuality as God hates homosexuality.

Homosexuality is not only a moral issue, but a political one, and it is largely the gay liberation advocates who have made it so. They have pushed, at the federal and state level and in counties and cities across the nation, for special laws recognizing them as a minority group and giving them special protection against discrimination. They have asked for the right to teach our children in public schools, at our expense. They have demanded that our public schools teach our children that homosexuality is an acceptable life-style. But homosexuality is not simply an individual matter; it affects society as a whole. It influences the entire moral strength and moral fibre of society. Furthermore, the more widespread homosexuality becomes, the greater the likelihood that homosexuals will recruit our children into homosexuality, voluntarily or involuntarily.

Homosexuality also constitutes an attack upon the family. Not only is homosexuality by nature contrary to the very purposes and functions of the family; in addition, as homosexuality comes "out of the closet" and is openly practiced and advocated in society, it tears families apart. Parents and children are alienated from one another when a child announces that he is a homosexual; marriages are torn apart at the seams when a spouse announces that he has become "gay." Parents are fearful of public schools, media, and other community agencies that teach their children that homosexuality is an acceptable life-style. And as increasing numbers of Americans adopt a "gay" life-style, or a "swinger" life-style, or any of the other alternatives advocated today, the traditional family declines in influence and number in society.

And homosexuality invites the judgment of God upon all of society. The great sin that brought destruction by fire and brimstone upon Sodom and Gomorrah was homosexuality (Genesis 19:5, 8). It is a mistake to suggest that the decision to become a homosexual affects no one but oneself.

Space does not permit a thorough discussion of the many political issues related to homosexuality. Should homosexual acts between consenting adults be prohibited by law? Should landlords be required to rent apartments to homosexuals? Should public schools be required to hire homosexual teachers? Should those homosexual teachers be allowed to tell our children that homosexuality is an acceptable sexual preference? These are difficult subjects, and they are very much political as well as moral and religious.

Kids' liberation. Women have been in the forefront of the women's liberation movement. Homosexuals have been leaders in the gay rights movement. But children's liberation is unique in that it is led entirely by adults. What kind of rights does this movement seek for children?

(1) Freedom from any kind of physical punishment. Sweden already has a law prohibiting spanking, and such laws have been proposed in the United States as well. (But see Proverbs 13:24; 22:15; 23:13, 14.)

(2) Freedom from religious indoctrination. Supposedly parents should not be allowed to compel children to attend church and Sunday school. (But see Deuteronomy 6:5-7; 11:18-21; Proverbs 4:1, 2, 10, 11; Ephesians 6:4.) Curiously, kiddie lib advocates do not seem very interested in freeing children from humanistic indoctrination in the public schools!

(3) The right to "divorce" one's parents. Amazing as it may seem, more and more authorities are arguing that a child should not have to live with his parents if he doesn't want to.[9]

(4) The right to birth control information and abortion without the parents' consent or knowledge.

(5) The right to choose one's own sexual preference and life-style.

(6) The right to participate in making any decision that affects the welfare or future of the child.

The irony is that children's liberation will not really free children at all. They need control, and most of them want control in the form of loving discipline from their parents. And when freedom is given to a group that can't handle freedom, a vacuum is created, and someone or something inevitably steps in to fill that vacuum.

Who will fill the vacuum if parents lose control of their children? The state! Children's liberation would remove them from the control of their parents and place them under the control of the state.

Public schools and social services are two such means of state control of children. Another, one which would reach children at a much earlier age than ever before, is comprehensive system of federally-funded and federally-controlled day-care centers. As reported in the *New York Times,*

> The creation of a national program of early childhood education reaching every youngster in the country, starting at three years of age . . . has emerged as a top priority among American teachers . . . the Child and Family Services Act of 1978 . . . is considered by education groups to be the opening wedge in their attempt to establish a universal education program beginning with (the) three-year-old.[10]

The 1970 Report to the President of the White House Conference on Children concluded, "Day care is a powerful institution . . . a day-care program that ministers to a child from six months to six years has over eight thousand hours to teach him values, fears, beliefs and behaviors."[11] Do we really want to give this kind of control to the government?

A tragic mistake of many who advocate state intervention in the family is the belief that once children are under the protection of the government they are in good and safe hands. Nothing could be further from the truth! We have already seen the problems inherent in foster-care programs, and when the state institutionalizes children its track record is even worse. Consider Martin Guggenheim's accusations in *Children's Rights Report:*

The State as an Abuser of Children

Regardless of the facts, people in the juvenile justice system cannot overcome the myth that state intervention is good for children. This is true despite the fact that the reality of the system has been graphically exposed time and again. Consider what the state of Texas had done to its children in the 1970's.

When new children (known as "fresh fish") were admitted to the Mountain View State School for Boys, they were regularly beaten by other boys at the facility as an initiation rite, under the supervision of the guards. Guards also employed a system of "racking": Boys were lined up against a wall with their hands in their pockets while a correctional officer punched each one in the stomach. Documented reports from Mountain View include the case of one boy who was hit and kicked by a guard until knocked unconscious and another boy who was knocked down and had tear gas sprayed in his face for not answering questions about why he had attempted suicide. Another boy struck by a guard ended up "with a hole going straight through" his eardrum.

Some of the less shocking situations included work details established by the institution. In one work detail, known as "picking," boys were forced to line up foot to foot with their heads down and were required to strike the ground with heavy picks swung overhead as the line moved forward. They did this for five hours at a time with three fifteen-minute breaks. During the breaks, all were required to sit with their heads between their legs looking down without talking. In a second detail, aptly called "grass pulling," boys were required to bend from the waist with their knees straight and pull grass out of the ground without talking or looking at one another for six hours a day. If they bent their knees they were "racked" or otherwise beaten. It is perhaps unnecessary to add that nothing was ever planted in these fields. The work was ordered solely for discipline . . . the Texas abuses can in no way be considered isolated, and they do condemn the entire system. . . .

Far from being isolated, state abuse of children is the most rampant problem we face. The state is, by far, the greater abuser of children in this country. And the abuse is imposed, it is to be remembered, not as punishment, but for the children's "own good."[12]

Defenders of the juvenile justice system will protest that these examples are exceptions rather than the rule. Hopefully that is the case, though there are recent indications that such abuse in juvenile institutions is more widespread than is commonly supposed.

But before we rush to institutionalize children, let us remember that parental neglect and abuse of children is likewise an exception rather than the rule. The vast majority of parents love their children very dearly and care for them very well. On the whole, parents do a far better job of raising children than does the state. That should not be surprising. God has placed children in the care of their parents, and he has created in parents a natural love for their children that far surpasses any love the state can give them.

The family is God's order for the human race. Let us preserve it at all costs, and let us carefully examine impending government legislation in the penetrating light of this question: Will this proposal strengthen or weaken the family?

15 Humanism

In the beginning was the Word, and the Word was with God, and
the Word was God. The same was in the beginning with God. All things
were made by him; and without him was not any thing made that was
made. In him was life; and the life was the light of men. And the light
shineth in darkness; and the darkness comprehended it not. (John 1:1-5)

Man is the measure of all things, of things that are that they are and of
things that are not that they are not. (Protagoras)

For me to live is Christ, and to die is gain. (Philippians 1:21)

These statements illustrate two of the three major faiths of America
today: theism and humanism. A third major religion, idolatry, has not
received public acceptance in America, though it is becoming more
popular than most of us realize. Nevertheless, theism and humanism
represent the two major faiths currently vying for our intellectual
assent.

What Is Humanism?
The term *humanism* is used imprecisely. Christians often use it as a
broad-brush term to describe anything and everything they find objectionable, from atheism to obscenity to liberal politics. One suspects
that often they are unable to give a clear definition of the term
because they do not really understand it.

The *American Heritage Dictionary* defines humanism as "a philosophy or attitude that is concerned with human beings, their achievements and interests, rather than with the abstract beings and problems
of theology." Humanism involves a preoccupation with man as the
center of the universe, the supreme value of the universe, and the sole
solver of the problems of the universe.

Humanism, therefore, is fundamentally at odds with Christianity. Christianity regards God, not man, as the supreme value of the universe and looks to God to solve the problems of the universe.

In 1933 a group of American humanists prepared a declaration of the philosophical and religious principles that were fundamental to humanism. They called it the Humanist Manifesto. Thirty-four leading humanists signed the Manifesto, among them educator John Dewey. A second manifesto was prepared forty years later, in 1973, and signed by one hundred and fourteen leading humanists and subsequently by many others. These manifestos are referred to as Humanist Manifesto I and Humanist Manifesto II.

An examination of Humanist Manifestos I and II reveals several basic principles of humanism:

God is either nonexistent or irrelevant to modern man. The sixth tenet of Humanist Manifesto I reads:

> We are convinced that the time has passed for theism, deism, modernism, and the several varieties of "new thought."[1]

Humanist Manifesto II claims:

> As in 1933, humanists still believe that traditional theism, especially faith in the prayer-hearing God, assumed to love and care for persons, to hear and understand their prayers, and to be able to do something about them, is an unproved and outmoded faith. Salvationism, based on mere affirmation, still appears as harmful, diverting people with false hopes of heaven hereafter. Reasonable minds look to other means for survival. (Preface)
>
> We find insufficient evidence for belief in the existence of a supernatural; it is either meaningless or irrelevant to the question of the survival and fulfillment of the human race. As non-theists, we began with humans, not God, nature, not deity. Nature may indeed be broader and deeper than we now know; any new discoveries, however, will but enlarge our knowledge of the natural.

Having rejected the existence or relevance of God, the second premise of humanism follows logically:

Man is the supreme value in the universe. When Lucifer rebelled against God, he declared, "I will be like the Most High" (Isaiah 14:14). And, having fallen from heaven, he seduced Eve with the same temptation: "Ye shall be as gods" (Genesis 3:5). The modern humanists offer man the same promise. Humanist Manifesto I, tenet 13 reads, "Religious humanism maintains that all associations and institutions exist for the fulfillment of human life."

Evolution is the unifying principle of all life. Christians regard man as a creature of God. He was created in an ideal state from which he fell and from which he continually degenerates and to return to which he stands in need of divine grace. The humanist sees man as moving in exactly the opposite direction. Instead of having been created in an ideal state and having fallen and degenerated thereafter, man's history is an upward progress of evolution from lower forms of life to his present state and greater things beyond.

Let's let the humanists speak for themselves on this point:
Humanist Manifesto II says,

> . . . [S]cience affirms that the human species is an emergence from natural evolutionary forces.

Evolution is far more than a mere corollary to humanistic thinking; it is a central cornerstone. It makes possible the humanist understanding of man as a purely biological creature, and facilitates a world view that leaves out God as the Creator.

Man is purely a physical or biological creature. Humanists view man as merely a highly complex animal; even the human brain is merely a physical organism which operates on electrical impulses like a highly complex computer.

Humanist Manifesto II reads:

> As far as we know, the total personality is a function of the biological organism transacting in a social and cultural context. There is no credible evidence that life survives the death of the body. We continue to exist in our progeny and in the way that our lives have influenced others and our culture.

No absolute morals or values exist. Since the humanist denies the possibility of God as a source of ultimate moral values, he turns to man as a source. Acts, morals, and values are good or bad only insofar as they operate for the benefit of human beings. Again, let us look at Humanist Manifesto II:

> Third, we affirm that moral values derive their source from human experience. Ethics is *autonomous* and *situational*, meaning no theological or ideological sanction. Ethics stems from human need and interest. To deny this distorts the whole basis of life. Human life has meaning because we create and develop our futures. Happiness and the creative realization of human needs and desires, individually and in shared enjoyment are continuous themes of humanism. We strive for the good life here and now. The goal is to pursue life's enrichment despite debasing forces of vulgarization, commercialization, bureaucratization, and dehumanization.

All of this makes sense if man is the highest value of the universe. But we reject the humanist value system because we recognize a higher value than man: God.

Man, through the use of his scientific reason, will solve his own problems. The humanist looks, not for the kingdom of God, but for the kingdom of man. Man, rising upward through the evolutionary process and through the achievements of science and human reason, will eventually perfect his world and create a paradise on earth. Humanist Manifesto II says,

> . . . [W]e can discover no divine purpose of providence for the human species. While there is much that we do not know, humans are responsible for what we are or will become. No deity will save us; we must save ourselves. . . .
> Reason and intelligence are the most effective instruments that human-kind possesses. There is no substitute: neither faith nor passion suffices in itself. The controlled use of scientific methods, which have transformed the natural and social sciences since the renaissance, must be extended further in the solution of human problems.

The Humanist Manifestos speak in magnificent terms about man and his future. But while purporting to glorify man, they actually debase him, for they rob man of the soul and spirit that distinguish man from the animals and that place him above the animals. They rob man of that unique feature by which he may claim to be created in the image of God. Instead, they relegate him to the status of a mere animal—a complex and intelligent animal, but an animal nevertheless. And by reducing him to a mere biological organism, they make him subject only to the laws of cause and effect. Making him the product of environmental determinism, they destroy his only basis for freedom. To the humanist, man is nothing more than a naked ape. Secular humanism could be better called secular animalism.

Government Promotion of Humanism

Humanists have a right to believe as they do. I do not wish to deny them their right to articulate and promote their beliefs. Shocking as their beliefs may be to many Christians, tolerance of different and at times unpopular beliefs is an essential ingredient of a free society.

My concern, however, is that humanism has become the official "party line" of our nation. In fact, all levels of government actively promote humanism. Let us consider several ways in which this is done:

Support for evolution. Federal, state, and local governments spend billions of dollars per year to promote the theory of evolution. If you doubt this, next time you go to a national park notice how much you and your children are exposed to the theory of evolution. How many books can you buy, how many displays can you view, how many presentations can you watch, and in how many tours can you participate without being presented with materials that either promote evolution or are based upon evolutionary premises? How many scientific or nature programs can you watch on television that are free of evolutionary influence? How many science courses in public schools and universities do not contain evolutionary thought?

Now, I don't mind being exposed to something I disagree with occasionally. But consider the public outcry that would arise were government to promote Christianity or creationism in this manner. Why should government ally itself with the faith of humanism?

The public schools. We have already seen the evolutionary influence in the public schools. But humanism does not start or stop there.

Begining with *Engel v. Vitale*[2] a series of Supreme Court decisions have severely limited the extent to which God may be recognized or worshiped in public school facilities.

Often public school officials defensively reply, "We don't allow our teachers to teach either for or against God. We're neutral!" But the message that comes across to the child is that God is not important enough to be mentioned. As the humanists say, he is either nonexistent or irrelevant to modern man.

Furthermore, much of the curricula used in public schools is based upon humanistic premises. Many of the materials used in values clarification classes teach that values and moral judgments are to be formed simply by human reason and the scientific method, not by reliance upon God's self-revelation in the Bible. Sex education materials often reject the Judeo-Christian ethic and teach or imply that premarital sex is perfectly acceptable so long as you don't hurt anyone, get venereal disease, or get pregnant. Sociology, psychology, and health courses often assume that man is a complex animal and the product of his environment and teach children to think accordingly. Materials used in history and civics classes often display a negative attitude toward America and the free enterprise system and advocate world government and Socialism instead.

Humanists themselves recognize the importance of the public schools in promoting their philosophy. As Paul Blanshard wrote in *The Humanist,*

> I think that the most important factor moving us toward a secular society has been the educational factor. Our schools may not teach Johnny to read properly, but the fact that Johnny is in school until he is 16 tends to lead toward the elimination of religious superstition. The average American child now acquires a high school education, and this militates against Adam and Eve and all the other myths of alleged history.[3]

In another issue of *The Humanist* a professor of English education said:

> Something wonderful, free, unheralded, and of significance to all humanists is happening in the secondary schools. It is in the adolescent-literature movement. . . . They may burn *Slaughterhouse Five* in North Dakota and

ban a number of innocuous books in Kanawha County but thank God [sic]
the crazies don't do all that much reading. If they did, they'd find that they
have already been defeated. . . . Nothing that is part of contemporary life is
taboo in this genre and any valid piece of writing that helps make the
world more knowable to young people serves an important humanistic
function. . . . None of the books are didactic, but all of them espouse the
humanistic ideals to which young people should be exposed.[4]

And another humanist leader adds,

I am convinced that the battle for humankind's future must be waged and
won in the public school classroom by teachers who correctly perceive their
role as the proselytizers of a new faith: a religion of humanity that recognizes and respects the spark of what theologians call divinity in every
human being. These teachers must embody the same selfless dedication as
the most rabid fundamentalist preacher, for they will be ministers of another servant, utilizing a classroom instead of a pulpit to convey humanist
values in whatever subjects they teach regardless of the educational level—
preschool daycare or large state university. The classroom must and will
become an area of conflict between the old and the new—the rotting
corpse of Christianity, together with all its adjacent evils and misery and
the new faith of humanism resplendent in its promise of a world in which
the never realized Christian idea of "love thy neighbor" will finally be
achieved.[5]

Dumphy's comparison of the humanist public schoolteacher to the
"rabid fundamentalist preacher" is most interesting. He is correct in
that each uses his pulpit or his lectern, his church or his classroom, to
promote his ideas. But he is wrong in suggesting that they are on the
same footing. For the fundamentalist preacher pays taxes to provide
the humanist teacher's salary and classroom. The teacher doesn't have
to contribute a dime to the preacher or his church if he doesn't want
to. Furthermore, the teacher has a captive audience. All parents must
send their children to public school unless they can provide other
means of education. But no one need attend church unless he wants to.

So you see what we are up against: a public school system that relies
upon compulsory attendance and public funds, relegates God to a
position of unimportance, and uses curricula that at times are based
upon humanistic assumptions.

The secularization of history. In the summer of 1982, while travel-
ing in the East, our family camped near the battleground of Manassas,
Virginia, where the Battle of Bull Run was fought. While there I
purchased a copy of the *Memoirs of Stonewall Jackson, His Letters
and Writings Compiled by His Widow Mary Anna Jackson.* As I read
through General Jackson's memoirs, I was fascinated by his public and
unabashed pronouncements of Christianity and the important place

Christianity held in his life. Describing the hanging of abolitionist John Brown, he says:

> I was much impressed with the thought that before me stood a man in the full vigor of health, who must in a few moments enter eternity. I sent up the petition that he might be saved. Awful was the thought that he might in a few minutes receive the sentence, "depart, ye wicked, into everlasting fire!" I hoped that he was prepared to die, but I am doubtful.

And he writes to his wife from Manassas on July 22, 1861:

> My precious Pet,—Yesterday, we fought a great battle and gained a great victory for which all the glory is due to God alone. . . . My preservation was entirely due, as was the glorious victory, to our God, to whom be all the honor, grace, and glory.[6]

Yet in the same bookstore on the same battlefield, I examined several contemporary books about General Thomas J. "Stonewall" Jackson, and not one of them even mentioned his religious faith.

George Washington has suffered much the same fate. Modern historians commonly ignore our first President's religious beliefs. In his book *Daily Sacrifice* he wrote beautiful prayers containing orthodox Christian theology. Consider his entry for one Sunday evening:

> O most glorious God . . . I acknowledge and confess my faults, in the weak and imperfect performance of the duties of this day. I have called on Thee for pardon and forgiveness of sins, but so coldly and carelessly that my prayers are become my sin and stand in need of pardon. I have heard Thy holy Word but with such deadness of spirit that I have been an unprofitable and forgetful hearer . . . but, O God, who art rich in mercy and plenteous in redemption mark not, I beseech Thee, what I have done amiss; remember that I am but dust, and remit my transgressions, negligences and ignorances, and cover them all with the absolute obedience of Thy Dear Son, that those sacrifices (of sin, praise, and thanksgiving) which I have offered may be accepted by Thee, in and for the sacrifice of Jesus Christ offered upon the Cross for me.[7]

The founders of our country were religious men. Most of them crossed the ocean for religious reasons, and their convictions shaped their lives. But modern history ignores or downplays their religious motivations. For example, the eight-hour CBS television drama "George Washington," aired April 8, 10, 11, 1984, virtually ignored the religious aspect of Washington's character and focused instead on unproven allegations concerning drunkenness and romantic attachments.

In this way, beginning in the late 1800s, a new, secularized version of history has been written. It is a grave distortion of reality.

The secular media. Certainly the media are among the most influential forces in our nation today. They occupy the minds and attention of most Americans for several hours a day. Their ability to communicate ideas, form opinions, and even shape personalities is staggering. Unfortunately, except for a few Christian stations, most of the media's influence is secular.

Newspapers usually give little coverage to religious news, unless it involves some type of scandal. In television dramas preachers are presented as bigots, Christians are portrayed as fanatics. Public television, financed by government funds, is supposed to present all sides of issues of public concern. But when was the last time you saw a program on public television supporting creation, or Christian morality, or the authority of the Bible, or the power of Jesus Christ to change people's lives?

Why is the government allowed to promote humanism?

In recent decades, humanists have sought the protection of the First Amendment. Concerned that their beliefs would not be given the same protection as Christianity, they wanted to establish themselves as a religion. They sent forth their creeds, they articulated their beliefs in religious terms, and they went to court to demonstrate their religious character. In 1961 a man sued the clerk of court for Montgomery County, Maryland. He argued that the clerk had violated his religious freedom by refusing to swear him in as a notary simply because he refused to affirm a belief in God. The U.S. Supreme Court ruled in the man's favor.

The Supreme Court expressly noted in *Torcaso* v. *Watkins*[8] that:

> Among religions in this country which do not teach but would generally be considered a belief in the existence of God are Buddhism, Taoism, Ethical Culture, Secular Humanism, and others.

In that decision humanism received official recognition as a religion, and humanists became entitled to free exercise of religion.

But remember, the First Amendment has two clauses—the establishment clause and the free exercise clause. Now, if humanism is a religion for purposes of the free exercise clause, it is also a religion for purposes of the establishment clause. Therefore, just as the government cannot actively promote Christianity, so also the government should not actively promote secular humanism.

A Christian Counterattack

In an attempt to remain neutral on religion, our courts and government officials have allowed the humanists to share their religion as the lowest common denominator. The result is government promotion of a religion or philosophy that violates the fundamental beliefs of orthodox Christians.

What should we do about it? Here are a few suggestions:

First, we should be aware of what humanism is and how it is manifested in various areas of public life: schools, the media, parks, public facilities, government grants, etc.

Second, tactfully but firmly, we should voice our objections when we see government funds or government facilities being used to promote humanism. Our objections can take two forms. We can ask that the humanistic materials be removed, or, and this is in my opinion often a better suggestion, we can ask that alternative views be presented, including those of orthodox Christianity. We should demand that public schools which teach evolution teach creation also. We should insist that libraries which contain humanistic books contain Christian books as well.

Third, we should defend the right of those who dissent from our humanistic culture to pursue alternative lifestyles: private and home schools, Christian radio and TV stations, even Christian communes or cooperatives (although I wouldn't want to live in one myself). The right of the individual to choose a God-centered environment for himself and his family must be defended at all costs.

Last, somehow the virtual stranglehold the secular media exercise over the minds of the American people must be broken. I do not advocate censorship or government control. But Christians should encourage the development of alternative sources of news and entertainment, such as CBN and CNN. Pat Robertson's CBN tries to broadcast from a Christian viewpoint, and Ted Turner's CNN at least tries to maintain objectivity in its news and decency in its programming. More effort is needed to develop Christian programming, including Christian drama and Christian fiction. The advent of cable TV, satellite reception, low-power television videotaping, etc., may provide expanded opportunities for this to be done.

16 Education

Education ranks with defense and welfare as one of the three major expenditures of government. No wonder education is a hot political issue in every part of the country and at every level of government.

Should the Christian support the candidate who favors the highest spending for education, or the lowest? Should he favor the candidate who wants to centralize control of education at the state or federal level, or the candidate who wants to maintain local control? Should a Christian support public education, or private education? And what about home schools? In short, what is the biblical position on education?

We will first examine certain myths which have arisen concerning education.

The First Myth: That Christianity is opposed to education. Nothing could be further from the truth. The value of learning and wisdom occupies a high place in Scripture. Both Solomon and Jesus praised wisdom (Proverbs 1:20; 8:5, 12, 14; Luke 7:35).

Furthermore, the synagogue and church were centers of learning in Old and New Testament times and throughout the church age. In the so-called "Dark Ages" the light of learning was kept alive mostly in the monasteries, and the universities that arose in the later Middle Ages were mostly founded and directed by the church. Most of the thinkers, writers, lawyers, philosophers, and scientists were churchmen also.

As Justice Frankfurter observed in *McCollum* v. *Board of Education,*[1]

> Traditionally, organized education in the Western world was Church education. It could hardly be otherwise when the education of children was primarily study of the Word and the ways of God. Even in the Protestant

countries, where there was a less close identification of Church and State, the basis of education was largely the Bible, and its chief purpose inculcation of piety. To the extent that the State intervened, it used its authority to further aims of the Church.

God is the author of all knowledge. God is the Creator of the human mind, and it is his will that we develop our minds to their fullest potential. Let us remember the words of the psalmist: "The fear of the Lord is the beginning of wisdom" (111:10).

The Second Myth: That education will solve all the world's problems. Solomon was the wisest man the world has ever seen. Solomon valued wisdom greatly, but also recognized that there were limits to what human wisdom can accomplish. He recognized that "Wisdom excelleth folly, as far as light excelleth darkness" (Ecclesiastes 2:13); but he also concluded that wisdom by itself is vanity and does not give lasting satisfaction (2:15). He despairingly concluded, "How dieth the wise man? as the fool" (2:16).

Horace Mann and other architects of the American system of public education passionately believed that education could improve human nature to the point where crime, poverty, and other evils could be virtually eliminated.[2] As he wrote in *The Common School Journal,*

> Let the Common School be expanded to its capabilities, let it be worked with the efficiency of which it is susceptible, and nine-tenths of the crimes in the penal code would become obsolete; the long catalog of human ills would be abridged; men would walk more safely by day; every pillow would be more inviolable by night; property, life, and character held by a stronger tenure; all rational hope respecting the future brightened.[3]

Mann and his followers have had their way with American education for the past one hundred and forty years. Their prophecies have not proven accurate.

In the 1930s Germany was perhaps the most highly educated nation in the world. We must remember that education can be used for wonderful things. But it has its limits, and if used in the wrong way, it has immense potential for evil.

The Third Myth: That education is the responsibility of the state. The directives of Scripture are clear: education is the responsibility of *parents.* Consider the words of Moses:

> Hear O Israel, the Lord our God is one Lord: and thou shalt love the Lord thy God with all thine heart, and with all thy soul, and with all thy might. And these words, which I command thee this day, shall be in thine heart: and thou shalt teach them diligently unto thy children, and shalt talk of them when thou sittest in thine house, and when thou walkest by the way, and when thou liest down, and when thou risest up. (Deuteronomy 6:4-7)

This command is clearly not directed to the state—not even to the church or synagogue. It is directed to parents.

Consider also the admonitions of Solomon in the Book of Proverbs:

> Hear, ye children, the instruction of a father, and attend to know understanding. For I give you good doctrine, forsake ye not my law. (4:1, 2)

> Hear, O my son, and receive my sayings; and the years of thy life shall be many. I have taught thee in the way of wisdom; I have led thee in right paths. (4:10, 11)

> My son, attend unto my wisdom, and bow thine ear to my understanding: that thou mayest regard discretion and that thy lips may keep knowledge. (5:1, 2)

> Train up a child in the way he should go: and when he is old, he will not depart from it. (22:6)

Paul gives a similar admonition in Ephesians 6:4:

> And, ye fathers, provoke not your children to wrath: but bring them up in the nurture and admonition of the Lord.

Parents, the message of Scripture is clear: the education of your children is *your* responsibility.

Some parents may choose to delegate to a public, private, or parochial school the authority to educate their children. But if those children are not raised in the nurture and admonition of the Lord, those parents cannot blame the schools. The responsibility is theirs; it cannot be delegated to anyone else.

The Fourth Myth: That public schools are the "American way." The public schools are respected institutions in America. In some parts of the country, particularly the upper Midwest, they are practically revered as the bastion of Protestant or American values. Private schools are at times and in some quarters viewed with suspicion.

This was not the attitude of our founding fathers. Education in early America was actually a mixture of home, private, and parochial schools, to some extent financed by local townships. Early colonial compulsory education laws simply reinforced the parental obligation to teach children; they did not envision state control of education. Today's concept of a state-controlled educational system was totally foreign to the thinking of our founding fathers. The modern system began in the 1840s when Horace Mann, Secretary of the Board of Education for the state of Massachusetts, fought for a secularized statewide public school system as a means of supplanting the Calvinist-dominated local schools of his day. His movement spread throughout the nation, and the modern public school system is the result. The movement was accompanied by compulsory education statutes passed in every state, requiring children between certain ages to attend school. However, even then the purpose of these statutes was not to abolish private or home education, but merely to make education available to all. As the Supreme Court of Massachusettses noted in *Commonwealth v. Roberts*,[4]

> The great object of these provisions of the statutes has been that all children shall be educated, not that they shall be educated in any particular way.

Still, some insist that all children should attend public schools because public schools are the general leveler and insure a quality of opportunity. The public school, it is argued, is therefore the guarantor of freedom.

I disagree. Freedom is best maintained, not by making sure everyone receives the same education, but rather by preserving diversity in education. The power to educate is the power to control thought and shape personality. The power to educate is the power to brainwash. No state should have an exclusive monopoly upon that power. And freedom and diversity are best assured if education takes place in many ways and comes from many sources: traditional and nontraditional, liberal and conservative, state, church, private, and home.

Exclusive state control of education is a blueprint for tyranny. Adolph Hitler declared in 1933,

> When an opponent declares, "I will not come over to your side," I calmly say, "Your child belongs to us already . . . what are you? You will pass on. Your descendants, however, now stand in the new camp. In a short time they will know nothing else but this new community."[5]

In 1936 Hitler abolished all Christian schools in Germany. In 1938 all public school teachers were ordered to resign from any denominational organization.[6] The state had complete control of education; Hitler's control of the mind of Germany was now complete.

The Fifth Myth: That the American public schools, founded by Horace Mann and others, lifted America out of a dismal ignorance. We are used to seeing stereotypes of ignorant, backwoods pioneers, devoid of the rudiments of any culture until the public schools brought learning and enlightenment to them.

In fact, however, colonial America enjoyed a very high degree of learning. Art, music, poetry, literature, philosophy, and political science flourished. Academic scholarship was at a much higher plane than today. For example, in colonial days, to be admitted to William and Mary College as an undergraduate freshman, the prospective student had to be able to not only read, write, and converse, but also to debate, in Greek. Our founding fathers were true scholars in a way that is most uncommon for politicians today.

Nor was American education in that day limited to the wealthy, the influential, or the privileged. Rather, it was the property of all. DuPont de Nemours, ancestor of the DuPont line of Delaware which later established DuPont Industries, was commissioned by Thomas Jefferson to survey and report upon American education around the year 1800. He wrote:

> Most young Americans . . . can read, write and cipher. Not more than four in a thousand are unable to write legibly—even neatly; . . .
> In America, a great number of people read the Bible, and all the people read a newspaper. The fathers read aloud to their children while breakfast is being prepared—a task which occupies the mothers for three-quarters of an hour every morning. And as the newspapers of the United States are filled with all sorts of narratives—comments on matters political, physical, philosophic; information on agriculture, the arts, travel, navigation; and also extracts from all the best books in America and Europe—they disseminate an enormous amount of information, some of which is helpful to the young people, especially when they arrive at an age when the father resigns his place as reader in favor of the child who can best succeed him.
> It is because of this kind of education that the Americans of the United States, without having more great men than other countries, have the advantage of having a larger proportion of moderately well-informed men; although their education may seem less perfect, it is, nevertheless, better and more equally distributed. But this does not mean that the general education cannot be improved.[7]

What an astounding claim! De Nemours says not more than four in a thousand are unable to write legibly and neatly. That's a literacy rate in the year 1800 of 99.6 percent!

Daniel Webster, speaking at Plymouth, Massachusetts in 1820, made a similar observation about American education:

> It is said that in England, not more than *one child in fifteen* possesses the means of being taught to read and write; in Wales, *one in twenty;* in France, until lately, when some improvement was made, not more than *one in thirty-five*. Now, it is hardly too strong to say that in New England *every child possesses* such means. It would be difficult to find an instance to the contrary, unless where it should be owing to the negligence of the parent; and in truth, the means are actually used and enjoyed by nearly everyone. A youth of 15, of either sex, who cannot read and write is very seldom to be found. [emphasis original].[8]

Alexis de Tocqueville, the French writer who visited America in the 1830s, wrote:

There has never been under the sun a people as enlightened as the population of the north of the United States. Because of their education they are more strong, more skillful, more capable of governing themselves and understanding their liberty; that much is undeniable.[9]

As we consider the quality of education in an age when Americans had so little to spend on it, our thoughts turn to the multibillion dollar educational enterprises of today. And we ask ourselves: what went wrong?

The Sixth Myth: That American public schools are providing quality education. For most of this century, Americans have boasted that they were the best educated nation in the world. The public school was thought to be the bastion of America values.

But in the last several decades there have been danger signs. Since 1963, Scholastic Aptitude Test scores have steadily declined, as have the results of other forms of standardized testing. Employers have complained that job applicants lacked basic skills: they could not write letters, spell and punctuate properly, or do simple math. The armed forces have been forced to institute special remedial reading programs because many of their recruits lack necessary academic skills. (Military manuals, formerly written at an eleventh-grade reading level, are now mostly written at a sixth-grade level.)

In May 1983 the report of the National Commission on Excellence in Education declared bluntly,

> If an unfriendly foreign power had attempted to impose on America the mediocre education performance that exists today, we might well have viewed it as an act of war. . . . The ideal of academic excellence as the primary goal of schooling seems to be fading across the board in American education.

The report noted surveys indicating twenty-three million adults, 13 percent of all seventeen-year-olds, and up to 40 percent of minority youth ". . . can be considered functionally illiterate," functionally illiterate being defined as being unable to read a want ad, bus schedule, or label on a medicine bottle. Another thirty-four million are just barely capable of simple reading tasks. The report warned:

> Our nation is at risk. Our once unchallenged preeminence in commerce, industry, science and technological innovation is being overtaken by competitors throughout the world. . . . The educational foundations of our society are presently being eroded by a rising tide of mediocrity that threatens our very future as a nation and a people.[10]

Going beyond academic content to the moral, social, and spiritual education our children are receiving, Josh McDowell reported in a recent letter,

In the next year, if current trends continue, the lives of more than 30 million young people will begin to fall apart. Here are the facts:

1. 500,000 will attempt suicide.
2. 1,000,000 kids will run away from home.
3. 1,200,000 teenagers will become pregnant.
4. 362,000 will give birth to illegitimate babies.
5. 434,000 girls under age 19 will receive an abortion.
6. 13 million unmarried teens will be active sexually.
7. 12 million will take some form of narcotic.
8. 4 million children will be beaten, molested, or otherwise abused by their parents.
9. 300,000 young people will have a serious drinking problem.
10. 5 million children will become victims of broken homes.

We need not go on endlessly citing the gory details. Nor need we deny that there are many excellent teachers in the public schools, including many who uphold traditional Christian values. But the evidence clearly reveals that as a whole public education today is in serious trouble.

The Seventh Myth: That without state regulation private schools will not provide quality education. Certainly I do not suggest that all private schools are good, any more than I would claim that all public schools are bad. But every study I have seen in recent years strongly indicates that on the whole private school children are performing better academically than their public school contemporaries.

In April 1981, a government-funded survey of 58,728 public and private high school seniors and sophomores drew nationwide attention. The survey, conducted by sociologist James Coleman's National Opinion Research Center, concluded:

> The students were tested on a 1½-hour battery of achievement tests prepared by the Educational Testing Service. On 20 reading questions, the average public school senior got 10.8 correct, the average Catholic school senior 11.9, and other private school seniors 13. On 27 vocabulary questions, the public sector got 12.9, Catholics 15.1, and other private 15.9. On 32 math questions, the scores were 18.9, 22.1, and 22.4 respectively.[11]

James Graley, Director of Curriculum Services for the Western Association of Christian Schools, has released a report on the recent Stanford Achievement Tests scores for students in schools belonging to that association. Test scores revealed that students in Christian schools belonging to the Western Association, grades 1-8, are achieving sixteen to nineteen months ahead of the national norm.

Dr. Raymond Moore, a development psychologist, former principal, superintendent, professor of education, and college dean and president, has extensively studied home schools and has concluded that, on the average, home school children do even better than their public and private school contemporaries.[12]

Nor can these statistics be explained away with the assertion that private school children come from elite, upper-class families. In my experience the reverse is true. Most Christian schools are operated by fundamentalist churches in which most of the parents come from lower middle-class, blue-collar backgrounds.

Rather, I am convinced, the success of private schools is due to the following factors: an emphasis on basic skills; teachers who view their work as a Christian calling and are therefore highly dedicated; stricter discipline standards; and parental interest and involvement.

Private schools have achieved their success with a fraction of the funding available to public schools. Frequently they meet in church basements, utilizing less than ideal facilities. Often their teachers teach for salaries much lower than public school teachers receive. And in almost all cases they function without government funds.

In most cases private schools function without much government regulation. However, government attempts to regulate private schools have taken several forms:

State licensing. Some states require that private schools attain a license from the state before they can operate. Many Christians object to such licensing requirements because they insist that the Christian school is a ministry of the church. For the state to require a Christian school to have a license, therefore, is equivalent to the state licensing the church. This, they say, is like Caesar licensing God!

Teacher certification. Other states require that private schools use only certified teachers. Some Christians object that such requirements are unnecessary and violate religious freedom. They advance the following arguments in support of their position: (1) *There is no evidence to indicate that teacher certification has any relationship to quality teaching.* (2) State teacher certification programs are based upon teacher education in state institutions which prepares teachers for teaching in the public schools but which is largely irrelevant to teaching in Christian schools. (3) Others argue that a requirement that they use only certified teachers limits their pool of prospective employees and makes it difficult for them to compete. Frequently they know of excellent teachers who are uncertified for various reasons, such as lack of particular course work, whom they would like to hire if the law would allow them to do so. (4) Others argue that the education to which state certified teachers must expose themselves contains much humanistic and anti-Christian indoctrination. Many would prefer that their teachers come from Christian institutions.

Curriculum requirements. In a few states, officials have attempted to impose curriculum requirements on private schools. They have tried to require that private schools use only certain texts approved by the state, or that private schools conform to a certain philosophy. Such requirements were struck down by the Ohio Supreme Court in *Ohio* v. *Whisner*[13] and by the Kentucky Supreme Court in *Kentucky State Board for Elementary and Secondary Education* v. *Rudasill*.[14] Christian schools have argued that such requirements violate their free exercise of religion and establish the religion of secular humanism.

Accreditation. Some states require that private schools be accredited. Others condition certain benefits upon accreditation. The problem is, these accrediting agencies often employ standards that violate the religious convictions of Christian people. The American Bar Association, for example, tried to deny accreditation to the law school at Oral Roberts University solely because the law school required a Christian commitment of its students and faculty, thus violating A.B.A. prohibitions against religious discrimination. Fortunately a federal court ruled that the A.B.A.'s requirement violated the university's right to free exercise of religion. A subcommittee of the Virginia State Board of Education voted to deny accreditation to the Education Department of Liberty Baptist College, solely because that department taught creationism instead of evolution. The board reversed the subcommittee's recommendation upon a showing that Liberty Baptist had revised its curriculum to give full treatment to evolution as well as creation. Isn't it strange that private schools (not financed by the taxpayers) have to give equal time to evolution, but state schools (financed by the taxpayers) do not have to give equal time to creation?

Nondiscrimination requirements. Efforts are under way by federal, state, and local civil rights agencies to force Christian schools to hire or enroll persons who are inimical to their religious viewpoint: homosexuals, atheists, Communists, and the like. Religious freedom is threatened when a Christian institution cannot maintain its integrity by hiring only those who support that institution's religious viewpoint.

Health and safety standards. Most Christians do not object to reasonable regulations designed to enforce sanitation, fire safety, etc. in Christian schools. They reason, according to the two-kingdoms concept, that Caesar has jurisdiction over certain things, but others are left to God. They insist, however, that these requirements be imposed fairly and be reasonably tailored to reflect the unique needs of smaller Christian schools.

Zoning. At times zoning restrictions have been imposed to shut down Christian schools. Typically these ordinances prohibit businesses in residential districts, but allow churches. Authorities sometimes reason that a Christian school is not a ministry of a church and therefore does not fit within the exemption for churches and cannot be allowed. The New Hampshire Supreme Court ruled that a Christian school was a ministry of a church in *City of Concord v. New Testament Baptist Church and Heritage Christian School,*[15] but other courts have reached different conclusions. Sometimes the case turns upon how closely the school is associated with the church, whether it is separately incorporated, etc.

Taxation. Long ago, in *McCulloch v. Maryland,*[16] the United States Supreme Court ruled that "The power to tax involves the power to destroy." Attempts to impose taxes upon Christian schools must therefore be regarded with grave apprehension.

These are just a few of the ways government attempts to regulate private schools. In a few instances such regulation may be necessary; the vast majority of it is not.

For private schools are largely self-policing. The parent who sends his child to a private school pays tuition, usually exceeding $1,000 per year per child. Yet if he were to send his child to the public school he could do so for free. Now, how many parents would forego the benefits of a free public education and spend thousands of dollars of their hard-earned money to send their children to private schools unless they were convinced their children were receiving superior education there? Ultimately, free market competition is the best guarantor of quality private schools.

The Eighth Myth: That education can be neutral about religion, morals, and values. Educators cannot merely teach raw facts. Inevitably education must give meaning to those facts. Educators are necessarily involved in the task of shaping ideas, personalities, morals, and values. And they cannot begin to teach these things without touching upon religion. Even those courses which most loudly claim to be divorced from religion, such as values clarification, are in fact teaching religion. They are in fact teaching children that values are based upon humanistic criteria such as experimentation, the scientific method, and consideration of utilitarian consequences, rather than by reliance upon God's revelation in the Bible.

The position of many public educators seem to be, "We want to be neutral about religion, and the best way to be neutral is simply not to talk about it." But the message that comes across to the child is that God is not important enough to be mentioned for most of the working day. The child learns that however important his religious beliefs may be in his church and private life, they are to be divorced from his academic and professional disciplines.

This is not what the Bible says. In all things, Paul tells us, Christ is to have the preeminence (Colossians 1:18). The fear of the Lord, the psalmist tells us, is the beginning of wisdom. All knowledge must be based upon God and his Word.

The early colonists in America recognized that education and religion were closely interrelated. The "Old Deluder Satan Act" of colonial Massachusettes (1647) ordered that every township of fifty householders or more was to appoint a schoolteacher to educate the youth "not only in good literature but in sound doctrine," and the reason for this education was that it was "one chief point of that old deluder Satan, to keep them from the knowledge of the Scriptures. . . ."[17] The 1784 New Hampshire Constitution declared that "morality and piety, rightly grounded on evangelical principles, will give the best and greatest security to government and '. . . is most likely to be propagated through a society by the institution of the public worship of the DEITY, and of public construction in morality and religion. . . .' " The New Hampshire Constitution therefore provided for the support and maintenance of "public, protestant teachers of piety, religion and morality. . . ."

Likewise, the Northwest Ordinance of 1787 linked religion with education. It declared: "Religion, morality and knowledge, being necessary to good government and the happiness of mankind, schools and the means of education shall forever be encouraged." As a result of the Northwest Ordinance, newly opened lands were set aside for schools—public, private, and parochial.[18] And the purpose of schools, as the Ordinance states, was to encourage "religion, morality, and knowl-edge."

Even after independence, and after the Constitution and First Amendment were adopted, public schools continued to teach religious doctrine. They could do so, because the First Amendment only applied to the federal government; it did not apply to the states or local communities: "*Congress* shall make no law respecting an establishment of religion or prohibiting the free exercise thereof. . . ." But in 1868, the Fourteenth Amendment was adopted, which states in part, "Nor shall any state deprive any person of life, liberty, or property, without due process of law; . . ." Rightly or wrongly, subsequent court decisions have interpreted the "liberty" clause of the Fourteenth Amendment as applying the First Amendment and most of the rest of the Bill of Rights to the states. Consequently, today all levels of government are equally prohibited from establishing religion or interfering with the free exercise of religion.

This being the case, the public school systems had two choices: (1) they could divorce themselves of their public school systems and turn them over to private hands; or (2) they could divorce the school systems from religious influence. Supposedly, they chose the latter.

In reality, religion and education have not been divorced from each other. The public schools have not divorced themselves from religion; rather, the religion of the public schools has changed. In the 1700s, the religion of American education was orthodox and mostly Calvinist

Christianity. In the 1800s this religion was replaced by a more liberalized version of Christianity bordering on Unitarianism. And in the twentieth century the religion of the American public schools appears to be something closer to secular humanism.

While Horace Mann's goal was to remove the schools from the control of Calvinist church authorities, he never intended to remove them from the influence of religion. However, his view of religion was much more liberal than that of his adversaries. A Unitarian, Mann piously believed in God, but also in the basic goodness and rationality of man. His biographer, Jonathan Messerli, writes of Horace Man's views:

> What the church had become for medieval man, the public school must now become for democratic and rational man. God would be replaced by the concept of the Public Good, sin and guilt by the more positive virtues of Victorian morality and conformity. . . .
>
> All of this was now possible if only reasonable men and women would join together to create a well managed system of schooling, where educators could manipulate and control learning as effectively as the competent new breed of engineers manage the industrial processes at work in their burgeoning textile factories and iron and steel mills. For the first time in the history of western man, it seemed possible for an intellectual and moral elite to effect mass behavioral changes and bring about a new golden age of enlightened ethics, humanism, and affluence.

Just as Horace Mann was the most influential educator of the 1800s, so John Dewey was the most influential educator of the 1900s. A signer of Humanist Manifesto I, Dewey was a thoroughgoing humanist. And for Dewey, religion played a clear role in American education:

> . . . The American people is conscious that its schools serve best because of religion in serving the cause of social unification; and that under certain conditions schools are more religious in substance and in promise without any of the conventional badges and machinery of religious instruction than they could be in cultivating these forms at the expense of the state consciousness.[19]

Humanists desire to use the public schools to promote a religion of secular humanism. As Sidney Meade writes,

> Of necessity, the state and its public education system is and always has been teaching religion. . . . The public schools in the United States took over one of the basic responsibilities that traditionally was always assumed by an established church. In this sense, the public school system of the United States *is* the established church.
>
> In this context one can understand why it is that the religion of many Americans is democracy—why their real faith is the "democratic faith"— the religion of the public schools.[20]

So religion is alive and well in the American public schools. But is it the religion to which Christians want their children exposed? Is it compatible with biblical Christianity? Martin Luther declared,

> Above all things, the principal and most general subject of study, both in the higher and lower schools, should be the Holy Scriptures. . . .
> *But where the Holy Scripture does not rule I certainly advise no one to send his child.* Everyone not unseasonally occupied with the Word of God must become corrupt; therefore we must see what people in the higher schools grow up to be. . . . *I greatly fear that schools for higher learning are wide gates to hell if they do not diligently teach the Holy Scriptures and impress them on the young folk.* [emphasis added][21]

The Ninth Myth: That private schools destroy diversity in education. A diverse and pluralistic America is best preserved when a wide variety of educational options are available: public schools, church schools of different denominations and varieties, private schools of different styles and philosophies, and home schools. Rather than give the state the right to control our children's minds, thus concentrating too much power in the hands of the state, diversity can better be preserved by allowing many forms of education.

Toward Freedom and Excellence in Education
What can a Christian do to make sure that his child receives a quality education? And what can he do to make sure that his child's education is compatible with Christian values? Here are several suggestions:

Private schools deserve our support. Whether you enroll your children in private schools or not, the right of parents to decide what type of education their children should receive is a fundamental constitutional right. That right is under severe attack today. In the United States of America of all places, pastors and parents are actually going to jail simply because they insist upon the right to educate their children in a Christian atmosphere free from government regulation. These courageous people deserve our prayers and support.

As we have seen, private schools are essential to the freedom of America, and without regulation and without much money they are outperforming the public schools. In those states where Christian schools are free from regulation, they should remain free. In those states where government regulates private schools, Christians should work for legislation that would free Christian schools from these regulations or at least make those regulations less burdensome.

If the state insists it must monitor the quality of private schools, there are much less restrictive means by which it can do so without dictating cirriculum choices, teacher certification, etc. For example, the state can require that public and private school children undergo periodic standardized testing to determine their educational progress. In Arizona, home school parents have been required to take competency tests—a better alternative than teacher certification, because it establishes how much a teacher knows rather than the extent to which that teacher has been formally educated. Many other means of insuring quality education in private schools can be employed if necessary. And if the state were to seek to improve private schools by working with them instead of trying to regulate them, its efforts would be much more productive.

We need to consider the thorny question of government aid to private schools. Many supporters of private schools argue that such aid is necessary to prevent an unjust situation created by "double taxaton." Private school parents are forced to pay taxes to support a public school system which they do not use and which is in many cases contrary to their religious beliefs, and also they are forced to pay tuition to send their children to private schools which are compatible with their beliefs. If all private school parents were to send their children to public schools, the burden to the taxpayers would increase substantially. By foregoing the public schools and using private schools, these parents save the taxpayers billions of dollars every year. It is argued that some of government aid is necessary to redress this imbalance and at least partially compensate the private school parent for the extra burden he bears and for the expense he saves the state.

Others argue that since most private schools are church-related or at least religious in character, government aid to these private schools would constitute an establishment of religion. The courts have rendered mixed verdicts on this issue. Such aid was struck down as unconstitutional in *Committee for Public Education and Religious Liberty* v. *Nyquist*[22] and in *Meek* v. *Pittenger*.[23] Other cases, such as *Everson* v. *Board of Education*[24] and *Mueller* v. *Allen*,[25] have upheld such aid.

The courts generally distinguish between the types of aid offered. First, they consider whether the aid furthers the clearly religious purposes of the school, or simply more secular purposes. For example, if the government supplies secular textbooks, that may be permissible; if it supplies Bibles, that would be struck down.

The court also distinguishes between direct and indirect forms of aid. A test seems to be: does the government program benefit primarily the school or the student and his parents? If it benefits the student or his parents, it is more likely to be indirect and therefore constitutional. Busing students to private schools, textbook loans, guidance counseling, speech help, remedial reading programs, and standardized tests have been held to be constitutional because they are secular in nature and because they aid primarily the students rather than the schools themselves. The recent case of *Mueller* v. *Allen* upheld a Minnesota law providing tuition tax credits for parents who incur expenses sending their children to public or private schools.

Proposals for government aid to private schools have taken many forms, in addition to those described above. Allowing tax credits or deductions for parents who send their children to private schools is one possibility, and the *Mueller* v. *Allen* case indicates this is constitutional so long as it applies to expenses incurred by parents in both public and private schools.

The "voucher plan" is another possibility. Under this proposal, the parent of every school-age child would receive a "voucher" or check from the state to cover the cost of that child's school tuition. The parent could take that check and present it to the public school when he enrolls his child there, or he could apply it to the tuition of a private school. If the private school charges more in tuition than the amount of the voucher, then the parent would make up the difference himself.

Others advocate a tax "check-off," which would allow taxpayers to designate on their tax return that the share of their taxes which goes for education should be paid to a private school designated by the taxpayer. All undesignated funds would go the public schools. A similar proposal would excuse taxpayers from that portion of their taxes which goes to public education upon a showing that that taxpayer has contributed an equal or greater amount to a private school.

I can understand why Christians dislike having to support a public educational system with which they disagree. I can also understand their excitement at the possibility of some type of government aid which would redress that imbalance. I am not impressed by the argument that such aid is unconstitutional; rather than establishing the religions of those churches which support private schools, it merely accommodates them by relieving them of the burden of double taxation, and recognizes the contribution these private schools make to the general welfare.

But I am concerned that government aid can lead to government control. If Christian schools want to remain free from government interference, they should be very hesitant about accepting government aid.

Let us suppose, for example, that the state were to institute a program of tuition tax credits or vouchers. What is to prevent the state from limiting the use of those vouchers to certain schools which conform to "public policy" as determined by the state?

Such control might begin with seemingly innocuous regulations that nearly everyone would support, such as prohibiting the use of vouchers or tax credits for schools that practice racial discrimination. But how about schools that practice sexual discrimination, or religious discrimination? What happens when the state tries to deny tax credits to parents who send their children to schools that refuse to employ atheists or homosexuals? Or schools that use uncertified teachers, or that teach "too much religion" in their curriculum? The dangers are obvious. Once you become accustomed to eating from the government's trough, it is hard to start foraging for yourself. Any proposals for government aid to private schools rather than to private school parents should be drafted very carefully to avoid the possibility of government control, and even then should be regarded with great caution.

We should work to improve the public schools. I know a fine pastor who has a Christian school in his church. When I asked for his assistance in an effort to promote balanced treatment for creation and evolution in the public schools, he refused. He said, "We have a Christian school in our church. That's where our children attend, so we don't care what the public schools do." Many Christians share that attitude. On the other hand, sometimes when Christians protest public school policies, they are told that since they don't send their children to the public schools, they shouldn't have anything to say about what the public schools do.

Much as I respect those who hold these viewpoints, they are wrong. Whether you have children in the public schools or the private schools, or even if you have no children at all, the public schools are your institution. As a citizen you own the public schools; as a taxpayer you pay for them. As a member of the community, you must live with the products of the public schools. Consequently you have as much right as anyone else to have a voice in how they are operated. In fact, if you are a private school parent you may have special insights that could be especially helpful in the public schools. And you may find that your input is appreciated more than you might expect.

Children who attend public schools should receive quality education, and Christians should work to make sure that quality exists. As you consider whom to vote for in school board elections, make sure the candidates you support are committed to quality education.

Obviously, no school board member will say he is against quality education. Christians should look more specifically at the candidate's policies. For example, does he support a renewed emphasis on basic skills such as phonics and mathematics, rather than nonessentials? Does he support efforts to improve the quality of teachers? Again, that might be easier said than done. Such proposals as merit pay and competency testing deserve careful consideration.

But academic excellence is not enough. A graduate can be academically excellent but morally and spiritually bankrupt. We need to consider these dimensions in education as well.

Given our pluralistic society and the way the courts presently interpret the First and Fourteenth Amendments, we cannot expect the public schools to provide Christian education. But we can at least expect the Christian child to be protected. We can at least ask that the public schools not deliberately exclude the Christian viewpoint or deliberately promote a different perspective.

Christians should therefore be on the alert for humanistic and other unchristian teaching in the public schools. Remember, to the same extent that the First Amendment prohibits the establishment of Christianity, it also prohibits the establishment of other religions. In *Malnak v. Maharishi Mahesh Yogi*,[26] the court held that Transcendental Meditation (TM) is sufficiently religious in character that the establishment clause forbids it from being taught in public schools.

Unfortunately some educators and lawyers, and even some judges, seem to think the establishment clause of the First Amendment prohibits only the establishment of Christianity, and the free exercise clause of the First Amendment protects everyone except Christians. This attitude reflects the hypocrisy of many modern liberals who are not truly liberal at all. This double standard needs to be exposed.

Christians can work to remove curricula which they find to be unduly offensive. Often, however, it is better to make sure that all viewpoints are given equal exposure—including the Christian viewpoint. Rather than working to eliminate the teaching of evolution, Christians are better advised to work for a two-model approach in which creation and evolution are given balanced treatment. Clarence Darrow, the attorney for John Scopes in the famous Tennessee "Monkey" trial, declared that "It is bigotry for public schools to teach only one theory of origins."[27] That's true regardless of which side is practicing bigotry at the present time.

In health and sex education courses, Christians could insist that students not be taught that premarital sex or homosexual life-styles are acceptable. But rather than asking that those viewpoints be banned, they might ask that the traditional Christian view of morality be presented as an option alongside these others.

The question of school prayer is difficult. In many ways it certainly seems unfair that one person can stop millions of students from praying together in a public classroom—especially if those who dissent are free to remain silent or leave the room. On the other hand, atheists are citizens too, and their constitutional rights deserve respect. Furthermore, many fundamental Christians might question the propriety of organized, state-written school prayers.

In the famous *Engel v. Vitale* case, the prayer in question read, "Almighty God, we acknowledge our dependence upon thee, and we beg thy blessing upon us, our parents, our teachers, and our country." Is this prayer truly addressed to the God of the Bible? Are you really sure you want a public school teacher who may not even be a Christian to lead your children in this prayer? I must confess that I am undecided about the issue.

A proposal which may make more sense is to allow silent meditation. A space of time is set aside in some school districts, sometimes commenced and terminated with a bell or chimes, during which the child is free to pray, meditate, think obscene thoughts, or do whatever he wishes in the privacy of his own mind and soul. This practice has been upheld by some courts and struck down by others, and the Supreme Court is presently considering it. I believe it is a valid accommodation of the free exercise rights of religious children and that it is an acceptable practice.

In several jurisdictions a genuine travesty of justice has occurred when religious student groups have been denied the right to meet in public school facilities. Groups such as Young Life, Youth for Christ, and others have been banned from high school and college campuses while secular groups are allowed to meet freely.

This is nothing but blatant discrimination. Not only does it violate the free exercise of religion; it also violates the First Amendment guarantee of free speech. If schools and universities are going to allow some student groups to meet, they cannot restrict those groups based upon the content of their speech. If these groups choose to talk about religion, they have as much right to do that in a student meeting as they have to talk about politics, homosexuality, literature, or any other subject. In the recent landmark Supreme Court case of *Vincent* v. *Widmar*,[28] the right of a Christian organization to meet on campus facilities for religious worship and discussion was upheld. By an 8-1 margin the Supreme Court ruled that the university's refusal to let a Christian group called Cornerstone meet on campus violated the students' right to freedom of speech. However, the Supreme Court has not yet determined whether this same right should apply to religious groups in public high schools, and the lower courts have reached conflicting decisions on that question. Several cases currently in the lower courts may reach the United States Supreme Court soon.

Christians should be aware that various groups such as the American Civil Liberties Union are working actively to remove religious influence from the public schools. Often they claim that the First Amendment restricts the right of school authorities to allow religious exercises more than it really does. Misinformed or dishonest persons have often led school boards to believe that such practices as nativity scenes, carols during Christmas programs, prayer at baccalaureate services, Bibles on teachers' desks, the expression of religious opinions by Christian teachers, etc. have been held unconstitutional by the Supreme Court when in reality they have not.[29]

Christians should not assume that school board members, administrators, and teachers are their enemies. Often they are willing to accommodate Christian beliefs and practices to the extent they can legally do so. Also, they sometimes do not understand why Christians insist upon certain practices or why Christians find certain other practices objectionable. Frequently a courteous meeting with school officials in which Christian concerns and requests are outlined and explained can be most productive.

However, there is also a time for firmness. Probably the greatest nightmare a school official experiences is the possibility that he might be sued. When a school official hears Christians politely requesting a Christmas program on the one hand, and the ACLU screaming about lawsuits on the other hand, he is likely to follow the path of least resistance. School officials should be made aware that Christians can and will go to court if necessary to protect their constitutional rights. Obviously it is therefore important that Christians be aware of their constitutional rights. Several good sources of information are *The Christian Legal Advisor* by this author (Milford Mich.: Mott Media, 1984); Lynn R. Buzzard, *Schools: They Haven't Got a Prayer* (Elgin, Ill.: David C. Cook, 1982); Lynn R. Buzzard and Samuel Ericsson, *The Battle For Religious Liberty* (Elgin, Ill.: David C. Cook, 1982).

Obviously, the individual citizen can have a greater impact on his school system at the local level than at the state level or federal level. Diversity and limited, representative government are best preserved if government is decentralized. For this reason education should be locally financed and locally controlled. State and federal aid and regulation should be kept to a minimum.

Take a personal interest in your children's education. Whether you teach your children at home, or delegate that duty to a public or private school, you are still responsible for the education of your children. Know what they are learning! Meet their teachers, examine their texts, discuss their courses with them. If your children are learning certain ideas at school, go to the library and find out about those ideas yourself. Be ready to reinforce ideas that are compatible with Christianity and be ready to intelligently discuss and combat those which are not. Otherwise your children will grow beyond you, you won't understand them, and they won't respect your views.

The fact that your children are going to school elsewhere does not mean they cannot learn at home. Remember again the biblical admonition:

And thou shalt teach them diligently unto thy children, and shalt talk of them when thou sittest in thine house, and when thou walkest by the way, and when thou liest down, and when thou risest up. (Deuteronomy 6:7)

Education does not have to take place in a formal classroom. This passage says parents should teach their children while they sit in the house, while they go for walks, and at other times of the day. A vacation can be a great learning experience in economics, history, geography, science, map reading, and (if you're unlucky) auto mechanics. A trip to the grocery store can be a lesson in arithmetic, nutrition, and home economics.

I vividly remember a walk I enjoyed with my four-year-old son David in some snowy meadows near our house in rural Fergus Falls, Minnesota. We got to talking about how the world was round, and to demonstrate that we made a huge snowball to represent the world. I traced an outline of the United States on the snowball. We pinpointed Minnesota, then pointed out where Russia would be, China, Norway, etc. Then I showed him the hills and valleys, rivers and forests on all sides of us, how vast the horizon was and showed how that whole area was a mere speck compared to the entire world. And I explained how God, the Creator of the universe, had to be infinitely greater even than that. David then asked, "But isn't Jesus God?" When I assured him that was true, David trapped me: "But Jesus was just as big as people!" Try explaining the hypostatic union to a four-year-old!

Know what your schools are doing, and what your children are learning. Regardless of where you send them to school, keep on teaching them yourselves. Not only will it help them learn; it will also help you to educate yourself.

17 Censorship and Pornography

In Gerrard, Pennsylvania, in 1982, a controversy over a book in use in the public schools attracted nationwide attention. Several students and their parents objected to the book *Working* by Studs Terkel, because of obscenities, profanities, and certain viewpoints expressed in the book.

Immediately the media and the educational establishment jumped to the defense of "academic freedom." Terkel himself went to Gerrard to defend the book against what he called "censorship." The protesting students and their parents were denounced as bigots, censors, narrow-minded, and generally stupid.

But wait a minute. A closer examination of the controversy reveals that the protesting students and parents were not trying to prohibit Mr. Terkel from writing or publishing his book. They did not object to the book being sold in the bookstores, displayed in the school library, or even used in class. All they had asked was that they be assigned an alternative book because Terkel's book violated their religious and moral beliefs.

Think about that! A teacher in a public school uses her authority to force students to read a book for a required class, even though she knows that book violates their religious beliefs. The students are denied the right to choose an alternative book, and are told that if they do not compromise their religious beliefs and read the objectionable book they will not be allowed to graduate. Only after they secured a lawyer who negotiated with school authorities were dissenting students finally allowed to receive their diplomas. But even then they were assigned F's for the course. And whom does the press label an enemy of the First Amendment? The students and their parents, of course![1]

Suppose the tables were turned. What if liberals were to protest the use of a textbook because it was too traditional, too conservative, too chauvinistic, or—heaven forbid!—too religious? The protesting student would be lauded as a free-thinking hero exercising his First Amendment rights, and school officials would be condemned as narrow-minded bigots trying to use the power of the state and the school system to enforce their views on others. Clearly the issue of censorship is more complex than most of us realize.

Regardless of which side is practicing censorship, what does the Bible say about it? Is censorship justified in Scripture? Let's look at some basic principles.

Ideas and beliefs are vitally important. Many, particularly those whose views tend to be more liberal, have difficulty understanding why beliefs are so important to Christians. Such people often feel that it really doesn't matter much what a person believes, and truth is relative anyway.

Christians, however, regard truth as absolute, God-given, and known through God's revelation in the Bible.

Furthermore, knowledge and acceptance of the truth of Jesus Christ's revelation determines one's eternal destiny in heaven or in hell.

> I am the way, the truth, and the life: no man cometh unto the Father but by me. (John 14:6)

> Believe on the Lord Jesus Christ, and thou shalt be saved, and thy house. (Acts 16:31)

> He that believeth on the Son hath everlasting life: and he that believeth not the Son shall not see life; but the wrath of God abideth on him. (John 3:36)

Therefore, for the Christian, the question of what one believes is vitally important.

Christians should not force their ideas on others. Christianity is both the most tolerant and the most intolerant of religions—tolerant in that God gives man the choice of accepting or rejecting the gospel; intolerant in that God holds man eternally responsible for his choice.

During his earthly ministry Jesus Christ preached forthrightly and fearlessly. He preached to individuals; he preached to groups. At times his preaching annoyed his listeners. But on no occasion did he use force to compel anyone to accept him as Lord and Savior. He laid his claims clearly before the rich young ruler; but when the young man walked away sorrowfully, Jesus let him go. Jesus knew that his heart was not ready to receive the gospel (Mark 10:17-22).

Christ used force to clear the temple of God of corrupt practices, but he did not force his ideas on others. Nor do his followers have authority to do so. Christians must earnestly contend for the faith (Jude 3), but they should not use the authority of the state to impose their viewpoints upon unwilling listeners.

Nevertheless, some censorship is inevitable. The American Library Association has joined with several other organizations to establish The National Coalition Against Censorship. Working together, these groups have placed ads in newspapers and magazines across the country warning people of the dangers of censorship and extolling the virtues of freedom of thought.

What they didn't tell you, however, is that among the principal censors in the nation are librarians themselves.

Only a tiny fraction of the books that are published in any given year ever make their way into local public libraries. Someone must decide which books will be purchased for the library and which books will not, which books will be retained on the shelves and which will be discarded. How do librarians make those decisions? They consider which books would be of the greatest value, interest, and benefit to the public. And in making those determinations, inevitably their own religious, moral, and value systems come into play.

Teachers are censors too. A teacher of American government cannot possibly use every text on American government that has ever been written. He must, of necessity, select some and reject others. And he will select the texts that in his opinion best present the facts, ideas, and values that he wants to convey to his students. This is censorship.

The same is true of reporters and editors. Recently I was interviewed on a local radio station. The reporter and I talked over a tape recorder for about forty minutes. Of this, a minute or less was actually used on the newscast. The reporter selected those portions of my comments which he thought were most important, aired those, and censored the others. And in doing so, he employed his own value systems in determining what was most important. Fortunately he did a good job of editing; it is not always so.

So you see, some censorship is inevitable. The question is not whether censorship will take place, but who will make censorship decisions and what criteria they will utilize in doing so.

In Texas, and in some other jurisdictions, citizen groups made up of parents and taxpayers have a right to review school textbooks and make recommendations. These groups are not advocating censorship. They simply recognize that somebody has to make decisions as to what texts are going to be used, and that such decisions inevitably are based on morals and values. These parents and taxpayers are simply asking to have a hand in the selection process so their beliefs will be considered along with those of teachers, librarians, and administrators.

A great difference exists between banning the publication of a book, or refusing to sell a book in your own bookstore, or refusing to carry a book in the public library, or refusing to assign the book to children in a required class. Some forms of censorship are repressive and even unconstitutional; others are necessary and even desirable.

Censorship is not practiced exclusively by the right. As we have seen, librarians, educators, editors, and media officials regularly practice censorship as part of their professions. Often these persons are much more liberal than the general public, and their censorship decisions reflect their more liberal values. Many attempts to suppress books were obviously not instigated by the Moral Majority. For example, *The Adventures of Huckleberry Finn* was barred from classroom use in, of all places, Mark Twain Intermediate School of Fairfax, Virginia, because it allegedly portrayed blacks in a demeaning fashion. John Wallace, a school administrator who opposed using Twain's novel, called it a "grotesque example of racist trash."[2]

An all-white, eleven-member committee in Davenport, Iowa, reached the opposite conclusion: they voted unanimously that *The Adventures of Huckleberry Finn* is not racist and is important for the study of American literature. However, the school did afford some relief; they allowed a complaining student to read another selection.[3]

Feminists have demanded the removal of material of magazines and books that, in their opinion, display women in traditionally "sexist" roles such as cooking, sewing, and mothering. As a result of this, under the Women's Educational Equity Act Program, hundreds of thousands of dollars have been spent to rewrite textbooks, curricula, and media packages to eliminate sexist stereotypes and promote the "unisex" view.[4]

The list goes on. Jewish Americans have protested Shakespeare's *The Merchant of Venice* because of the portrayal of Shylock. Mexican Americans have protested materials which depict them as the villains at the Alamo.[5]

Probably no group is more often the subject of repression and censorship than traditional Christians. With the blessings of the courts and their distorted interpretation of the First Amendment, and at times going beyond what the court has directed, religious materials have often been banned from public school classrooms and even from public school libraries.

Perhaps the most absurd example of censorship in history occurred at Lake Worth Community High School in suburban West Palm Beach, Florida. A Bible club had met in a school classroom for about twenty-five years, but in the spring of 1983 principal David Cantley told the group they could no longer meet in school facilities. Not only that, he ordered his staff to sit down with razor blades and cut the club's picture out of the school's yearbook![6] The student group sued, and the case is currently in the courts. Isn't it strange that the national media did not deem this incident worthy of comment?

Another notable example is the current creation/evolution controversy. I know of no creationist who wants to ban the theory of evolution from the public schools, despite what the media often claim. But I know of many evolutionists who want to ban creation; very few evolutionists believe creation should be given balanced treatment. Isn't this censorship?

As an attorney who specializes in First Amendment religious freedom cases, I have received numerous complaints in recent years about discrimination against creationists in academic circles: creationist professors fired or denied tenure, government grants denied to creation scientists, academic honors denied, graduate degrees refused, doctoral dissertations rejected, etc. Occasionally the evolutionary establishment has been careless enough to openly admit that they have acted against a creationist because of his convictions. Usually they have been subtle and clever and have disguised their discrimination with other reasons.

A most blatant example of discrimination occurred early in 1983 at Iowa State University, where a student was dismissed from class for having complained about the professor's dogmatic teaching of evolution (the university later reinstated the student). Professor John W. Patterson expressed amazement that students who have publicly rejected biological evolution and who believe the universe is only 10,000 years old are nevertheless allowed to pass science courses and graduate from the university. He declared,

> I suggest that every professor should reserve the right to fail any student in his class, no matter what the grade record indicates, whenever basic misunderstandings of a certain magnitude are discovered. Moreover, I would propose retracting grades and possibly even degrees if such gross misunderstandings are publicly espoused after passing the course or after being graduated.[7]

Professor Patterson later insisted that his ideas did not amount to condemning students for their beliefs, but his statement speaks for itself. Such bigotry would be downright comical, were it not for the tragic violation of civil liberties involved.

In 1947 Dr. Immanuel Velikovsky wrote *Worlds in Collision* and sold it to Macmillan Publishers. Velikovsky's book did not endorse special creation, but it did cast serious doubt upon the assumptions of uniformitarian geology and evolutionary science. His book created a veritable scientific storm. A distinguished Harvard professor wrote to Macmillan, urging the publisher not to venture into the "black arts" and implying that Macmillan's reputation in the academic community would suffer as a result. When Macmillan refused to back down, a number of professors at prestigious universities organized a boycott of Macmillan. They refused to submit works to Macmillan for publication and refused to order works published by Macmillan for their classrooms. Dr. Gordon Atwater, Curator of the Hayden Planetarium and Chairman of the Department of Astronomy, supported Velikovsky to the extent of asking that his views be given fair consideration; for this he was fired from both positions. Bowing to this pressure, Macmillan was forced to transfer its publishing rights to Doubleday, even though *Worlds in Collision* was at the time Number 1 on the *New York Times* nonfiction best-seller list. Don't these antics seem strange coming from professors who in almost any other context would prate self-righteously about academic freedom?[8]

This is not to say that boycotts are always wrong. I find fault with these professors, not for their boycott, but for their hypocrisy—for pretending to be open-minded scientists though they are really zealots for a narrow point of view. These are the same professors who in nearly any other circumstance would protest censorship and violations of academic freedom.

Boycotts themselves may be legitimate expressions of First Amendment dissent and protest. Take, for example, the Rev. Don Wildmon. Wildmon was concerned with excessive sex and violence in television programming. He therefore organized the Coalition for Better Television and took steps to implement a nationwide program of rating television programs and boycotting the products sold by companies that sponsor objectionable programs.

The media reacted predictably. They accused the Coalition of advocating censorship, ignoring the First Amendment, reviving the Inquisition, and many other silly things. TV Producer Norman Lear began a campaign to "counter the intolerant messages and anti-democratic actions of moral majoritarians"[9]—apparently unaware that Moral Majority had not joined in the boycott.

But Lear's remarks reveal that he understands neither tolerance, democracy, nor the Moral Majority. The Coalition never asked that any television programs be banned. They never asked the government to interfere with television at all. All they said was that they, as a group, would not buy the products of the companies that sponsored the objectionable programs. Wildmon said in effect, "Broadcast anything you choose, but we're not going to pay for it." That isn't undemocratic. That's democracy in action, letting the law of supply and demand determine what will and will not be shown on television.

Do you see the double standard? Do you see the chronic tendency of liberals to assume they have a monopoly on the First Amendment? The same First Amendment that gives Normal Lear the right to produce whatever he wants gives Rev. Wildmon the right to say he doesn't like what Normal Lear produces. And the First Amendment also gives Wildmon the right to freely associate with others to advance his beliefs. Properly applied, boycotts are a legitimate First Amendment weapon.

Christians can take action consistent with the First Amendment to insure that their views are treated fairly. As we have seen, censorship in the sense of government banning the publication, sale, or reading of certain books is generally to be avoided. But censorship in the sense of citizen input in the public purchase and use of books in libraries and classrooms is necessary and to some extent desirable. Christians should respect the First Amendment, but they should not allow their opponents to use the First Amendment as a barrier to block them from asserting their views.

In several states, special committees exist at the state or local level to review textbooks and make recommendations concerning them. This isn't censorship in the derogatory sense of the term. It simply insures that citizens at all levels—parents, taxpayers, teachers, and librarians—all have input into the selection of textbooks that affect all our children. Christians should support the formation of such groups, and should eagerly participate in them.

Sometimes it may be necessary to insist that certain objectionable materials not be presented in class. At the very least, children who find a book objectionable for religious or moral reasons should be allowed to read another book instead. A teacher may believe that students should be exposed to such a viewpoint, but the teacher has no right to force that belief on the child or his parents.

Often, however, it is better to insist that curricula be broadened to include the Christian or conservative viewpoint, than to ask that the liberal or humanist viewpoint be suppressed. Rather than demanding that evolutionary books be thrown out of the library, we should insist instead that creationist books be included. And certainly we should demand that the Christian viewpoint be given an equal position on the marketplace of ideas.

Cal Thomas said it well:

All we are asking for is balance. I would like to think that I could walk into a public library and find not only works by Gloria Steinem but also those of Phyllis Schlafly. I would like to think that a teenager could be taught in sex education that a serious alternative to abortion is teenage abstinence, or should pregnancy occur, that adoption might be preferable. I am not trying, as the ads say, to shove religion down anyone's throat. But I do think that everyone has a right to speak, and that the Christian voice is being choked off.[10]

I think all Christians, and all fair-minded people, can say amen to that!

A Special Word About Pornography

The Bible strongly condemns the sin of lust. Christ, in the New Testament, places that sin on a plane with adultery itself (Matthew 5:28). And adultery, of course, is a capital offense in Scripture (Leviticus 20:10; Deuteronomy 22:22). The same is true of many other sexual sins: incest and other unnatural sex (Exodus 22:19; Leviticus 20:11, 14, 16); rape (Deuteronomy 22:25); and some forms of unchastity (Deuteronomy 22:21, 23, 24; Leviticus 21:9).

Pornography, with its blatant appeal to lust and its encouragement of sexual sins, is to be strongly condemned.

The state also has a right to regulate pornography because pornography has a negative effect upon the well-being of others in society. Neil Gallagher, in his excellent book *How to Stop the Porno Plague*,[11] cites numerous examples of violent crimes which apparently were influenced by pornography. He cites the example of Houston, Texas, in the summer of 1973, when police dug up the bodies of twenty-two teenage boys who had been sexually abused and murdered. In the apartment of the accused murderers, police found sex torture devices sold in pornography shops. Gallagher cites other examples from "The Report of the Commission on Obscenity and Pornography":

> Two persons who tortured and murdered three young persons and tape recorded the events; pornographic literature was found in the possession of one of them.
> An Oklahoma case in which seven teenage youths raped and sodomized a 15-year-old girl. They admitted they had been incited to commit the act by reading obscene magazines and looking at lewd photographs.
> A 15-year-old boy sexually molested a 9-year-old girl in San Antonio, Texas. He said that his father kept pornographic pictures in his dresser drawer and that each time he looked at them the urge would come over him.
> A rape in Cleveland, Ohio in which the man was reading obscenity in his panel truck just prior to the attack.

Government regulation of pornography is different than other forms of censorship. Here we are not talking about the suppression of ideas and their expression. We are not talking about the infringement of people's First Amendment rights. Pornography is in a separate class.

At least since *Roth v. Goldman*,[12] the courts have agreed that that which is truly obscene is outside the protection of the First Amendment. The issue is not whether obscenity is protected; it is not. The issue is, what is obscene? Are topless photos obscene? Is a literary masterpiece obscene because it contains a few sexual overtones?

The courts have wavered somewhat on this question, but the current doctrine of the courts was set forth in *Miller v. California.*[13] In *Miller* the Supreme Court said the following three-part test must be followed in determining whether a work is truly obscene:

> (a) Whether or not "the average person, applying contemporary community standards" would find that the work taken as a whole, appeals to the prurient interest, . . . (b) whether the work depicts or describes, in patently offensive way sexual conduct specifically defined by the applicable state law; and (c) whether the work, taken as a whole, lacks serious artistic, political, or scientific value.

As you can see, this test is in many ways vague. Several things are plain, however. The test to be applied involves "contemporary community standards." These standards may vary in different parts of the country. What is obscene in Orange City, Iowa, might not be obscene in Atlanta, Georgia; and what is obscene in Atlanta might not be obscene in New York City.

Furthermore, in determing whether or not the work has serious "artistic, political, or scientific value," one must look at the work as a whole. As the Court said in *Kois v. Wisconsin,*[14] "A quotation from Voltaire on the flyleaf of a book [does not] constitutionally redeem an otherwise obscene publication."

While this standard leaves a lot of unanswered questions, it does provide communities with some freedom to regulate obscenity.

Christians should work to prohibit obscenity within the limits the courts have set forth. And they should also work to enforce obscenity ordinances by cooperating with local law enforcement officials and prosecutors.

Here are several types of ordinances which would probably be upheld by the courts if they are properly drawn.

(1) The outright prohibition of hard-core pornography is constitutional. Gallagher, in his book, has drafted several excellent model ordinances which might be helpful.

(2) In *Young v. American Mini-theaters Inc.,*[15] the Supreme Court upheld two Detroit zoning ordinances which prohibited adult theaters within five hundred feet of a residential area or within one thousand feet of other regulated establishments such as taverns.

(3) State laws prohibiting indecent exposure, indecent massage parlors, and live sex acts on stage have generally been upheld.

(4) The state has more freedom in regulating pornographic or semi-pornographic materials as they relate to minors. In *Ginsberg v. New York,*[16] the Supreme Court upheld the constitutionality of a state law prohibiting the distribution to minors of sexually explicit materials, even though those materials might not be considered obscene as relat-

ed to adults. In other words, states and cities can probably prohibit the sale of *Playboy* to minors even though *Playboy* is probably not obscene under the *Miller* test.

(5) "Kiddie porn" is probably the most disgusting form of pornography one can possibly imagine. Such material exploits children and causes them lifelong emotional scars. It appeals only to perverts and could trigger violent sexual attacks on children. The production, promotion, distribution, and display of kiddie porn should be a felony and should be strictly enforced. *New York* v. *Ferber*[17] indicates that such law would be upheld as constitutional.

(6) "Block bidding" should be prohibited. This is the practice whereby movie wholesalers require local motion picture theater owners to bid for a "block" or large number of movies as a whole to show in their theaters. Often local theater owners cannot pick and choose which movies they want; the theater owner either has to buy all of them or get none at all. Thus he is practically forced to buy some R-rated or X-rated movies along with the G and PG movies. Some theater owners claim that they would like to show only wholesome entertainment, but because of block bidding they cannot. Legislation prohibiting block bidding is desirable. It could be of considerable value in cleaning up the movie industry, and it might also improve the overall quality of the theater since theater owners could not then be forced to show mediocre films.

(7) Laws requiring that sexually explicit materials be kept under the counter or behind plain wrappers would probably be upheld. The purchase of pornographic literature is generally the result of impulse buying, and Gallagher points out that when such legislation is placed into effect, pornography sales to adults drop 75 to 95 percent.[18]

But even the strongest laws against pornography will not be effective unless they are actively enforced. We must insist that our leaders support them. Only with proper enforcement can this blight be removed from our society and from the society our children will inherit.

18 The Right to Life

It is no accident that humanists tend to favor abortion. Abortion, euthanasia, infanticide, geriatricide—all are inherent in the humanist view of man.

For while humanists claim to glorify man as the supreme value in the universe, they in fact reduce man to an animal. For they remove that which separates man from animals—the conviction that man is created in the image of God.

If man is nothing but a complex animal, his value and worth are relative. An individual human being may be sacrificed for the common good, just as one sheep may be sacrificed for the good of the flock. Hence, the unwanted child may be aborted because his or her birth would be inconvenient, expensive, or otherwise undesirable. The elderly parent may be "terminated"—a nice antiseptic term—because he has "outlived his usefulness." For that is the ultimate test of human worth in the humanist scheme of values—how "useful" is this person to society?

That is not the biblical view of human value. The Bible attributes infinite value to each individual human being, not based on his usefulness to society, not even based on his usefulness to the Kingdom of God, but based on his creation in God's image.

So God created man in his own image, in the image of God he created him; male and female he created them. (Genesis 1:27)

The psalmist tells us,

For thou hast made him a little lower than the angels, and hast crowned him with glory and honor. (Psalms 8:5)

170

Because God places infinite value upon each individual human being, he places a very severe penalty upon the willful taking of human life.

Whoso sheddeth man's blood, by man shall his blood be shed. (Genesis 9:6)

But let's finish the verse, for it gives the reason for the severe penalty:

. . . for in the image of God made he man.

God values human life so much that he has ordained capital punishment for those who wrongfully destroy human life.

These commands of God confer by implication a right to life. God's negative command, "Thou shalt not kill (murder)" (Exodus 20:13) conveys by implication the right to live. And by authorizing civil government to punish those who take human life, God has given civil government the responsibility of protecting human life.

This is the basic fallacy of the prochoice position. Government cannot be neutral on this question. If government has the responsibility of protecting human life, government must determine at what point that protection begins, and at what point it ends.

Is there not a similarity among the following statements?

"I personally would never own a slave, because I don't believe in slavery. But I have no right to impose this moral judgment of mine upon the good people of the South. After all, many fine and well-educated people consider blacks to be less than human, and the Supreme Court has said blacks are not protected by the Constitution."

"I personally would never have an abortion because I don't believe in taking innocent life. But I have no right to impose this moral judgment of mine upon others. After all, many fine and well-educated people do not consider the unborn child to be human, and the Supreme Court has ruled that unborn children are not protected by the Fourteenth Amendment."

"I personally would never gas a Jew because I consider it inhumane. But I have no right to impose this moral judgment of mine upon the good people of the SS. After all, many fine and well-educated Nazis believe Jews are lower on the evolutionary scale than Aryans, and the German courts uphold the Nazi position."

By supposedly adopting a prochoice policy, government has in effect determined that the protection of the right to life begins only at birth. But the logical point at which to begin the protection of the right to life is the point at which human life begins.

When does human life begin? Again, our determination should be based, not primarily upon legal, historical, or even medical considerations, but upon God's Word. What saith the Scriptures?

When Does Human Life Begin?[1]

I believe the various passages of Scripture which touch upon this question, when taken as a whole, compel a prolife answer. Let us look at what the Scripture has to say.

First of all, the languages used in the Bible make no distinction between the unborn child and children who are already born. Let us consider the various words which are used in the Bible for the unborn child. *Brephos* is a Greek word used for baby. The term is used for "babe" in Luke 1:44, where Elizabeth says of her unborn child, John the Baptist, "the *babe* leaped in my womb for joy." In the next chapter the angel says to the shepherds, "Ye shall find the *babe* wrapped in swaddling clothes, lying in a manger" (Luke 2:12). Again the word is *brephos.*

Paul uses the same word in 2 Timothy 3:15 when he says of Timothy, "From a *child* thou hast known the holy Scriptures. . . ." Note that the authors of Scripture make no distinction in the use of the word *brephos.* It is used for an unborn child in Luke 1 and for a child already born in Luke 2, and used again for a young child in 2 Timothy.

Huios is commonly used for son in the New Testament. In Luke 1:36 the angel tells Mary, "And, behold, thy cousin, Elisabeth, she hath also conceived a *son,*" using *huios.* Five verses earlier, in Luke 1:31, the angel told Mary, "Thou shalt conceive in thy womb, and bring forth a son," again using *huios* for the child conceived and a child brought forth. And two chapters later, God the Father says to the Lord Jesus Christ, "Thou art my beloved *Son*" (Luke 3:22). At this time Jesus was a young adult. Again, the New Testament makes no distinction between an unborn child and a child already born in the use of the word *huios.*

Ben is an Old Testament Hebrew word commonly translated son or child. It appears hundreds of times in Scripture, normally for a child already born, but not always. In Genesis 25:21-24 we read of Jacob and Esau in the womb of their mother, Rebekah: "And the *children* struggled within her. . . ." The word used for children is *ben.* We also see the word *ben* used for Ishmael when he was thirteen years old (Genesis 17:25) and for Noah's adult sons (Genesis 9:19).

"Let the day perish wherein I was born, and the night in which it was said, There is a *man child* conceived" (Job 3:3). The word here is *gehver.* It is used approximately sixty-five times in Scripture, usually for a man or men.

In Job 3:16 Job expressed the wish that he could have been miscarried, "as *infants* which never saw light." Clearly, in that context infants are unborn children—children who never were born, but who were miscarried. The word used is *gohlahl*. We find this word on twenty occasions in Scripture, and in each other instance it is used for a child already born. For example, in Lamentations 4:4 we read, "The young children ask bread," and again the word is *gohlahl*.

These linguistic factors are significant. The authors of Scripture, writing under divine inspiration, do not refer to the unborn child as a fetus, or as tissue, or in some other subhuman capacity. They use the same terminology for the unborn child as for the child already born. That indicates that they regard him as a human being.

Secondly, the biblical authors identify themselves with the unborn child. In Psalm 139:13-16 David says, "Thou hast covered *me* in my mother's womb." He does not say, Thou hast covered the fetus that became me, or thou hast covered my embryo. Rather, he identifies himself with the unborn child in the womb: "Thou hast covered *me.*"

We see a similar reference in Isaiah 49:1: "The Lord hath called *me* from the womb." Note also Jeremiah 1:5: "before *thou* camest forth out of the womb I sanctified *thee*, and I ordained *thee* a prophet unto the nations." God, the speaker in the above passage, sanctified and ordained Jeremiah while Jeremiah was still in the womb! And Jeremiah identifies himself with that unborn child in the womb.

Thirdly, the Bible speaks of the death of the unborn child. Job says in Job 10:18, 19, "Wherefore then hast thou brought me forth out of the womb? Oh that I had given up the ghost, and no eye had seen me! I should have been as though as I had not been; I should have been carried from the womb to the grave."

Jeremiah expresses a similar desire in Jeremiah 20:15-18, "Cursed be the man who brought tidings to my father, saying, A man child is born unto thee; making him very glad . . . because he slew me not from the womb; or that my mother might have been my grave, and her womb to be always great with me. Wherefore came I forth out of the womb to see labour and sorrow, that my days should be consumed with shame?"

The authors of Scripture speak of the unborn child as dying. How can one die if one is not alive?

Fourthly, the Bible affords legal protection to the unborn child. Exodus 21:22-25 is probably the passage of Scripture which speaks most directly to the question of abortion. However, many shy away from the use of this passage because in many English translations it seems ambiguous. After a thorough study of this passage, however, I am convinced that the passage affords legal protection to the unborn child.

In the King James Version, the passage reads as follows: "If men strive, and hurt a woman with child, so that her fruit depart from her, and yet no mischief follow: he shall be surely punished, according as the woman's husband will lay upon him; and he shall pay as the judges determine. And if any mischief follow, then thou shall give life for life, eye for eye, tooth for tooth, hand for hand, foot for foot, burning for burning, wound for wound, stripe for stripe."[2]

The key phrase is in verse 22: "her fruit depart from her." Some translations, including the *New American Standard*, render this passage as "miscarriage." But an analysis of the words used clearly demonstrates this translation to be in error. The word for fruit is *yehled*. *Yehled* is found eighty-nine times in the Old Testament. In every other place it is translated as a human being—a child, children, a boy, or a young man. In no other passage is it used for fruit or for fetus or anything less than human.

Second, the word for depart is *yatsah*. In every other passage where this verb appears in connection with childbirth, except possibly Numbers 12:12 which may refer to a stillborn child, it is used for a live birth (Ecclesiastes 5:14, 15; Jeremiah 20:18; Genesis 25:23-26; 38:28-30). If Moses had wanted to speak about a miscarriage, there are at least two distinctive Hebrew words which mean miscarriage and which he could have used. He could have used the word *shakol*, a word which he used for miscarriage just two chapters later in Exodus 23:26, and which also appears in Hosea 9:14. Or he could have used *nephel*, a word which is used for miscarriage in Job 3:16, Psalm 58:8, and Ecclesiastes 6:3. But Moses chose not to use those words. Instead, he used the word *yatsah*, which normally means live birth. Why? I am convinced that Moses, writing under the inspiration of the Holy Spirit, knew what he was saying and meant exactly what he said: "her fruit (children) depart from her"—a premature but live birth.

The word used later in the passage for "mischief" is *ahsohn*. The term simply means mischief or harm, and could refer to anything from death to a sore finger. Some have understood the mischief of this passage to refer only to harm to the mother; but, as we have seen, since the passage contemplates a live birth, there is no reason to think that the mischief cannot pertain both to the mother and to the child.

When properly translated, the meaning of the passage is clear. If men are involved in a fight and hurt a pregnant woman so that she delivers her child prematurely, but there is no injury to the mother or child, the husband is to be compensated only for his time, expenses, inconvenience, etc., and perhaps pain and suffering as well. But if the mother or child is injured as a result, or if either die as a result, the *lex talionis*, or law of like punishment, applies: eye for eye, tooth for tooth, life for life.

The clear meaning of this passage is that the unborn child is a human being whose right to life is protected just like anyone else's right to life. The criminal penalty for causing the death of the unborn child is death!

Fifthly, the Bible ascribes sin to the unborn child. In Psalm 51:5 David says, "Behold, I was shapen in iniquity; and in sin did my mother conceive me."

David does not mean that the act of conceiving him was sinful; there is no suggestion that David was illegitimate. Rather, he means that the child has a sin nature from the point of conception.

This naturally raises the question, does the sin nature reside in the human body, or in the soul or spirit? Ezekiel 18:4, 20 state, "the soul that sinneth, it shall die." This indicates that the sin nature probably resides in the soul/spirit, not in the body. In any event, the fact that a sin nature is attributed to the unborn child clearly establishes that the unborn child is a person, not a mass of tissue.

Sixthly, the unborn child shows signs of personhood. In Luke 1:44 Elisabeth says, "the babe leaped in my womb for joy" when she (Elisabeth) came into the presence of Mary, who was carrying Jesus in her womb. Elisabeth's child, John the Baptist, leaped for joy in the womb! It is hard to imagine a mere glob of tissue leaping for joy. This is an expression of emotion, and therefore a sign of personhood.

In Genesis 25:22 we read that Esau and Jacob "struggled together within her"—i.e., within the womb of Rebecca. This again is a sign of personhood.

The medical evidence supports this viewpoint. For the Christian who regards the Bible as the authoritative Word of God, the medical evidence is secondary. When the Word of God speaks clearly, the Word of God controls. But it is reassuring to know that the medical evidence largely supports the view that human life begins at conception.

Consider the medical facts. When the sperm and egg come together to form a fertilized zygote, from that moment on the newly formed child has a different genetic makeup from that of his mother and father, a genetic makeup that is uniquely his and that will remain fixed throughout his life. If we could analyze that genetic makeup, we would know from conception the child's sex, future hair color, bone structure, skin color, and many other traits. From that time on, the genes, chromosomes, DNA, and RNA are fixed and do not change. It is appropriate to say that from that time on the unborn child is not a "potential human being," but rather a human being with potential.

Many people are amazed to learn how quickly the unborn child develops. Two weeks after conception, the child already has a blood supply and blood type. His blood and his mother's blood come into contact through a membrane, but they do not mingle. By the end of the third week, the heart is beating and a body rhythm has been established that will last all the child's life. By the fourth week, the brain, arms, legs, kidneys, liver, and digestive tract have begun to take shape. By the end of four weeks, the embryo is already ten thousand times larger than it was at conception. By the end of the second month, the child is still less than one thumb's length in size, but everything—hands, feet, head, organs, brain—is in place. The child even has fingerprints!

During the third month of pregnancy, the palms of the hands become sensitive, as do the soles of the feet. The child will grasp an object placed in his hand and can make a fist. He swallows, his lips part, his brow furrows, and he is capable of moving to avoid light or pressure. His eyelids even squint. By the end of the third month, the baby has fingernails, sucks his thumb, and recoils from pain. After the third month, the development of the unborn child consists largely of growth and strengthening. All of the vital organs are already present.[3]

Not only does the unborn child have the physical characteristics of a human being; scientific evidence indicates that he has personality characteristics as well. He is able to react to pain; if the womb is touched with a sharp instrument, the infant will draw away from the instrument. He is able to move; and some move more than others, indicating different personality traits among individual unborn children. At times, he even tries to make sounds as early as the third month.[4]

Alternative positions as to the beginning of life are wholly unsatisfactory. There are basically four alternative positions as to the beginning of life. The first is that human life begins at birth, the second that human life begins at viability, the third that human life begins at quickening, and the fourth that human life begins at implantation. Let us analyze each of these in the light of Scripture and logic.

Birth: The primary (and usually the only) Bible passage cited in support of this position is Genesis 2:7—"And the Lord God formed man of the dust of the ground, and breathed into his nostrils the breath of life; and man became a living soul." From this passage it is sometimes argued that one is not completely human until he begins breathing—that is, at birth. However, an analysis of this verse does not support that position.

First, this is a unique, one-time event. The formation of Adam does not answer the question of whether human life begins in the womb, because Adam was never in a womb. He was the first man, and he was formed out of the dust as an adult, mature human being. Obviously God had to give him a soul/spirit, because there was no other way he could get one. Never has anyone else been formed out of dust, not even Eve! And nowhere are we told that God breathed into Eve the breath of life. The probable reason is that Eve was formed out of living, organic matter, Adam's rib. Before God had breathed into

Adam the breath of life, Adam was still dust, inorganic matter— perhaps something like a clay statue. This has been true of no one since that time.

Second, even if we conceded that in order to be human one must breathe air, the fact still remains that the unborn child uses oxygen. He simply takes in oxygen in a different manner before birth—through the placenta. There are certain medical procedures by which air is inserted into the womb, and occasionally the unborn child will take a gulp of air during that procedure. Does that make him human?

In the final analysis birth is simply a change of environment in which one acquires the ability to breathe for himself. This by no means makes him any more or less human than he was before.

Viability: This means the ability of the child to sustain life outside the womb. Many argue that the unborn child becomes human at the point of viability.

First, let us note that this position has no scriptural support whatso- ever.

Second, viability varies with time. A generation or so ago viability was generally thought to be about the sixth month after conception. But because of modern medical procedures the child born premature- ly much younger than the sixth month is often capable of surviving— at the fifth month, or possibly even younger. Does this mean that children become human sooner today than they did a generation ago? As medical science advances, will children become human even sooner still?

This is a very subjective test. In many cases there is no way of knowing whether the child, given adequate medical treatment, could have survived outside the womb. It is left to the subjective opinion of the doctor.

Finally, what does viability have to do with being human? The child who is already born can survive for a few hours or a few days at most without someone to care for him. Does this mean that he is not human?

In short, viability is no basis for determining whether or not the unborn child is human. The viability test simply cannot stand up in the light of Scripture or common sense.

Quickening: Some argue that the unborn child becomes human at the point of quickening. Quickening is sometimes used interchange- ably with viability, but it actually has a different meaning. It refers to the point at which the mother first feels the unborn child move within her womb.

First, we should note that, like viability, the idea that a child be- comes a human at the point of quickening has no scriptural support whatsoever.

Second, quickening is a very subjective test because it depends upon the mother's feeling rather than actual movement. A baby may move long before he is large enough or strong enough for his mother to feel his movement. In fact, there is cellular activity from the point of conception.

Third, quickening varies with individual babies. Some begin moving more quickly than others. And throughout pregnancy some are simply more active than others. This does not mean that some babies become human sooner than others.

Like the test of birth and the test of viability, the test of quickening lacks a scriptural support and has no basis of logic or common sense. It must therefore be rejected as a test of humanness.

Implantation: Still others look to implantation, the point at which the fertilized egg becomes fastened to the wall of the uterus, usually a few days after conception. After implantation, the embryo can no longer divide into identical twins. How, it is asked, could this embryo be human if it can divide into twins?

One suggestion is that God creates two human souls at conception and causes them to temporarily reside in one embryo. Another might be that God creates one human soul at conception and another at twinning.

Apart from that difference, there is no reason to look to implantation as the beginning of human life. It is a position without support in Scripture, science, or common sense.

We may summarize as follows:

1. The authors of Scripture make no linguistic distinction between unborn and born children.

2. The biblical authors identify themselves with the unborn child.

3. The Bible speaks of the death of the unborn child.

4. The Bible affords legal protection to the unborn child.

5. The Bible ascribes sin to the unborn child.

6. The Bible shows the personality of the unborn child.

7. The medical evidence supports the above analysis of Scripture.

8. Other positions—birth, viability, quickening, and implantation—lack support in Scripture, evidence, and logic.

9. Therefore, human life begins at conception.

10. Therefore, the unborn child is a living human being.

Is Killing the Unborn Child Justifiable?

We have established that the unborn child is a human being; therefore, killing him constitutes the killing of a human being. But to establish that abortion violates Exodus 20:13, we must also inquire whether or not the killing of that unborn child is justifiable. Let us, therefore, examine some of the commonly advanced justifications for abortion.

Should a mother have control over her own body and the right to choose whether or not to bear a child? For the most part I agree that a woman should have control over her own body. But as the above evidence has demonstrated, the unborn child is not part of her body; he or she is a separate and distinct human being.

Should abortion be allowed for cases of rape or incest? First, let us place this problem in its proper perspective. While pregnancy resulting from rape is extremely serious for the persons involved, it happens far less frequently than is commonly supposed. A study reported in the *Illinois Medical Journal* found that there were no pregnancies resulting from rape in a nine-year period in Chicago.[5]

Other reports show no pregnancies resulting from rape in over thirty years in Buffalo, New York,[6] none in over ten years in St. Paul, Minnesota,[7] and none in Philadelphia in a decade. Pregnancies resulting from incest are similarly rare, and those pregnancies which result from incest and which are subsequently aborted are even more rare.[8]

Since they are very rare, pregnancies resulting from rape and incest should not be used to justify abortion-on-demand. If abortion is to be allowed for rape and incest, statutes should be narrowly drawn to limit abortion to those circumstances only, and such laws should have adequate safeguards to insure that the pregnancy has indeed resulted from genuine rape or incest and that this charge is not being used simply as an excuse to obtain an abortion solely for reasons of convenience.

However, I would oppose a law allowing abortion even for rape or incest. For one thing, the unborn child still has the right to life. It is wrong to punish an innocent child for the sin of his father (Deuteronomy 24:16).

Furthermore, abortion does not undo the harm of rape or incest. While having to bear an unwanted child can certainly be traumatic, there is reason to believe that abortion can be equally traumatic, if not more so. And the woman has a further option—she can give up the child for adoption.

Should abortion be allowed for the sake of the mental health of the mother? Again I answer no.

First, there is little evidence that abortion contributes to mental health. In fact, a study done at the University of British Columbia's Department of Psychiatry, as reported in the March 3, 1978, issue of *Psychiatric News*, demonstrated that abortion often increases a woman's psychological stress. The abortion may be more detrimental to the woman's mental health than bearing the child and putting him up for adoption.

I have read numerous accounts of mothers who have gone through abortions, only to report they are haunted by psychological trauma, guilt, and regret thereafter.

Second, even if we were to concede that abortion could heal the mental health of the mother, we would then be faced with a conflict of rights: the mother's right to mental health versus the child's right to life. I would argue that the child's right to life is paramount.

Should abortion be allowed to prevent child abuse and unwanted children? First, I note that we do not "mercifully" kill unwanted and abused children that are already born. Why should society do so before these children are born?

Second, there is no evidence that unplanned or unwanted pregnancies result in the higher proportion of unwanted or abused children. In fact, as abortion statistics have skyrocketed over the past decade, instances of reported child abuse have similarly increased.

Should abortion be allowed for birth defects? Before answering this question, let us consider an alternative proposal. Why not wait until the child is born and we can observe more clearly the nature and extent of his defects, and then put the child to death if he is overly defective? Or better yet, wait until the child is several years old and then put him to death if his defects are serious and uncorrectable?

"That's barbaric!" you say. And I agree. But if you accept the premise that the unborn child is a human being, what is the difference between killing him before birth and killing him after birth? Any argument for abortion based upon birth defects can be made with equal or greater force—and is in fact being made today—for infanticide!

The plain fact is, in most instances we cannot predict with any reasonable medical certainty whether a child will be defective or the extent of his defects. Retardation, for example, may be extreme, slight, or nonexistent. Furthermore, many persons with birth defects, such as Helen Keller, have lived happy and meaningful lives and have made valuable contributions to society.

Useful or not, wanted or not, "normal" or not, even the defective child has the right to life.

What Is the Present State of the Law?

Based upon the foregoing analysis, one might think that abortion would be illegal in the United States, except perhaps to save the life of the mother. And this was the law in nearly all states until 1973.

But in 1973 a landmark U.S. Supreme Court decision, *Roe* v. *Wade*,[9] effectively struck down all antiabortion statutes as unconstitutional. The Court reasoned that the "life, liberty and property" clause in the Fourteenth Amendment guaranteed to a pregnant woman the privacy right to determine for herself whether or not to terminate a pregnancy.

In that case, the State of Texas argued that the Fourteenth Amendment guarantee that no state shall deprive any person of life, liberty, or property without due process of law also protects the unborn child's right to life. But the Supreme Court ruled that the term "person" as used in the Fourteenth Amendment was not intended by its authors to include unborn children.

The Court conceded that the state may have some legitimate interest in regulating abortion after the first trimester of pregnancy for health and safety reasons; however, such restrictions can only be for the purpose of health and safety, such as requiring that abortions take place in hospitals, under sterile conditions, by licensed physicians. The Court also ruled that after the second trimester—that is, after the sixth month of pregnancy—the states may have a legitimate interest in protecting "potential life," and may therefore restrict abortions in the third trimester of pregnancy except where abortion is necessary to preserve the life or health of the mother. However, since many pro-abortion doctors will readily certify any patient as needing an abortion for the sake of her mental health, the practical effect of *Roe* v. *Wade* is to allow abortion-on-demand.

I believe the Supreme Court was wrong in *Roe* v. *Wade*—tragically wrong.

First, the Court's conclusion that the authors of the Fourteenth Amendment did not mean to include unborn children in the term "person" ignores the fact that the Fourteenth Amendment was passed and ratified during the same period of time (1868) when most of the nation's antiabortion statutes were passed. And the prochoice argument that these statutes were passed primarily to protect the mother from dangerous surgery is utterly wrong; all surgery in that day and that time was dangerous, yet there were no laws preventing appendectomies. Furthermore, the term used in the Iowa statute, and probably others as well, for abortion was "foeticide," the Latin term for killing *(cedo)* an unborn child *(fetus)*.

Second, even if we accept the Court's conclusion that "person" in the Fourteenth Amendment does not include unborn children, that does not mean the state has no compelling interest in protecting their right to life. Animals are not persons under the Fourteenth Amendment; yet we have laws preventing cruelty to animals. Strangely enough, livestock have more protection under the law today than do unborn children!

There is an interesting parallel between *Roe* v. *Wade* and the *Dred Scott* decision of 1857[10] and the *Antelope* decision of 1828.[11] These latter cases concluded that blacks were not "persons" as defined by the Fifth Amendment. Even still, this did not mean that blacks could be legally killed, and a person who killed a black could be tried for murder. In other words, personhood is not to be equated with the right to life.

Since *Roe* v. *Wade,* there have been an estimated 15,000,000 abortions in the United States, and further court decisions have expanded the right to abortion. In *Planned Parenthood in Central Missouri* v. *Danforth,*[12] the Court struck down a Missouri law requiring that a married woman have the written consent of her spouse for an abortion, that an underage minor have the written consent of her parents for an abortion, and that a physician use due care and skill to preserve the life and health of the fetus insofar as that is possible.

In *Bellotti* v. *Baird,*[13] the Court again struck down as unconstitutional a state statute—this time from Massachusetts—requiring parental consent for an abortion on an unmarried minor. But two years later, in *H. L.* v. *Matheson,*[14] the Court upheld as constitutional a Utah statute which required a physician to "notify, if possible" the parents or guardian of a minor upon whom an abortion is to be performed. And in *Harris* v. *McRae,*[15] the Supreme Court upheld as constitutional the Hyde Amendment which prohibited most federal funding for abortions. However, several state supreme courts have struck down laws prohibiting state funding of abortions on the ground that such prohibitions violate the equal rights amendment provisions of the respective state constitutions.

And while the prochoice argument is that abortion should be a private and voluntary matter, the fact is that government coercion is still involved. Despite *Harris* v. *McRae,* government funding of abortion remains a reality in many areas, and taxpayers who oppose abortion are thereby required to subsidize an operation which they regard as murder. There have even been several instances in which courts have considered ordering minors to undergo abortions "in their best interest" against their will![16] To my knowledge, however, no such involuntary abortion has ever been carried out.

Many are, however, forced to subsidize abortion through group insurance policies that include abortion coverage. And in a few recent cases, doctors have been held liable for the expenses and inconvenience of raising a child in "wrongful life" actions in which a plaintiff has alleged that she is saddled with an unwanted child because her doctor failed to counsel her to obtain an abortion.

And while the legal and political battles rage on, the national holocaust continues—one and a half million abortions per year, over 15,000,000 since 1973!

What Can Be Done?
Those who fight for the life of the unborn child often become discouraged. Eleven years have passed since *Roe* v. *Wade;* yet it often seems

that nothing is being done, that no progress is being made.

However, I believe more people are coming to realize that the unborn child is in fact a human being, and that his right to life deserves protection. Let us remember that the battle to abolish slavery took over sixty years, and the battle for full racial equality is still being waged a century later. But few would deny that progress has been made and victories have been won.

I believe there is much that can be done to restore legal protection to the unborn child. Let me suggest several steps:

(1) The most basic necessity is for a human life amendment which would declare that life begins at conception and which would thereby extend the right to life to the unborn. The practical effect of this amendment would be to overrule *Roe v. Wade* and make abortion illegal once again.

(2) So far efforts to pass a human life amendment have not been successful. For this reason, many have seen hope in the "Hatch Compromise" offered by Senator Orin Hatch of Utah, which is basically a state's rights position. The Hatch amendment would not totally prohibit abortion, but would reserve to each individual state the right to do so.

(3) Christians should continue working for what they call a human life bill, by which Congress would declare that life begins at conception. In *Roe v. Wade* the Supreme Court did not rule that life does *not* begin at conception; rather, the Court held that there is insufficient basis for declaring with certainty when life begins. The Court noted a lack of consensus among churches and past civilizations on the question of the begining of life. The authors of the Human Life Bill hope that such a declaration by Congress, supported by expert medical testimony in the Congressional committees, will provide that basis and cause the Court to rule differently in future cases. It is possible (but by no means certain) that if President Reagan appoints a conservative majority in the Court, that majority could use the Human Life Bill as justification for overruling or modifying *Roe v. Wade*. I believe Christians should work for the Human Life Bill, but they should not stake all their hopes on it.

(4) Other steps can be taken short of outright prohibition of abortions. A statute which required parental notification before an abortion was upheld in *Matheson,* and similar statutes should be upheld in other states. Some lower court decisions indicate that a parental consent requirement might be upheld despite *Danforth* and *Belotti,* if it were drawn to require consent either by a parent or a judge.

(5) Laws providing that employers who provide health coverage for their employees need not include abortion coverage in those policies should also be upheld by the courts, and Christians should work for

such laws in their respective states. One form of such legislation would provide that no insurance policy shall include abortion coverage unless said coverage is added as a special rider. This protects the general public from having to underwrite the cost of abortions through their insurance premiums.

(6) Despite *Harris* v. *McRae,* public funding of abortion continues in many localities. In most jurisdictions such funding could be eliminated by simple legislation, and this by itself would eliminate many abortions.

(7) Laws providing that hospitals may refuse to allow abortions and protecting medical personnel from liability for refusing to perform abortions or advise abortions are sorely needed in many localities.

(8) While we must protect the life of the unborn child, we must also be concerned about the expectant mother. Her trauma, financial pressure, and other problems are very real. We must do more than just prohibit abortion; we must provide the expectant and troubled mother with the emotional, psychological, educational, financial, and spiritual support she needs to carry her child through pregnancy and deliver the child successfully.

Fortunately, there are several organizations which do exactly that. One is Birthright, loosely affiliated with the National Right to Life Committee, Inc. Another is the Save-A-Baby program recently established by the Old-Time Gospel Hour of Dr. Jerry Falwell—often branded by proabortionists as an enemy of pregnant mothers. Our government's double standard is reflected in the strange fact that these organizations receive no government funds while the proabortion Planned Parenthood agencies receive millions from the public treasury. Save-A-Baby and Birthright both deserve our support.

(9) We can work as individuals or we can work as organized groups. The National Right to Life Committee, Inc., is a well-organized group which works for the rights of unborn children. Those wishing to work against abortion could probably increase their effectiveness by uniting with National Right to Life. Its address is: Suite 402, 419 7th Street NW, Washington, DC 20004, telephone (202) 638-4560. We need to work, not only on the legislative front, but also as individuals, one-on-one, to educate our fellow-citizens as to the right to life. If one pregnant mother can be persuaded not to have an abortion, a human life is saved.

And the King shall answer and say unto them, Verily I say unto you, Inasmuch as ye have done it unto one of the least of these my brethren, ye have done it unto me. (Matthew 25:40)

Fetal Experimentation

Closely related to the issue of abortion is the travesty of fetal experimentation. For once it is determined that the unborn child has no human rights, he may be treated simply as an animal.

In fact, the unborn child has less rights than an animal. We have laws to guarantee the humane treatment of animals, and even their humane slaughter. No such protection exists for the unborn child.

Doctors can readily establish that the unborn child is capable of experiencing pain. Yet no laws exist to protect him or her from painful forms of abortion. Among those are saline abortions whereby solution is injected into the uterus; the baby breathes and inhales it, then slowly dies from salt poisoning, dehydration, and cerebral hemorrhage. The baby's skin is often stripped off in the process. Another is the suction method whereby a hollow tube with a knifelike edged tip is inserted into the womb, tears the baby into pieces, and sucks the parts into a container. The dilation and curettage (D&C) involves the insertion of a loop-shaped knife that cuts the baby into pieces and scrapes them out of the womb. Sometimes hysterectomies are used whereby the baby is lifted out of the womb and the umbilical cord is clamped; the child usually struggles for awhile and then dies.

In most jurisdictions, no laws exist to prohibit experimentation on live fetuses. As John Whitehead reports:

> The research of Dr. Peter A. J. Adam, an associate professor of pediatrics at Case Western Reserve University, shows how far a Supreme Court decision can be taken. Six months after *Roe* v. *Wade* Dr. Adam reported to the American Pediatric Research Society on research he and his associates had conducted on twelve babies who had been born alive by hysterotomy abortion up to twenty weeks. These men took the tiny babies and cut off their heads—decapitated the babies and cannulated the internal carotid arteries (that is, a tube was placed in the main artery feeding the brain). They kept the diminutive heads alive, much as the Russians kept the dogs' heads alive in the 1950s. Take note of Dr. Adam's retort to criticism:
> "Once society's declared the fetus dead, and abrogated its rights, I don't see any ethical problem. . . . Whose right are we going to protect, once we've decided the fetus won't live?"[17]

Not only do such experiments frequently take place; other developments are becoming commonplace which are nothing short of macabre.

Donald DeMarco, associate professor of philosophy at Canada's St. Jerome College, University of Waterloo, writes:

> A few years ago, Reuters News Agency reported the story of a Lebanese man who was impotent, and had a testical transplant from a fetus aborted at six months. (Nick Thimmesch, "Strange Tales of Fetal Life and Death," *Human Life Issues,* Jan. 1983, Vol. 9, No. 1, p. 4.) Clearly, the transplanted organ was deemed not only a human part of a human being, but one capable of infusing the impotent beneficiary with a masculine power that

his own human physiology has failed to provide. Wordsworth, who viewed the child as "the father of the man," could not have known that the child in the womb could provide the manhood of the father. Whether the operation proved successful is beside the point. What is pertinent here is the belief demonstrated by the patient and the surgical team that the human fetus is indeed human and in fact can supply human parts for its homologue who lacks them.

Another case, reported in the Hastings Center Report, concerns a 28-year-old engineer who found life on a dialysis machine intolerably restricting. Since he had been adopted as an infant and did not know his natural family, an ordinary kidney transplant had been ruled out. The novel solution was agreed upon: The man's wife would get pregnant and, after five or six months, have an abortion. The kidneys from their own pre-born child would then be transplanted to the husband. Here again, the point is that the fetus, being human, offers real hope (sometimes the only hope) for other humans who suffer from some physiological dysfunction. But it raises the prospect of using the uterus as an organ farm, and the fetus as an organ bank. While based on the recognition that the fetus is human, it denies the right of unborn children not to be exploited as a means for some other human's end.

In Australia, serious consideration is being given to deliberately growing human embryos to provide organs for transplantation in children. Mr. Justic Kirby, chairman of Australia's Law Reform Commission, has expressed his belief that a majority of the populace might see this as better than simply burying the aborted fetuses. (Quoted from the Australian in *The Human*, April 1982, p. 4.) The inequity of allowing some fetuses to live and consigning others to arbitrary and premature death does not disturb some people as much as the "waste" involved in not using aborted human fetuses to improve the health of other human beings. As a spokesman for the medical faculty of Adelaide University puts it: "In Adelaide alone there are over 4,000 fetuses a year. It seems a waste if they are not going to be used."[18]

Dead babies have other uses, too. Bodies of aborted babies are reportedly used by American·businesses to produce collagen, a gelatinous substance found in connective tissue, bones, and cartilage. Collagen is used in shampoos and hand creams. Dr. Olga Fairfax says that unless the beauty product specifies "animal collagen" or "bovine collagen," it possibly contains unborn human collagen. She adds, "Since there are 1.5 million abortions every year, there is an abundant source for commercial use." She quotes one abortionist as saying, "A baby is becoming property. We kill, keep or sell the property."[19]

These practices sound like the gruesome climax of a horror movie, but they are very real. Regardless of the validity of *Roe v. Wade*, Congress and/or the state legislatures have authority to prohibit practices such as these. Even animals are entitled to humane treatment, and society has a right to protect itself against practices which brutalize and dehumanize. Laws requiring the adminstration of painkiller to the unborn child prior to an abortion should be upheld with little difficulty. Those who oppose such laws would find themselves in a difficult position: they could oppose the idea, thereby giving the unborn child less protection than an animal; or they could support it, thereby conceding that the unborn child does have certain rights. And many mothers might think twice about an abortion, knowing that the unborn child is capable of feeling pain.

Legislation prohibiting experimentation upon live fetuses, prohibiting trafficking in the bodies of unborn children, or requiring doctors to use medical diligence to save the lives of babies who are aborted alive deserve our support.

Infanticide

Several decades ago, as the debate over legalization of abortion waxed hot, prolife forces argued that abortion would lead to infanticide. Proabortion advocates called the idea ridiculous.

Today, eleven years after *Roe v. Wade*, what do we have? Consider the case of *Infant Doe*.

Born on Good Friday (April 8) in Indiana, Infant Doe was afflicted with Down's Syndrome and also needed corrective surgery so his stomach could receive food properly. Doctors believed the chances for successful surgery were good to excellent, and there was no way of knowing with certainty what degree of retardation, if any, would result from the Down's Syndrome. But the parents opted to refuse corrective surgery, intravenous feeding, or other life support—in other words, they chose to starve their baby to death.

The hospital contacted the local courts, but they refused to intervene, since the parents had made their decision after consultation with medical personnel. The Monroe County Prosecutor's Office and the legal guardian for Infant Doe then appealed to the Indiana Supreme Court, asking that Infant Doe be temporarily removed from the custody of his parents so that medical treatment could be performed. On Wednesday, April 14, the Indiana Supreme Court voted 3-1 to refuse the request.

The prosecutor and guardian then appealed to the U.S. Supreme Court, joined by a couple who sought to adopt Infant Doe. But the next day, before the Supreme Court acted, Infant Doe died of starvation and related complications.[20]

The unique feature of cases like this is that they achieve national publicity. Many doctors claim that what happened to Infant Doe is standard operating procedure in hospitals and clinics across the country.

And it is not surprising. Almost any argument that can be made for abortion can be made with at least equal force for infanticide. For example, if one is concerned that his child may be deformed or retarded, it would make more sense to wait until the child is born, examine fully the extent of the defects, and then "terminate" if the child doesn't meet our expectations. Many of the societies which Justice Blackmun cited in *Roe v. Wade* as practicing abortion also practiced infanticide. In Rome and Greece, for example, unwanted children were "exposed," or left on a hillside to die.

This is the logical consequence of the humanist "quality of life" ethic. Consider the words of biomedical ethicist Peter Singer in *Pediatrics:*

> Once the religious mumbo-jumbo surrounding the term "human" has been stripped away, we may continue to see normal members of our species as possessing greater capacities of rationality, self-consciousness, communication, and so on, than members of any other species; but we will not regard as sacrosanct the life of each and every member of our species, no matter how limited its capacity for intelligence or even conscious life may be. If we compare a severely defective human infant with a nonhuman animal, or dog or a pig, for example, we will often find the nonhuman to have superior capacities, both actual and potential for rationality, self-consciousness, communication, and anything else that can plausibly be considered morally significant. Only the fact that the defective infant is a member of the species Homo sapiens leads it to be treated differently from the dog or pig. Species membership alone, however, is not morally relevant. Humans who bestow superior value on the lives of all human beings, solely because they are members of our own species, are judging along lines strikingly similar to those used by white racists who bestow superior value on the lives of other whites, merely because they are members of their own race.[21]

And it makes perfect sense to say that species membership is not morally relevant—unless one accepts the Judeo-Christian ethic which teaches that man is different from all other species in a very profound way: he is created with a soul and spirit, in the image of God.

Regardless of *Roe v. Wade*, it is clear that the state may prohibit infanticide. In fact, infanticide already constitutes murder under current laws. All that is necessary is for these laws to be properly interpreted and vigorously enforced. To accomplish this, Christians must vigilantly watch what is going on and report actual or potential cases of infanticide to the authorities.

Euthanasia

So far, we have been talking about killing at or near the beginning of life. What about the other end of the life spectrum?

This issue attracted nationwide attention in the *Matter of Quinlan.*[22] Karen Quinlan, an eighteen-year old girl, was rendered comatose by an accident. Doctors concluded there was no reasonable likelihood that she would ever regain consciousness and live a "meaningful" life.

The Supreme Court of New Jersey concluded that a terminally ill patient has a right under the Fourteenth Amendment to refuse extraordinary care—life supports, respirators, etc. And if the patient is comatose, like Karen Quinlan, and unable to make that decision for herself, her guardian may make that decision for her, in conjunction with doctors and other advisors.

The case generated much comment. I recall listening to a talk program on a Christian radio station during the time. Caller after caller echoed the same theme: If God wants to keep Karen Quinlan alive, he doesn't need life support to do it.

True, I thought. But at the same time, if God has determined that it is time for Karen Quinlan to die, life supports will not prevent him from accomplishing his will. God can save lives without cardio-pulmonary respiration, surgery, medicine, or even bandaids. And he can end life regardless of our best efforts.

The question is, what role should the doctor assume? Should he work to take life, or preserve it—recognizing, of course, that the final outcome rests with God.

"Reasonable medical certainty" is not all that certain. Karen Quinlan is now thirty years old, and still she lingers in her coma. Yet persons have been comatose for as long as sixteen years and awakened to normal life. Doctors can be wrong. New medical techniques could be discovered to treat comatose persons who today cannot be treated. And of course there is always the possibility of divine intervention.

And who really knows what, if anything, the comatose person is thinking and feeling? Some persons have recalled that, while comatose, they could hear doctors and nurses discussing them as though they were dead. Others believe some comatose persons can hear, feel, and think, but do not remember anything when they regain consciousness.

Is the comatose person thinking, "Please turn off that respirator! Let me die with dignity!" Or is he thinking, "No! Please don't kill me! I want to live!" Or is he thinking nothing at all? The fact is—*we don't know.*

And how do we know when someone is alive or dead? What test do we use? Some states have recently changed the legal definition of death. They frequently stress "brain death" (the absence of brain waves on an electroencephalogram) instead of "heart death" (the absence of heartbeat on an electrocardiogram). The scriptural test is set forth in James 2:26—". . . as the body without the spirit is dead. . . ." But what doctor, what minister, can determine when the soul or spirit has left the body?

This presents a special problem with organ transplants. Donating one's organs to another person is a commendable practice. The problem is—to be useful, organs must be removed from the body as soon after death as possible. But what test should doctors use in determining when to remove organs? Brain death? Cessation of heartbeat? The danger exists that doctors, in their zeal to save a human life, may destroy another life in the process. They may be tempted to do so because the organ donor is "certain" to die or because he has no reasonable prospect of any "quality" of life. But what doctor has the right to decide that one life is worth more than another—even a comatose or terminally ill person? The humanist view of measuring the value of life by its "usefulness" is once again apparent.

The dilemma is not getting easier; it is getting more difficult. New medical techniques may soon make it possible to keep human bodies technically alive almost indefinitely. Under what circumstances must extraordinary means be used, and when may artificial life supports be disconnected? Does the desire of the patient make a difference? How does he express his desire if he is comatose or terminally ill? If he has expressed a desire previously, is that binding? If not, may a guardian make the decision? These decisions must often be made when one is least emotionally ready to do so.

How much weight must be given to financial considerations? It is easy to say that money is secondary to human life. But what of the man who has saved all his life so he would have something to pass on to his children? Must he use up all his savings—perhaps even his house or farm—while he lingers on a respirator for a month?

And how much pain must he be forced to endure before he may choose to die? These are difficult questions, and I'm not sure I have all the answers.

Once we decide to treat a person for disease or deformity, what type of treatment is appropriate? Many believe in seeking help through prayer or faith healers rather than medical professionals. It is difficult to deny that such methods of healing have worked in many instances where medical science has failed.

Does the government have a right to require medical treatment instead of prayer or faith healing? By doing so, isn't the government adopting an official establishment position that prayer and faith healing are not effective?

Or what about other alternative forms of treatment? Some choose vitamin therapy. Some choose laetrile. Some seek help from holistic health practitioners, others from chiropractors. Still others choose osteopaths, whose training equals or exceeds that of other doctors in many respects, but who are in some areas less accepted by the medical profession.

Should the state require that all treatment be performed by a regular, licensed doctor? Or should freedom of choice in therapy be allowed? If we allow an adult person to exercise freedom of choice for himself, may he exercise the same freedom of choice for his child?

These are difficult questions, and I don't have a definite answer. I suggest, however, that the legal status of a person who in good faith provides alternative treatment for his child (including faith healing) should perhaps be different from the legal status of a person who utterly neglects his child's health.

One thing I am sure of: God has sovereign control of human life. No human life is conceived against his will, and no person dies until God has determined it is time.

Each person dies when God's earthly plan for him is finished. It follows, then, that as long as a person is alive, God has a plan for that person's life and a reason for keeping him alive.

Why is God keeping Karen Quinlan alive? I don't know. Perhaps he is using Karen to teach her family something. Possibly he is working in Karen's mind and soul and spirit, even in her comatose state. Or maybe he plans to restore Karen to consciousness, to show forth his power and impress upon us the sanctity of life. I am not sure what God's purpose is. I am sure he has one.

It is difficult to know what the human role should be in God's plan. Is the doctor working with God when he tries to save a life God has created in his image? Or is he fighting God when he uses extraordinary means to preserve a life God has ordained should die? I have no precise answer, but I would say this: any moral doubts in this area should be resolved in favor of preserving human life.

War and Capital Punishment

Prolifers are sometimes accused of being inconsistent. They are prolife on issues such as abortion and euthanasia, but antilife on war and capital punishment.

The apparent inconsistency exists on both sides, of course. Those who oppose capital punishment and war often justify or excuse abortion and euthanasia. And there are some who, out of respect for life, oppose *all* taking of life—whether by abortion, euthanasia, war, or capital punishment.

The issues of war and capital punishment are covered in Chapters 9, 19 and 20. Suffice it to say at this point that these issues need not be linked. To be against abortion and euthanasia, one need not also be against capital punishment and defense.

As we have seen, Exodus 20:13 properly understood prohibits murder—the intentional and unjustified killing of a human being. It is possible to distinguish between killing an innocent child and killing a convicted murderer. The Bible forbids the former but authorizes the latter (Genesis 9:6). It is innocent life that may not be taken.

Six things doth the Lord hate; yea, seven are an abomination unto him: a proud look, a lying tongue, and hands that shed innocent blood. . . . (Proverbs 6:16, 17)

19 Crime and Punishment

"Let's have law and order in this country! Let's stop coddling criminals! After all, we are to obey the law."

"Christ says we should forgive those who wrong us, and we should visit those who are in prison. We must overcome evil with love."

Christians, like all other citizens, are concerned about crime, and the above quotations represent the views commonly expressed on the subject. It seems Christians generally fall into two camps: those who want to lock up all the criminals and throw away the key, and those who want to forgive all the criminals and let them go. And there is the Christian who, in C. S. Lewis's words, is used to "having a dozen incompatible philosophies dancing about together inside his head," who alternately expresses both positions without realizing their possible inconsistency.

Are these views compatible? Should we punish criminals or forgive them? Can we do both at the same time? Is there a middle ground between these extremes? What does the Bible say?

Obviously in an area as sensitive as this we have to be careful to interpret the Bible correctly and in context. Let's examine what the Bible says about crime and punishment.

The Root Cause of Crime Is Sin

From whence come wars and fightings among you? come they not hence, even of your lusts that war in your members? Ye lust, and have not: ye kill, and desire to have, and cannot obtain: ye fight and war, yet ye have not, because ye ask not. (James 4:1, 2)

In context, James is speaking about conflicts among Christians. He enlarges his statement to include killing and fighting, and the principle could apply to crime in general. What does James say is the cause of trouble? It comes from the "lusts that war in your members"—that is, the sinful drives within us. James attributes these problems not to external causes, but to our basic sin nature. Paul makes a similar observation:

> Now the works of the flesh are manifest, which are these, adultery, fornication, uncleanness, lasciviousness, idolatry, witchcraft, hatred, variance, emulations, wrath, strife, seditions, heresies, envyings, murders, drunkenness, revelings, and such like: of the which I tell you before, as I have also told you in time past, that they which do such things shall not inherit the kingdom of God. (Galatians 5:19-21)

Like James, Paul attributes crime to our sinful nature.

Knowing what the root cause of crime is helps us to know what it is not. Social scientists today look to many other causes of crime. But while these may occasionally be contributing factors, they are not the ultimate cause of crime.

Environmental determinists often assume that a bad environment is the cause of crime, and therefore the way to reduce crime is to improve the environment, and the way to reform criminals is to place them in a new environment. But Adam and Eve sinned in a perfect environment, the Garden of Eden. Certainly man's environment affects him, but man has the capacity to rise above it, free himself from it, and even control it. Ultimately, therefore, he cannot blame his environment for his crimes.

Nor is poverty the cause of crime. Crime in America today is much higher than during the depths of the Depression; it is many times higher than in the poor nations of the world such as India, China, and Africa. Poverty is at most a contributing factor to crime; it is not the ultimate cause.

Some argue that ignorance is the cause of crime, and that the solution is education. As Horace Mann wrote:

> Let the Common School be expanded to its capabilities, let it be worked with the efficiency of which it is susceptible, and nine-tenths of the crimes in the penal code would become obsolete; the long catalog of human ills would be abridged; men would walk more safely by day; every pillow would be more inviolable by night; property, life, and character held by a stronger tenure; all rational hope respecting the future brightened.[1]

But has Mann's prophecy come to pass? If education is the solution to crime, then something is sadly wrong with American education!

Crime in America is much higher than in the undeveloped, less educated parts of the world, Men commit crimes not because they don't know any better, but because of an evil heart.

Still others blame the crime wave on the increase in firearms and seek the solution in gun control. But this notion simply ignores the facts. All kinds of crimes are increasing, from murder to larceny to tax evasion to overtime parking. Considering felonies alone, firearms are involved in less than 1.5 percent of all crime. It is ridiculous to blame the entire crime wave on guns. It is difficult to find any connection between gun control laws and crime prevention.[2] While on rare occasions the presence of a firearm may facilitate the commission of a crime, guns are not the root cause of crime and gun control is not the solution. The problem is the human heart.

God Has Delegated to Human Government the Authority to Punish Crime

Private citizens are to leave vengeance to God. While they may defend themselves, they may not seek to execute vengeance themselves. "Vengeance is mine, I will repay, saith the Lord" (Romans 12:19). "To me belongeth vengeance and recompense," God says in Deuteronomy 32:35; see also Psalms 94:1 and Hebrews 10:30. Christians, Paul says in Romans 12, are to "recompense to no man evil for evil" (v. 17), but as much as possible to "live peaceably with all men" (v. 18). Christians are commanded to "avenge not yourselves" (v. 19) and to "be not overcome of evil, but overcome evil with good" (v. 21).

But in the very next verse (13:1), Paul informs us that God has ordained civil authority. He goes on to say that civil magistrates have authority from God to punish evildoers.

> For rulers are not a terror to good works, but to the evil. Wilt thou then not be afraid of the power? do that which is good, and thou shalt have praise of the same: for he is the minister of God to thee for good. But if thou do that which is evil, be afraid; for he beareth not the sword in vain: for he is the minister of God, a revenger to execute wrath upon him that doeth evil. (13:3, 4)

Note that civil magistrates are authorized by God to punish evildoers. Private citizens do not have that right, but civil powers (judges, policemen, prosecutors, and the like) do.

Peter likewise tells us that governors are "sent by him (God) for the punishment of evildoers, and for the praise of them that do well" (1 Peter 2:14). And Paul assures us in 1 Timothy that one reason we pray for those who are in authority over us is so "that we may lead a quiet and peaceable life in all godliness and honesty" (2:2). As government officials keep the criminal element under restraint, the safety and freedom of law-abiding citizens is preserved. This also facilitates the spread of the gospel.

This authority to punish criminals did not begin with the book of Romans, however. It began with the Noahic covenant of Genesis 9, a covenant which God made with all generations and all nations (Genesis 9:9, 10, 15-17). Included in this covenant was civil authority to punish evildoers.

> And surely your blood of your lives will I require: at the hand of every beast will I require it, and at the hand of man; at the hand of every man's brother will I require the life of man. Whoso sheddeth man's blood, by man shall his blood be shed: for in the image of God made he man. (Genesis 9:5, 6)

So civil government has authority to punish evildoers. And it does so, not out of meanness, but to safeguard human life and human freedom. According to Genesis 9:6, the reason God has directed that those who shed man's blood shall have their own blood shed is that "in the image of God made he man." Since man is in the image of God, his life is of infinite value; therefore those who take his life must be punished severely.

Why punish criminals for their crimes? Why not just find them guilty, admonish them, and let them go? There are basically five reasons for criminal punishment.

The first is simple *justice,* or as some call it, retribution. Most of us feel that if a person commits a serious crime and gets away with it, an injustice has been done. Crime demands punishment. That is a New Testament concept as well as an Old Testament concept. Paul tells us in Romans 13:4 that the civil ruler is the "minister (servant) of God, a revenger to execute wrath upon him that doeth evil."

Second, we punish criminals to *deter* others from committing crimes. The knowledge that criminals are severely punished tends to cause others to obey the law. Some perhaps obey the law because they want to, others because they know it is right. But some obey the law only because they fear they will be punished otherwise. That is why Paul tells us in Romans 13:3 that "rulers are not a terror to good works, but to the evil." By "terror" he means deterrent. We are told repeatedly in the Old Testament that the purpose of a punishment such as stoning was that "all Israel shall hear, and fear" (Deuteronomy 13:11; 17:13; 21:21).

A third reason for punishing a criminal is *restraint*—to physically prevent him from committing further crimes. As long as he is in chains or behind bars, he won't be committing any more crimes—

except upon other inmates (a problem which also needs to be dealt with).

A fourth reason is *rehabilitation*. It is hoped that punishment will have a beneficial effect, causing the offender to repent of his evil ways and become a better person, or at least learn to obey the law in order to avoid punishment. I know of no specific verse of Scripture that speaks about punishment for rehabilitative purposes in a criminal justice context, but the many passages in Proverbs which speak about punishing a child for correction (13:24; 22:15; 23:13, 14) may be applicable for criminal justice purposes as well.

A final purpose is to *prevent private vengeance*. If society does not take action against criminals, the victim or his relatives will. In fact, in some early systems of justice such as viking law, once the court found a defendant guilty, it was up to the victim's relatives to carry out the sentence. The result was often bloodshed and civil war, especially if the offender had relatives of his own. The cities of refuge that we read about in Numbers 35:25-28 and other passages appear to have been established in part to prevent private vengeance.

Before Instituting Punishment, Precautions Are Necessary to Protect the Innocent

The Bible passages that command the trial and execution of prisoners do not connote a "lynch mob." Rather, they call for an orderly system of justice. Judges were instituted (Exodus 18:13-16; cf. Deuteronomy 1:16, 17; 19:15-21), along with a multi-tier judicial system with (to use modern terminology) a justice of the peace over every ten families, a local magistrate over every fifty families, a district court judge over every hundred families, a circuit court of appeals over every one thousand families, and Moses himself as the Supreme Court. The judges were commanded to be honest and not to take bribes or favor the rich (Exodus 23:1-8)—a charge they repeatedly violated, as we see from the prophets (Isaiah 1:23; Jeremiah 5:28; Micah 3:11). Nor were they to show special favoritism to the poor: "Neither shalt thou countenance a poor man in his cause" (Exodus 23:3). Everyone was entitled to equal justice before the law—neither more nor less.

A person accused of a crime was presumed to be innocent until proven guilty, and at least two witnesses were necessary to convict:

> At the mouth of two witnesses, or three witnesses, shall he that is worthy of death be put to death; but at the mouth of one witness he shall not be put to death. (Deuteronomy 17:6; cf. 19:15; Numbers 35:30)

It was recognized that a single witness could lie or be mistaken. Of course, it is also possible that two witnesses could lie or be mistaken, but it is less likely. And the law provided a severe penalty for perjury: the witness who testified falsely in a criminal prosecution received the same penalty the defendant would have received had he been found guilty. In other words, the penalty for perjury in capital cases was death (Deuteronomy 19:16-21).

Extrabiblical Jewish law provided many other protections for the defendant: the right to counsel, the requirement of a quorum of the judges of the Sanhedrin (high court), the requirement of a unanimous verdict in capital cases, and a second deliberation before imposing capital punishment. These and many other protections made the Jewish law the most enlightened legal system of the ancient world, rivaled only by the Roman system which was, in part, based upon it. And this should be little cause for surprise, for its author was God himself.

Still, even the best legal system can be abused when run by fallen men, and the Jewish law was often abused. The most classic example of that abuse was the trial of our Lord Jesus Christ.

In an era of soaring crime rates, many are frustrated and impatient with the endless protections granted to the accused. It seems the system is stacked in favor of the criminal and against law enforcement, and the one who suffers most is the criminal's innocent victim.

But many who believe this may change their tune when they themselves or one of their loved ones is under prosecution. When a person sees the awesome power and resources of the state—prosecutors, police officers, detectives, investigators, experts, and the like—arrayed against him, he feels very helpless indeed. And he must pay for his own defense, unless he is indigent, while the state has all the taxpayers' resources at its command. That being the case, the framers of our Constitution and Bill of Rights decided to give the accused certain protections to even the balance. Their decision was wise and just, and in accordance with God's law.

Certainly our system can be abused. The endless delay tactics by defense attorneys, sometimes for unethical reasons, do not serve the cause of justice. The exclusionary rule, under which illegally obtained evidence is generally not admissible in court, occasionally allows a guilty defendant to go free. Overcrowded court dockets frequently require plea-bargaining that may lead to the defendant getting off lighter (or possibly heavier) than he deserves.

But on the whole we should be thankful for the protections our criminal justice system affords. One hallmark of a free society is that a man is innocent until proven guilty. That being the case, he should be treated like a free and innocent man until he is duly convicted in a court of law.

This should include the right to remain free until convicted and sentenced, unless compelling reasons exist for pretrial confinement, such as the danger of violence or fleeing prosecution. The bail system in existence in most states today is patently unfair, because it requires a criminal defendant to pay for the privilege of remaining free, even though he is legally presumed innocent until proven guilty.

For example, let us suppose Charles is arrested on a charge of burglary. The judge releases him on $25,000 bail. In most states, that means Charles has to fork over $25,000 to the court, and the court will return it to him after his case is over, provided he has attended all court sessions. The trouble is, Charles probably doesn't have $25,000. That means he must either remain in jail or find a bondsman to post bond for him. The bondsman will do that, but only for a fee—usually about 10 percent, or in this case, $2,500. And none of this $2,500 is refundable. So Charles, or his relatives, somehow scrape together $2,500, and Charles is released on bail. Note that during this entire time Charles has been convicted of nothing and the law presumes that he is innocent.

Now let us suppose that the very next day the real burglar confesses, and the whole case turns out to be mistaken identity. The charges against Charles are dropped and he is free to go—but he is still out his $2,500!

Illinois has recently adopted a much more equitable system. There, instead of posting 10 percent with a bail bondsman, the defendant posts his 10 percent with the court directly. After his trial, if he has attended all court appearances, he receives his 10 percent back, minus a small administrative fee.

Similar bail reform bills are being considered in many states. If properly drafted, they deserve our support.

Once the Defendant Has Been Found Guilty, Punishment Is in Order

Scripture clearly authorizes government to punish criminals. Various forms of punishment are set forth in Scripture.

Capital punishment. Whenever an execution is about to take place, groups of people assemble to protest capital punishment. Usually clergymen are among the leaders of these protests, and that is understandable. To those who are trained to be compassionate and forgiving and to respect human life, an execution may well seem cruel and unchristian.

But distasteful though executions may be to some Christians, the Old Testament clearly authorizes capital punishment. It is true that Exodus 20:13 says, "Thou shalt not kill." But the Hebrew word is better translated "murder" and does not include all forms of killing. In the very next chapter, God's Word commands that a murderer be executed:

He that smiteth a man, so that he die, shall be surely put to death. (Exodus 21:12)

Many crimes in Scripture carry the death penalty: murder (Exodus 21:12); striking and reviling a parent (Exodus 21:15-17); blasphemy (Leviticus 24:14, 16, 23; 1 Kings 21:10); Sabbath-breaking (Exodus 31:14; 35:2); witchcraft and occult practices in general, including false prophecy (Exodus 22:18; Leviticus 20:27); some forms of unchastity (Deuteronomy 22:21-24; Leviticus 21:9); rape (Deuteronomy 22:25); incest and other unnatural sex (Exodus 22:19; Leviticus 20:11, 14, 16); man-stealing (kidnapping and selling into slavery) (Exodus 21:16); idolatry (Leviticus 20:2; Deuteronomy 13:6-10; 17:2-7); perjury in capital cases (Deuteronomy 19:16, 19); and according to my interpretation, abortion (Exodus 21:22-25). And at least in cases of murder capital punishment is found not only in the Mosaic Law, but also in the Noahic Covenant (Genesis 9:6).

But many Christians argue, "That's the Old Testament! The New Testament is a new dispensation of love and forgiveness. Christ has died on the cross to pay for everyone's sins, including those of the murderer."

Certainly Christ's death on the cross is full payment for the sin of the world (Isaiah 53:6; John 1:29; 1 John 2:2), even the sin of a condemned murderer. But God has still delegated to civil government the authority to punish criminals for societal purposes. Let us remember that the principal passage dealing with civil authority is Romans 13, and Paul wrote Romans 13 *after* Christ died on the cross, rose, and ascended into heaven. He wrote those words to the church at Rome, indicating the passage is normative for the church age. Paul said:

. . . he (the civil ruler) beareth not the sword in vain: for he is the minister of God, a revenger to execute wrath upon him that doeth evil. (13:4)

The word used for sword is *machaira*, which refers not only to a sword used in battle, but also to a sword used in executions, as when Herod killed James, the brother of John, in Acts 12:1, 2.[3] This would certainly indicate that capital punishment still applies today.

Students of criminal justice disagree on whether capital punishment deters crime. Comparing crime rates in states which do have capital punishment with those which do not, it is difficult to conclude that capital punishment is a specific deterrent. On the other hand, it cannot be denied that as capital punishment has become less common over the past several decades, the crime rate has correspondingly increased. But that does not show a clear cause-and-effect relationship.

My own belief is that capital punishment does act at least to some extent as a deterrent. Not only do people instinctively fear death, but in addition, by imposing capital punishment society demonstrates its abhorrence of the crime committed. Probably few defendants specifically think about the penalty when they commit the crime—some are insane, some commit crimes of passion, and others are convinced they won't get caught. But over a period of time the use of punishment impresses upon the citizenry the seriousness of the crime.

This does not mean I approve the way capital punishment is administered today. The two-witness rule of Scripture is no longer applied, and in recent years a few executions have taken place where the guilt of the accused was at least questionable. And of the thousands of murders committed every year, only a handful result in executions. Those few who are sentenced to death, and that tiny handful upon whom the death sentence is ultimately carried out, are not necessarily those criminals most deserving of death. Also, most of those who have been executed since 1977 have killed only a single person (granted, enough by itself to merit the death penalty), while mass murderers receive life sentences or less. So much depends upon the whim of the local judge, jury, or prosecutor, or the personality of the defendant or his attorney or his victim. Some means is needed to ensure that the death penalty is imposed on those most deserving of death, rather than the "roulette-wheel" system that applies today.

Restitution. The most common punishment in Scripture was restitution:

> . . . life for life, eye for eye, tooth for tooth, hand for hand, foot for foot, burning for burning, wound for wound, stripe for stripe. (Exodus 21:23-25; see generally Exodus 21—23)

This is commonly called the *lex talionis,* or law of like punishment. It is not a harsh principle. It was a most enlightened principle for its day, and a fair and effective principle for today as well. Stated simply, it means just this: let the punishment fit the crime. Unlike other ancient societies in which one could be tortured to death for the pettiest of crimes, Israel followed the law of like punishment.[4]

Nor does the principle of *lex talionis* involve maiming or mutilation. It does not mean that if Jones cuts off Smith's hand, Smith is entitled to cut off Jones's hand and mount it on his wall and contemplate with satisfaction that he has been avenged. Rather, it means Jones must pay restitution to Smith for the *value* of his lost hand—in medical expenses, lost wages, pain and suffering, etc. Actual mutilation took place only in a few cases where ritual cleansing was necessary, such as possibly Deuteronomy 25:11; 12.

Unfortunately the American legal system has, until recent years, largely neglected restitution. While the offender goes to prison or pays a fine to the state or serves on probation, the victim usually goes uncompensated for his loss. Fortunately more states are instituting restitution programs, either in the form of restitution or requiring the offender to perform a specific number of hours of community service. Not only does this save prison costs and benefit society and the victim; it also has a rehabilitative effect upon the offender himself.

As a juvenile court referee, I once required a juvenile, as a condition of his probation, to perform a specified number of hours of community service with a charitable organization to be selected by agreement between him and his probation officer. He chose the YMCA. When his period of service was finished, he informed us that he had enjoyed the work, that he wanted to continue, and that he was considering YMCA staff work as a career. Clearly, this community service had opened up a whole new horizon for him.

Judge William D. Bontrager describes a case in which he required a convicted criminal to split firewood for the family he had burglarized. The first day he came to split wood, his victim came and heaped vicious epithets upon him. The second and third time the victim was a little more civil. The next time the weather was cold, and the victim lent the offender his jacket. The next several times the victim came out and split wood with the offender, and finally the victim invited the offender to spend Christmas with him. In this case both the offender and his victim needed healing, and God's system of justice brought healing to both.

Other punishments. Other punishments found in Scripture include forfeiture of property (Ezra 10:8), involuntary servitude as part of restitution (Exodus 22:2, 3), and scourging with a limit of forty blows (Deuteronomy 25:3).

Can you imagine that! Scourging, corporal punishment, is endorsed in the Word of God!

The early Puritans used the whipping post, the ducking stool, the stocks, and other forms of corporal punishment. But in our "enlightened" age, such punishments would be decried as barbaric and struck down by the courts as cruel and unusual and thus in violation of the Eighth Amendment.

But think for a moment. Is whipping or any other reasonably mild and humanely administered form of corporal punishment really more barbaric or inhumane than the way we treat criminals today—putting them in prison? And might it not be more effective, as well as cheaper? Think about it.

Prisons. In our discussion of biblical forms of punishment, we examined capital punishment, restitution, forfeiture of property (fines), involuntary servitude, and corporal punishment. You might have noticed that the cornerstone of the American judicial system is not directly mentioned in the biblical system of justice. I refer to our jails and prisons.

Old Testament law makes no provision for prisons. It is true that Joseph was jailed in Egypt and Daniel was confined in Babylon, but not in Israel itself. In the later monarchical period, Michaiah was put in prison by King Ahab (1 Kings 22:27) and Hanani by King Asa (2 Chronicles 16:10); but this practice appears to be adopted from foreign countries. When Jeremiah offended the local authorities, they tried to keep him quiet by placing him in a cistern—apparently because they had no prisons. We do find prisons in the New Testament, but they were introduced by a foreign element, the Romans, during the first century B.C. They are not clearly endorsed by biblical law (though one need not conclude from this that there should be no prisons).

The same is largely true of early America. The Puritans used corporal punishment, restitution, and other such means for lesser offenses, and banishment or execution for more serious offenses. Jails existed for temporary incarcerations, but the idea of long-term prisons was relatively unknown.

How did our prison system begin? Charles Colson offers the following explanation:

> Imprisonment as a primary means of criminal punishment is a relatively modern concept. It was turned to as a humane alternative to the older patterns of harsh physical penalties for nearly all crimes. Quakers introduced the concept in colonial Pennsylvania.
>
> The first American prison was established in Philadelphia when the Walnut Street Jail was converted into a series of solitary cells where offenders were kept in solitary confinement. The theory was that they would become "penitents," confessing their crimes before God and thereby gaining a spiritual rehabilitation. Hence, the name "penitentiary"— as a place for penitents. In 1790, the State of Pennsylvania enacted laws making imprisonment the ordinary punishment for crimes.
>
> There were problems with this approach from the beginning: many early "penitents" locked in their solitary cells went mad and there was little evidence that this treatment produced any rehabilitation. Even so, the idea caught on and by 1850, all states had adopted similar laws. The concept of imprisonment as a principal form of punishment has since been exported from the United States to almost all Western nations.[5]

Today the American prison population is enormous, and it is skyrocketing. According to the U.S. Department of Justice, 412,303 persons were prisoners in "the land of the free and the home of the brave" in 1982. This is 170 prisoners per 100,000 population, and represents an 11.6 percent increase over 1981. Furthermore, the figure includes only convicts serving sentences longer than one year. Only two nations in the entire world—Soviet Russia and the Union of South Africa—have a higher percentage of their population in prison than does the United States.[6] The cost of maintaining an inmate in prison is well over $10,000 in state prisons and $13,588 in federal prisons as of 1980. (Some estimates run as high as $25,000.) These figures do not include all related costs, and they are probably substantially more than it would cost to send those inmates to Harvard.[7] Building a new prison in the United States today costs from $50,000-$80,000 per bed—more than the cost of building many modern houses.

And the result is a colossal failure. Along with our high imprisonment rate, the United States also has the highest crime rate in the Western world.[8] Prisons are largely ineffective in deterring crime, and in fact seem to promote crime. Inmates are brutalized by guards and fellow-inmates, subjected to homosexual rape and enticement, and often given a life of idleness.[9] They become bitter, and other hardened criminals in the prison teach them the tricks of the trade, so they simply come out smarter criminals. A prisoner's family often suffers more than he does. The wife is deprived of a husband, the children are deprived of a father, and the entire family is deprived of its breadwinner. The families of many prisoners go on welfare, and many families break up.

And what happens to the prisoner when he is released? In many Oklahoma prisons, he is given $50 and a bus ticket home. He reenters society untrained and unskilled, with no job, no property, perhaps no family, and to top it off, a criminal record. What does he do when his money is gone? You guessed it—all too often, he returns to crime. According to the FBI, 74 percent of the offenders released from prison are rearrested within four years.[10]

David Chilton put it well:

> The Bible does not allow imprisonment (except for a man held for trial or execution). The thief was not caged up at taxpayers' expense and treated like an animal; he labored productively in an evangelical family context, and made proper restitution to the victim for his crime. He earned back his self-respect, and restored what he owed to his victim. (If those who so fervently desire "social justice" wouldn't mind a suggestion, here's one: Work to implement "structual change" in our criminal and penal codes, and bring back restitution. Whoops—that would mean slavery! Oh, well. Better to keep the status quo, and to let the victims of theft live with their losses while supporting their attackers in tax-financed penitentiaries. Better to pin up the criminal with murderers and homosexuals in an "impersonal" environment than to have him work in a godly home.)[11]

To put it bluntly: the American prison system is unbiblical, inhumane, ineffective, inefficient, and idiotic. It needs to be replaced with something more effective.

We have suggested alternatives: community service, restitution, even mild forms of corporal punishment. And I am pleased that increasing interest is being shown in some of these alternatives.

But in the meantime, the prison system is likely to remain part of the American criminal justice system for a long time to come. It is therefore that we consider ways of improving the system while also looking for alternatives to it.

Work-release programs are one possibility. Under such programs, prisoners work at their regular jobs during the day and return to the prison at night. This enables them to support their families while in prison, or possibly accumulate some savings in anticipation of their release.

Similarly, the possibility of contracting with private enterprise to establish industries in prison should be considered. This could provide job training, teach good work habits, occupy time constructively, and provide prisoners with means of raising money for their release or for their families.

Educational programs, job-training programs, and opportunities for therapy should be made available, and prisoners should be encouraged to use them.

Conjugal visits, in which wives or husbands of prisoners may visit them and even spend the night with them in apartments located at or near the prison, should be encouraged. This is good therapy for the prisoners and helps to preserve the family unit.

A long-term inmate named Jim, serving three hundred and eighteen years for kidnapping, armed robbery, and two double-murders, describes his earlier life: "I was an animal. I should have been executed." But while in prison he has accumulated three years of college credits with a 4.0 average, is writing a novel, works in the prison as a teacher's aide, and teaches illiterates to read. His views of prison reform are worth noting:

> Do contract sentencing. Set goals for a prisoner when he comes in, that he will earn time off for getting so many years of education, for working at Alcoholics Anonymous, for self-improvement programs. Now you get good time for nothing, just for not making trouble. There's no incentive.
>
> We don't have prisons run by sadists. What we have are prisons run by people who are totally apathetic. The public must remember that 97 percent of all men who enter pens return to the free world. If we have guards calling us names, bad food, poor medical treatment, there's nothing we can do about it here. So when we get out, some innocent member of society suffers for the anger we bottle up in the pen. I came out of prisons in Indiana and Kansas truly vicious. I hated everybody and myself. I took

off on a small reign of terror. That's why the free world should care about what happens here. Their lives will depend on it.[12]

Individually, we should show concern for those in prison:

I was in prison, and ye came unto me. . . . Inasmuch as ye have done it unto one of the least of these my brethren, ye have done it unto me. (Matthew 25:36, 40)

Many churches and communities have prison ministries that visit prisoners, counsel them, witness to them, lead Bible studies, and otherwise help supply their spiritual and physical needs. If your community has such a ministry, I encourage you to work with it. If not, I encourage you to establish one. You might consider working with Charles W. Colson's Prison Fellowship (P.O. Box 40562, Washington, D.C. 20016; 703/759-4521). In this difficult time of their lives, many prisoners realize their sinful condition and their need for salvation. It is an optimal time to disciple people for Christ.

And let us not forget to minister to the offender who has just been released. He may find himself penniless, friendless, and jobless. At that time he may need our help more than ever before.

Current Problems In Criminal Law

We have discussed such issues as bail reform, capital punishment, restitution, and imprisonment. Several other problems need to be addressed.

Delays and miscarriages of justice. Judge William D. Bontrager maintains that swiftness and sureness of punishment are the most important factors in deterring crime. Severity and length of punishment run a distant third.

Unfortunately justice in the United States is neither swift nor sure. According to *U.S. News and World Report:*

Cases that do not end in plea bargains before trial rarely go to trial quickly. A survey of 32 metropolitan areas by the National Center for State Courts showed that the median time from filing of charges to trial ranged from 42 days in Portland, Oregon, to nearly a year in Buffalo.

Court backlogs are only one reason for delays. Defense lawyers often seek to postpone trials in the hope that prosecution witnesses will decide not to testify or will perhaps forget details of the crime. "The world's greatest defense attorney is Father Time," says Tulsa lawyer Patrick Williams.[13]

We would do well to remember the admonition of Solomon, wisest of all judges: "Because sentence against an evil work is not executed speedily, therefore the heart of some of the sons of men is fully set in them to do evil" (Ecclesiastes 8:11). Delays break the connection between crime and punishment, and the deterrent effect is therefore weakened.

And when trial finally does take place, very few criminals ever receive significant punishment. Of every five hundred reported crimes, four hundred remain unsolved. Of the one hundred which result in an arrest, thirty-five are juveniles—thirty of these are dismissed or placed on probation; only five are institutionalized. Of the sixty-five adults, twenty-five are never charged, and in six cases charges are dismissed. Of the thirty-four that go to trial, two are acquitted. Of the thirty-two convicted, twelve are placed on probation and twenty are imprisoned. These twenty adults and five juveniles constitute only 5 percent of the total five hundred reported serious crimes.[14]

Our criminal justice system needs to be streamlined to make justice more swift and sure. In some localities, more judges and court personnel are needed to eliminate the backlog. Better trained police investigators with more sophisticated equipment can help make sure the guilty are convicted and the innocent are freed from suspicion. And more programs by which young, first-time, and nonviolent offenders can be handled outside the criminal justice system can do more to rehabilitate such persons and, at the same time, free the courts to give better attention to more serious cases.

Juvenile justice. The juvenile justice system needs an overhaul. Started in the late 1800s as a reaction against the old system which treated children as adult criminals, juvenile justice sees the state as every child's ultimate parent and operates not to punish, but to effectuate the best interest of the child. As a result, juvenile court does not impose prison sentences or fines, but it can impose probation, counseling, therapy, foster care, or institutionalization.

It is generally agreed that the system has not worked out as well in practice as it sounds in theory. Juvenile crime rates are soaring and the ranks of juvenile offenders are reaching down to younger and younger children. Even preteens are occasionally charged with drug abuse or such serious crimes as armed robbery and murder. Teens seem aware that juvenile courts cannot impose serious punishment; consequently the juvenile court is no deterrent. Police officers report that juveniles commonly taunt them, "You can't do anything to me; I'm under eighteen."

In many states there is a drive to extend the authority of the adult criminal court to include children under eighteen for certain crimes. And in most states juveniles over a certain age can be transferred to adult criminal court under certain circumstances. But this does not really solve the problem. Placing the juvenile in prison with adult offenders will only make him into a hardened criminal.

Instead, I suggest giving the juvenile court some "teeth." Give the juvenile court the authority to impose reasonable fines, restitution, community service, mild corporal punishment, or—if we are going to be stuck with the prison system—brief jail terms so long as they are separated from adult offenders. I do not necessarily suggest that we abolish the "best interest of the child" concept. But I do suggest that at times punishment may be in the child's best interest.[15]

The cost of obtaining justice. Through carefully safeguarding the rights of criminals, we have created a criminal justice system which, for all its faults, is probably the best in the world. An accused defendant is more likely to get a fair trial here than anywhere else I can imagine.

But in so doing, we have placed the cost of obtaining criminal justice above the reach of the average person.

Court costs, attorney fees, expert witnesses, transcripts, and the like are so expensive that a criminal trial can wipe out an average person's savings. The truly indigent person will receive court-appointed counsel, and the wealthy man can afford it. But the middle-class or working-class person can ruin all his plans for financial security, just by trying to prove himself innocent in court.

For this reason, a criminal defendant on a minor charge may decide to plead guilty even though he thinks he has a good defense. It makes more sense to accept the conviction and pay a $50 fine than to pay an attorney $1,000 to represent him in a jury trial.

We must simplify the criminal justice system. Pretrial intervention, deferred sentencing, community dispute settlement, and perhaps even a return to justice of the peace courts (with right of appeal, of course) may help return justice to an affordable level.

Respect for police. A policemen's job is one of the hardest and most dangerous in the world. He must be a judge, lawyer, psychologist, public-relations expert, teacher, medic, social worker, traffic engineer, and crime-stopper. And for this he usually receives very little training, very little compensation, and very little thanks.

Training for policemen should be greatly upgraded. Police officers should be given opportunities to obtain advanced degrees in criminal justice or related subjects at public expense. And to attract qualified personnel, their salaries should be enhanced considerably.

More than that, they deserve our respect. Not only are they doing a difficult and necessary job, but they are called by God to do it. They are his magistrates, his ministers, his servants, just as much as the President, the governor, or the judge. They deserve our cheerful obedience and our willing respect.

20 *International Relations*

International relations seem very remote to the average American. Afghanistan seems as distant as the far side of Neptune.

But Planet Earth is smaller than most of us think. If you live in Brownsville, Texas, you are closer to the fighting in El Salvador than you are to Los Angeles or Minneapolis. And it is getting closer. More than anything else we do, what happens in international relations may affect our taxes, our prosperity, our liberty, and even our very lives and those of our children.

Strangely enough, churches and clergymen frequently find themselves on the wrong side when they speak about foreign policy— probably more so than with any other issue we have discussed in this book. After all, Christians are for peace and international cooperation, right? That means Christians must be against war, against defense, for the freeze, for cooperating with Communism, and in favor of world government, right?

Not necessarily. I mean no disrespect to church leaders or church tradition. But the Word of God must govern. And my analysis of Scripture tells me that in many instances the position taken by some churches and clergymen on issues of international importance is contrary to that of the Word of God.

Let us turn to the Word of God and examine eight cornerstones of a Bible-based foreign policy.

The First Cornerstone: Nationalism
During the past couple of decades, it has been fashionable to downgrade nationalism as a chauvinistic anachronism. Nationalism, it is thought, breeds war and hatred, has no place in the modern world, and leads to world cooperation and ultimately to world government.

Some churches and clergymen have been in the forefront of the movement for world government. Often their motives have been lofty. They have seen world government as a means of ending hatred and war, ushering in world peace, eradicating poverty, and paving the way for the kingdom of God. This was particularly true of the "social gospel" movement of the late nineteenth and early twentieth centuries.

Just think. If all worldly power were concentrated in one world government, the potential to do good would be unlimited.

Possibly true. But equally unlimited would be the potential for evil.

Let's review a moment. We saw in Chapter 1 that the most basic reason God ordained human government is the spreading cancer of human sin. Government exists to check and restrain human sin. We also saw in Chapter 11 that the danger of granting too much power to government is that rulers themselves are sinful and can abuse their God-given authority and become tyrannical and oppressive. For this reason, government power is to be kept in check by separating it among various branches of government, dividing it among various levels of government, and restraining it with constitutional guarantees of individual liberties. Human nature being what it is, we cannot rely upon government officials to exercise good faith. We must always guard against the potential for abuse. As George Washington observed, "Government is not reason; it is not eloquence; it is force! Like fire, it is a dangerous servant and a fearful master."[1] He and the other framers of the Constitution therefore established a separation of powers whereby the various branches of government check and balance each other.

In a similar way, nations are a check upon each other's power. Each nation's freedom to act is limited somewhat by the interests and desires of its neighbors. The Soviets may persecute their subjects and their satellites only so far, because they respect the power of the United States and its allies. The reverse is true also.

A world government would have no such check. One who rules the world could do as he wants. Constitutional limitations and guarantees would be meaningless, because there would be no one to protect them if the government decided to abolish them. World government has the potential for world tyranny.

I believe it is largely for this reason that God divided the world into nations.

> By these were the isles of the Gentiles divided in their lands; every one after his tongue, after their families, in their nations. (Genesis 10:5)

But in Genesis 11 we read of an attempt to build the world's first "united nations" building:

And they said, Go to, let us build us a city, and a tower, whose top may reach unto heaven; and let us make a name, lest we be scattered abroad upon the face of the whole earth. (Genesis 11:4)

What's wrong with power like that? Several things: It was a picture of salvation by works, reaching heaven by one's own efforts; one of its probable purposes was astrology or Satan worship, as with the ziggurat towers in ancient Babylonia; it was based on pride and self-exaltation. In addition, its purpose was to keep the people together in a one-world government instead of spreading them out into national entities as God had intended. The Jewish historian Flavius Josephus, writing shortly after the time of Christ, says:

Now it was Nimrod who excited them to such an affront and contempt of God. He was the grandson of Ham, the son of Noah—a bold man, and of great strength of hand. He persuaded them not to ascribe it to God, as if it was through His means they were happy, but to believe that it was their own courage procured that happiness. He also gradually changed the government into tyranny,—seeing no other way of turning them from the fear of God, but to bring them into a constant dependence upon his power. He also said he would be revenged on God, if He should have the mind to drown the world again; for that he would build the tower too high for the waters to be able to reach and that he would avenge himself on God for destroying their forefathers.

3. Now the miltitudes were very ready to follow the determination of Nimrod, and to esteem it a piece of cowardice to submit to God; and they built a tower, neither sparing any pains, or being in any degree negligent about the work; and by reason of the multitude of hands employed in it, it grew very high, sooner than anyone could expect; for the thickness (?) of it was so great, and it was so strongly built, that thereby its great height seemed, upon the view, to be less than it really was. It was built of burnt brick, cemented together with mortar, made of bitumen, that it might be liable to admit water. When God saw that they acted so badly, He did not resolve to destroy them utterly, since they were not growing wiser by the destruction of the former sinners; but He caused a tumult among them, by producing in them diverse languages; and causing that, through the multitude of those languages, they would not be able to understand one another. The place wherein they built is now called Babylon; because of the confusion of that language which they readily understood before; for the Hebrews mean by the word babel, confusion.[2]

As we can read in Genesis 11:5-9, God frustrated the building of the tower by causing the people to speak different languages. God then reaffirmed nationalism: "And from thence did the Lord scatter them abroad upon the face of all the earth" (Genesis 11:9). God further reaffirms nationalism in Deuteronomy 32:8 and Acts 17:26. National entities will continue even during Christ's millennial rule on earth

(Isaiah 2:4; 66:18; Revelation 12:5; 20:3, 8), and perhaps even in heaven (Revelation 21:24, 26). Nationalism is God's order for the human race.

However, internationalism must be regarded with suspicion as Satan's attempt to unite the world under himself—a feat which he will accomplish during the Tribulation (Revelation 13).

This does not mean some forms of international dialogue and cooperation are impossible. Certainly they are to be encouraged, so long as they do not infringe on national sovereignty. But we must recognize our nation as God's order for our age. We have already discussed the importance of patriotism in Chapter 8.

The Second Cornerstone: Integrity
George Washington warned his countrymen against "entangling alliances." He declared,

> Observe good faith and justice toward all nations. Cultivate peace and harmony with all. Religion and morality enjoin this conduct. And can it be that good policy does not equally enjoin it? . . . Against the insidious wiles of foreign influence—I conjure you to believe me, fellow citizens—the jealousy of a free people ought to be constantly awake; since history and experience prove that foreign influence is one of the most baneful foes of republican government. . . . If we remain one people, under an efficient government, the period is not far off when we may defy material injury from external annoyance; when we may take such an attitude as will cause the neutrality we may at any time resolve upon to be scrupulously respected;when belligerent nations, under the impossibility of making acquisitions on us, will not likely hazard giving us provocation; but we may choose peace or war, as our interests, guided by justice, shall counsel. Why forego the advantages of so peculiar a situation? Why, by interweaving our destiny with that of any part of Europe, entangle our peace and prosperity in the toils of European ambition, rivalship, interest, humor or caprice?[3]

Our nation should be wary about making treaties, commitments, and alliances with other nations. But when we do make such agreements, we should honor them.

Unfortunately, America in the twentieth century has done the exact opposite.

The Soviet Union, it is true, has a sorry record of keeping commitments. But this is understandable, for treaty-breaking is intrinsic to Communist philosophy, which teaches no absolute morality or absolute truth except the promotion of the Communist state. Lenin himself declared, "Promises are like pie crusts, made to be broken." But the Soviet Union, while regularly breaking its agreements with its enemies, has been remarkably consistent in its support for its friends.

We have done the exact opposite. For the most part we have kept our commitments to our enemies right down to the last detail. But we have shamefully betrayed our friends. Consider Cuba. Consider Vietnam. Consider Laos. Consider Cambodia. Consider Taiwan. Consider Nicaragua.

Is it any wonder El Salvador is worried? Is it any wonder our other allies are nervous about our support? Other nations will not trust a country that does not keep its promises.

Imagine that you are the president of a small country somewhere in the underdeveloped world. You are basically opposed to Communism, but you want the best for your nation. And the Communists are pressuring you and threatening you with insurgency unless you make concessions to them and ally yourself with the Communist powers. Are you likely to ally yourself with the United States, knowing America's tendency to turn tail and run when the going gets tough?

We must stand by our commitments to our allies even when it is no longer advantageous for us to do so. Israel's greatest king asked:

> Lord, who shall abide in thy tabernacle? who shall dwell in thy holy hill? . . . He that sweareth to his own hurt, and changeth not. (Psalms 15:1, 4)

The Third Cornerstone: Compassion
God has blessed America more abundantly than he has ever blessed any nation in history. These blessings entail a responsibility to help the poorer nations of the world.

In Chapter 13 we discussed social responsibility. Many of the same principles which apply to helping the poor in our nation may apply to helping other nations as well. As with helping the poor here, it is generally true in foreign relations that education and technology will provide more long-range assistance than outright grants of money.

Space does not permit the detailed discussion of all the ramifications of foreign aid. But two principles should be noted in passing.

First, we should not aid Communist nations or other enemies of the United States. While it is true that many of those nations are in dire need of help, aid to Communist nations merely strengthens the hand of their Communist oppressors and enables them to divert funds toward arms build-up and international subversion. We have plenty of friendly nations who need and deserve our help instead.

Second, we should not give aid in such a way that we dilute our own economic base so that we cease to be economically strong. If we do that, we will then be able to help no one.

The Fourth Cornerstone: Freedom
As we saw in Chapter 11, the Bible extols freedom as a desirable condition (Leviticus 25:10; 2 Corinthians 3:17).

We have also seen that there is a difficult balance between liberty and authority. That balance is difficult enough when we are talking about domestic problems here at home. But when we are talking about foreign relations, the issue becomes even more complicated. Our diplomats have to walk a tightrope. On the one hand, they must respect other nations' rights to self-determination; on the other hand, we try to make clear that we favor human freedom and human rights. But what do we do when another nation chooses to ignore human rights?

All too often the media and the academic community employ a double standard here. They vociferously condemn human rights violations in anti-Communist nations such as Chile, Argentina, El Salvador, the Philippines, or South Korea. But they have a blind spot toward far more blatant human rights violations in Communist nations. One reason is that most anti-Communist nations are generally open to the press and to fact-finding commissions, whereas Communist nations are closed to them. Out of sight, out of mind.

Soviet leaders once criticized Augusto Pinochet, president of Chile, for holding political prisoners, many of whom were Communists or Communist sympathizers. Pinochet responded by offering to exchange his prisoners for Christians imprisoned in the Soviet Union. He never got an answer. He made a similar offer to Premier Castro of Cuba. Cuban officials responded they would consider the offer. Pinochet remarked that he didn't need time to fatten his prisoners up for release.

The opposite double standard applies as well. Conservative Americans are accused, with some justification, of focusing on human rights violations in Communist nations while ignoring the sins of our allies. While there is truth in this charge, I suggest that several considerations are appropriate.

First, America must consider its own national security. Whatever its sins, South Africa has no designs of aggression against the United States. The Communist powers do.

Second, many of our anti-Communist allies are involved in struggles for their very existence. When Communist insurgents encourage and carry out terrorism, sabotage, assassinations, and guerrilla warfare, the possibility of maintaining civil liberties is very limited. (President Lincoln placed the United States under martial law during our Civil War.) In El Salvador, for example, the best way to promote freedom is to first of all win the war, then work for human rights.

Third, President Carter's outspoken pronouncements on behalf of human rights in allied nations irritated many of our allies, may have driven them further from American influence, and did little if anything to bring about any actual improvement in human rights in those nations. By establishing close relationships with these nations, we may be able to make more progress in human rights through quiet, backdoor methods.

Fourth, while some of our allies have flawed records on human rights, the alternative may be far worse. Cuban dictator Battista was far from perfect, but there was much more freedom under his rule than today under Castro. Diem and Thieu may have abused human rights in South Vietnam, but their regimes did allow some measure of freedom, and that has totally vanished today. Unquestionably the Shah of Iran was repressive, but his rule was probably preferable to that of the Ayatolla. Somoza was probably a heavy-handed dictator in Nicaragua, but less so than the Marxist Sandinistas. When we look at the human rights records of our allies, we need to ask, "What is the alternative?" Usually the choice is limited freedom under an anti-Communist ruler, or no freedom at all under Communism.

Fifth, the best means of promoting human freedom abroad might be our own example, a society that is free, yet strong and orderly.

A further matter should be of special concern for Christians: the persecution of our Christian brethren behind the Iron Curtain.

Several decades ago everyone knew that Christians in Communist countries were subject to imprisonment, harassment, intimidation, and even death. But in the late 1950s and early 1960s, the belief arose and became popular that the Communist rulers had mellowed and now allowed religious freedom. Accounts of persecution by refugees were thought to be lies, distorted anti-Soviet propaganda, or, at best, relics from the bygone Stalinist era.

When Rev. Richard Wurmbrand, a Lutheran minister who spent fourteen years in prison for his faith in Communist Romania, was released in 1964, and described in vivid detail the horrors of Christians suffering for Christ in Communist prisons, his accounts were greeted with skepticism, even by American Christians.

But hosts of others soon corroborated his account. Sergei Kourdakov, who had been a high-ranking Communist youth leader in the Soviet Union before becoming a Christian, described how he had personally led brigades in inflicting terror upon Christians.[4] Rev. Georgi Vins testified before Congress as to the persecution he faced.[5] In 1977 Anita and Peter Deyneka, Jr. wrote *A Song in Siberia*, describing persecution of the church in Russia.[6] And when Nobel Prize-winning author Alexander I. Solzhenitsyn reached the secular media and the academic community with his famous *The Gulag Archipelago*,[7] and described in minute detail even the locations of the Soviet concentration camps, the critics were put to silence.

Even so, the plight of Christians in the Soviet Union is largely ignored today, even by American Christians. We read about it, we emote about it, and then we forget about it. They deserve our daily prayers and our regular support. Numerous organizations exist to support them. One is Richard Wurmbrand's Jesus to the Communist World, Inc., P.O. Box 2947, Torrance, California 90509. Another is Georgi Vins' International Representation for the Council of Evangelical Baptist Churches of the Soviet Union, 300 East Jackson Boulevard, Elkhart, Indiana 46514. Another is Underground Evangelism, P.O. Box 250, Glendale, California 91209. And still another is the Slavic Gospel Association, P.O. Box 1122, Wheaton, Illinois 60187.

> Remember them that are in bonds. (Hebrews 13:3)

The Fifth Cornerstone: Anti-Communism

Strangely enough, in many circles today to be called an anti-Communist is a worse insult than to be called a Communist! Even in some Christian circles, a charge of anti-Communism dredges up memories of perceived excesses of an earlier era. Some Christians have even drawn parallels between Jesus Christ and Karl Marx, portraying both as social reformers trying to usher in a better world, and persecuted by the ruling classes for their efforts.

The informed Christian will realize that Communism is totally at odds with Christianity and is the greatest evil of the twentieth century. A biblically based foreign policy—indeed, the policy of any freedom-loving nation—must be one of absolute and uncompromising opposition to Communism.

Why should a Christian oppose Communism? Let me suggest several reasons:

Communism is atheistic. Communist leaders do not just "happen" to be atheists. They do not indoctrinate schoolchildren in atheism just as a matter of personal preference. They do not persecute churches and torture Christians just to indulge their sadistic lusts. Atheism is the central core of Communist philosophy; it is the cornerstone upon which the Communist ideological structure rests.

Marx titled his philosophy "dialectical materialism." *Dialectic* refers to Hegel's view of truth as a utilitarian process by which theses and antitheses develop into syntheses through a process of tension and conflict, in contrast with absolute and unchanging truth based upon God's revealed Word. In Marx's view man and the universe are purely material—there is no God, no spirit, no soul.[8] Marx wrote,

> Religion is the sigh of the oppressed creature, the feelings of the heartless world, just as it is the spirit of unspiritual conditions. It is the opium of the people. . . .
> The people cannot really be happy until it has been deprived of illusionary happiness by the abolition of religion.[9]

Marx also relied heavily upon the theory of evolution. He declared to Friedrich Engels that "Darwin's book is very important and serves me as a basis in natural science for the class struggle in history."[10]

Marx believed that since man could find no hope in an afterlife, he must create his paradise on earth. Rather than blaming his problems on original sin, man was a product of the environment that he himself—or his ruling classes—had made. Marx's economic interpretation of history, his advocacy of worldwide revolution to overthrow the ruling classes, his conception of a dictatorship of the proletariat to establish a worldwide classless society, and his prediction of the gradual withering and disappearance of the state as man is "reeducated" to live in a classless, Communist society—all is based on Marx's idea of man, freed from God, building his own kingdom on earth.

Communism's antipathy toward religion, and particularly toward Christianity, continues today. Anatole Lunacharsky, former Russian Commissar of Education, declared,

> We hate Christianity and Christians; even the best of them must be regarded as our worst enemies. They preach love of one's neighbor and mercy, which is contrary to our principles.
> Christian love is an obstacle to the development of the revolution. Down with love of one's neighbors. What we need is hatred. . . . Only thus shall we conquer the universe.[11]

Whittaker Chambers, a high-ranking Communist intellectual who broke with Communism after he found God, wrote in his book *Witness:*

> Communists are bound together by no secret oath. The tie that binds them across the frontiers of nations, across barriers of language and differences of class and education, and defiance of religion, morality, truth, law, honor, the weaknesses of the body and the irresolutions of the mind, even unto death, is a simple conviction: It is necessary to change the world. Their power, whose nature baffles the rest of the world, because in a large measure the rest of the world has lost that power, is the power to hold convictions and to act on them. It is the same power that moves mountains; it is also an unfailing power to move men. Communists are that part of mankind which has recovered the power to live or die—to bear witness—for its pain. And it is a simple, rational faith that inspires them to live or die for it.
> It is not new. It is, in fact, man's second oldest faith. Its promise was whispered in the first days of the Creation under the Tree of the Knowledge of Good and Evil: "Ye shall be as gods." It is the great alternative faith of mankind. Like all great faiths, its force derives from a simple vision. Other ages have had great visions. They have always been different versions of the same vision: The vision of God and man's relationship to God. The Communist vision is the vision of Man without God.

It is the vision of man's mind displacing God as the creative intelligence of the world. It is the vision of man's liberated mind, by the sole force of its rational intelligence, redirecting man's destiny and reorganizing man's life in the world. It is the vision of man, once more the central figure of the Creation, not because God made man in His image, but because man's mind makes him the most intelligent of the animals. Copernicus and his successors displaced man as the central fact of the universe by proving that the earth was not the central star of the universe. Communism restores man to his sovereignty by the simple method of denying God.[12]

Communism suppresses human rights. On September 1, 1983, the world gasped in horror when the Soviet Union shot down Flight 007, killing all one hundred and eighty-seven persons on board. The Soviets were branded as insensitive, callous, violators of international law, and murderers.

No one seemed to recognize, however, that this action by the Soviet Union was totally consistent with the Communist view of morality and the Communist view of man.

In the Communist view, the individual means little. He has no soul, no spirit, no eternal worth. He is nothing but a highly complex ape. He has no rights, only such privileges as the state chooses to give or take away. As such, his interests may at any time be subject to those of the larger community, and even those of the community may be subordinated to the "best interests" of the future of the human race as a whole. And of course those who know best what is good for the future of the human race are the leaders of the Communist party, for they are working to bring about the classless society, the workers' paradise on earth.

Lenin declared,

> We repudiate all morality that is taken outside of human, class concepts. . . . We say that our morality is entirely subordinated to the interests of the class struggle. . . . At the root of Communist morality, there lies the continuation and completion of Communism.[13]

Hence the individual occupants of that South Korean aircraft, even communities, groups, or classes, may be sacrificed or liquidated if the good of the human race requires it. In fact, to refuse to liquidate them would be an immoral act, for it would hinder the class struggle.

Because of their view of morality and of the nature of man, the Communist bloc nations have the worst human rights record in the history of the world. Wherever they have taken power, a blood bath has followed. Not only political opponents, but all who might possibly question Communist doctrine are liquidated or imprisoned or pressed into forced labor camps. Dr. G. Stewart-Smith, totaling all of the peacetime deaths for which the Communist bloc powers are responsible, including liquidation of the Kulaks, executions, purges, concentration camps, deportations, forced labor, etc., has estimated the total deaths to be eighty-three million betwen 1917 and 1964. Add the millions killed in Communist China's "cultural revolutions," and the blood baths in Vietnam, Laos, and Cambodia, and the figure today would approximate 100 million.[14] Solzhenitsyn and others consider this figure conservative and estimate the number to be 110 million in the Soviet Union alone. Such actions seem monstrous, but they are entirely consistent with the Soviet morality. For as the *Soviet Encyclopedia* states, the only scientific criterion of morality is the defense of the victory of Communism.[15]

This disregard for the right to life carries over to other rights as well. Lack of privacy, absence of property rights, denial of due process of law in court, imprisonment without trial, suppression of free speech, and of course suppression of religious freedom are commonplace in Communist countries where the state is totalitarian—that is, where the state intrudes into every aspect of life. Human rights are nonexistent, because there is no God to guarantee human rights according to the Marxist perception.

Communism is expansionist. Karl Marx closed his *Communist Manifesto* with the stirring words,

> The Communist disdain to conceal their views and aims. They openly declare that their ends can be attained ony by the forceable overthrow of all existing social conditions. Let the ruling classes tremble in a Communist revolution. The proletarians have nothing to lose but their chains. They have a world to win.
> Working men of all countries, unite![16]

When Marx published the *Manifesto* in 1848, his only followers were a few political outcasts and malcontents. Today, one hundred and thirty-six years later, his disciples control roughly one third of the world's land mass and one half of the world's population.

Thirty years ago Americans were worried. They realized that Communist rulers wanted world domination and were making substantial progress toward that goal. How long, it was asked, before the Red flag flies over America?

But today Americans laugh at the threat of Communist domination. Communism has mellowed. The Communists don't want to take us over anymore—if they ever did—which is doubtful. Thus reassured, the American Christian lets his mind wander to other problems or falls asleep.

But wait a minute. Let's think about it. What leads you to believe the Communist bloc nations have mellowed? Has anyone presented any evidence to convince you of that? Or do you believe it simply because the liberals in the media and the academic community have said it so often that you assume it must be true?

I believe the evidence clearly establishes that the Communist leaders still have designs on the United States and the entire world. Let us consider that evidence objectively.

First, the Communist rulers still claim this as their goal. Ever since Lenin set forth his blueprint for world conquest, Communists have echoed his words. Communist officials at the Politburo and the Communist Party meetings consistently call for the conquest of the world and the destruction of the capitalist powers. Ever since Khrushchev declared, "We will bury you," no Communist leader of any stature has ever repudiated that goal.

Second, they have made substantial progress toward that goal. Here is how John Stormer summarizes Lenin's blueprint:

> First, we will take Eastern Europe, then the masses of Asia, then we will encircle the United States, which will be the last bastion of capitalism. We will not have to attack. It will fall into our hands like an overripe fruit.[17]

Look at what happened since. Lenin's blueprint has been followed almost to the letter:

1917: Communists seize Russia as power base
1945: Czechoslovakia, Hungary, Romania, Bulgaria, Albania, Yugoslavia, Mongolia, and North Korea fall to Communism
1948-1949: Fall of Mainland China
1954: Fall of North Vietnam
1958: Fall of Cuba
1975: Fall of South Vietnam, Cambodia, and Laos
1976: Fall of Angola
1979: Fall of Nicaragua and Afghanistan
1984: What's next?

Somehow, as Whittaker Chambers says, "This movement, once a mere muttering of political outcasts, became this immense force that now contests the mastery of mankind."[18]

Third, Communist rulers' current actions are consistent with this goal. Over the past two decades, the Soviet Union has engaged in the most massive military buildup the world has ever seen, as we will demonstrate under the seventh cornerstone. They are endangered in subversion in many parts of the world, including Southeast Asia, the Middle East, Southern Europe, Africa, and South and Central America. Were it not for President Reagan's quick action, the strategic island of Grenada would have been added to the Soviet orbit in 1983.

The current "hot spot" is El Salvador, and most Americans are aware that the Communist war for El Salvador threatens to engulf Costa Rica, Honduras, and Guatemala as well. Most Americans are unaware that sporadic guerrilla warfare is currently going on in all of those nations, and is even taking place right now in certain parts of Mexico![19] The consequences to the United States of Mexico going Communist become ever clearer when we consider the illegal alien problems of our southwestern United States. Add to that the waves of refugees that flee from every nation taken over by Communists, and we are faced with what has been termed the "invasion of the feet people." What if a Communist Mexican government were to infiltrate the United States with spies, terrorists, and saboteurs coming across the river as illegal aliens? The next step would be guerilla warfare in the United States.

Some will object that the Communists no longer believe their own rhetoric, that while the Communist powers are strong and aggressive, Communism as an ideological force is virtually dead. Note that it is American liberals who make this claim, not the Communist themselves. The example of Grenada indicates that that view is sadly mistaken:

Washington (AP)—American experts say they are surprised by how far the Soviets and Cubans went to indoctrinate Grenadians in Marxist philosophy during the four-year association between the two communist countries and Grenada's leftist leadership.

"I've had to revise my view of the Soviet Union in this regard," said Michael Ledeen, a historian recruited by the State Department to analyze the documents captured by American forces in the invasion of Grenada.

"I had thought the Russians were as bored with Marxist-Leninism as the rest of the world seems to be," he said. "But instead I discovered they devoted an enormous amount of money and manpower to the indoctrination of Grenadians, and they have done it passionately and diligently, down to the last detail."[20]

Others shrug off the Communist threat by pointing to the split between the Soviet Union and China as proof that Communism is no longer a monolithic worldwide conspiracy.

But the issue is not whether Communism is monolithic. The issue is whether Communism is expansionist. Neither the Soviet Union nor China has renounced the goal of world domination. They both want to bury us; they simply disagree as to who should do it and how and when it should be done. For some reason I take little comfort in that.

Certainly Communism appears to be divided, just as Christians are divided. But that does not mean they have lost their ideological fervor, or their desire to win the world for Communism. The divisions in the

Communist bloc should be carefully watched and exploited for maximum American advantage. But they should not lull us into any false sense of security.

Some will shrug off these pages by saying, "Aw, he's just trying to scare us!" Yes, I certainly am! I would also try to scare you if there were a king cobra under your table, poised and ready to strike. Before you dismiss what I'm saying as "far-out," check out the facts I have presented and determine whether they are true.

Given the anti-Christian character of Communism and the threat it poses to the free world, foreign policy considerations that affect the Communist bloc nations cannot be considered in a theologically neutral context. Issues such as aid to El Salvador, giving away the Panama Canal, arms agreements, trade with Communist countries,[21] or aid to Taiwan must all be carefully considered in light of the basic question, Do these policies give support or encouragement to the Communist enemies of Christianity?

The Sixth Cornerstone: Peace If Possible

> If it be possible, as much as lieth in you, live peaceably with all men. (Romans 12:18)

We all know the horror and devastation that results from war—especially nuclear war. For this reason our fervent desire should be for peace. Our nation should strive to be at peace with other nations, and as a world leader America should be available to try to settle disputes between other nations, even when we are not directly involved.

The Seventh Cornerstone: Peace with Strength

Churches and clergymen have always been in the forefront of the peace movement. They marched with the "ban-the-bomb" crusade of the 1950s and 1960s; they led the "get-out-of-Vietnam" campaigns of the sixties and early seventies. Now the issue is nuclear freeze.

Unfortunately peace advocates often portray the issue as peace versus war. Since they are for peace, it logically follows that those who oppose them must be in favor of war.

But the issue isn't that simple. The fact is, no sane person in this country wants war—least of all those who are in military service and will have to place their lives on the line should war occur.

The issue, rather, is: How can peace best be preserved—by a nuclear freeze, or through military strength?

For reasons which were made clear in Chapter 9, I am not a pacifist. I hold to the just war position of Augustine, Luther, and others in the church, because I believe that position to be biblical and logical.

Furthermore, considering the avowed intention of our Communist enemies to wipe out all vestiges of Christianity, the arms race between the Soviet Union and the United States clearly has profound spiritual implications.

Peace is indeed a virtue, and war is always a tragedy. But peace is not the only virtue, and death in war is not the worst tragedy that can occur. Justice and freedom are also virtues, and sometimes their violation is worse than war. Peace is not to be obtained at the price of chains and slavery.

Furthermore, disarmament and appeasement are not necessarily the best means of preserving peace. When you give in to the neighborhood bully, he simply becomes bolder and makes more demands. The same is true of an aggressive nation like the Soviet Union. Military strength is likely to deter aggression and preserve peace, whereas military weakness is likely to encourage aggression and threaten peace. Chamberlain's futile attempts to appease Hitler prior to World War II are a case in point.

This, of course, does not mean we give the Pentagon everything it wants in terms of military expenditures. But we do need to remember that a sound national defense costs money, and this defense may be essential to our survival.

In determining how much we need to spend for defense, we need to examine our defenses in comparison with those of the Soviet Union. The fact is, the Soviet Union has engaged in an unprecedented arms buildup over the past two decades. Despite economic difficulties, in 1983 the USSR allocated an estimated 15 percent of its gross national product to its military buildup, a substantial increase from the 12-14 percent reported in 1981. This reflects a general increase over the past twenty-one years.[22] By contrast the U.S. spends a much smaller percentage of its GNP on national defense, and that percentage has steadily declined over the last twenty years, except for the Vietnam years.[23] There is considerable truth in the statement, "The United States has a military-industrial complex. The Soviet Union is one."[24] As a result of this increase in the Soviet Union and decrease in the United States, by 1980 the Soviet Union was spending 50 percent more for military forces than the U.S.[25]

At the close of World War II, the United States was the greatest military power in the world. Thirty-nine years later, we can no longer make that claim.[26] The following chart depicts the current situation:

Table 20.1
The Shifting Balance of Military Power

	United States	U.S.S.R.
	Intercontinental Satellite Missiles	
1968	1,054	858
Today	1,048	1,398
	Submarine-Launched Missiles	
1968	656	121
Today	520	989
	Anti-Ballistic Missiles	
1968	0	0
Today	0	32
	Surface-to-Air Missile Launchers	
1968	3,300	10,000
Today	0	10,000+
	Nuclear Warheads	
1968	4,300	1,300
Today	9,268	10,000+
	Strategic Bombers	
1968	640	180
Today	344	450
	Tactical Aircraft	
1968	5,100	4,000
Today	3,500	5,500
	Interceptor Aircraft	
1968	1,000	3,600
Today	508	3,500
	Major Surface Combatant Ships	
1968	360	230
Today	203	290
	Tanks	
1968	8,500	32,400
Today	12,130	50,000+
	Troops	
1968	3,500,000	3,400,000
Today	2,100,000	4,300,000[27]

One thing is clear: we have lost our advantage. The Soviet Union is rapidly overtaking us, if they have not done so already. And the momentum is on their side.

Some argue that it doesn't really matter how many arms each side has, since the Soviet Union and the United States could already destroy each other many times over. But that argument is too simplistic. It ignores the fact, first, that a nuclear warhead is effective only so long as it can be delivered to its target. If the other side has an antimissile missile to knock it out, it loses its effectiveness. Second, the extra megatonnage is of great importance, because it allows a larger margin of error. The fact is, we do not know for sure how reliable our missiles are, because they have never been tested.

Others protest that it is wrong to spend so much for defense when domestic needs are of greater importance. I must respond that, first, the preservation of American liberty is of fundamental concern, and for this a strong defense is essential. Second, money spent on national defense is not wasted in regard to domestic purposes. Rather, it supplies jobs, thereby alleviating unemployment. And many young men from poor families or minority groups have found military service to be their ticket out of the ghetto and into the mainstream of American life. Possibly the money could have achieved more economic benefit had it been used in a different capacity. But I mention this to emphasize that money spent on defense is not a total economic waste.

Still others contend that reliance upon nuclear weapons betrays a lack of trust in God. Not necessarily. God normally uses practical, earthly means of carrying out his will on earth. Just as God used Medo-Persian military power under Cyrus to free the Jews from the Babylonian captivity, so today he uses American military power to preserve the freedom of Americans and the rest of the non-Communist world. Relying upon a strong military defense no more betrays a lack of trust in God than does relying upon seat belts to protect us from auto accidents or relying upon fire alarms to warn us of fires. God does protect us, but he uses natural means to do so.

This does not mean that the Christian should oppose all forms of disarmament. I favor disarmament, so long as it is mutual, does not give the Soviet Union an unfair advantage, and an adequate means of inspection is provided to be sure the Soviet Union keeps its word. However, I cannot support disarmament without these safeguards, nor can I support a nuclear freeze at this time without such safeguards. Unfortunately the nuclear freeze movement seems to aim its propaganda only at the United States. There is no comparable movement in Moscow. If the nuclear freeze advocates have their way, the likely effect will be unilateral disarmament (of the United States, not the Soviet Union) and a weakening of the position of the United States relative to the Soviet Union.

Finally, let us remember that one avowed goal of our Communist enemy is the eradication of all vestiges of Christianity. That being the case, national defense and the nuclear arms race have clear spiritual implications. For they affect the freedom of Christians, not only in this country but in the entire world. The fact is, like it or not, the Christian world looks to the United States for leadership and for protection. And to those who reject this role for the United States, it may fairly be asked: To whom else would you suggest they turn? Richard Wurmbrand, who spent fourteen years in Communist prisons in Romania, said it well:

> Every freedom-loving man has two fatherlands; his own and America. Today, America is the hope of every enslaved man, because it is the last bastion of freedom in the world. Only America has the power and spiritual resources to stand as a barrier between militant Communism and the peoples of the world. It is the last "dike" holding back the rampaging floodwaters of militant Communism. If it crumples, there is no other dike, no other dam; no other line of defense to fall back upon. America is the last hope of millions of enslaved peoples. They look to it as their second fatherland. In it lies their hopes and prayers. I have seen fellow-prisoners in Communist prisons beaten, tortured, with 50 pounds of chains on their legs—praying for America . . . that the dike will not crumple; that it will remain free.[28]

The Eighth Cornerstone: Support for Israel

God called Israel out from the nations for a special purpose: to be the bearers of his Word, and to carry the lineage for his Son, the Lord Jesus Christ. He established a special covenant with them, and he gave them the land of Canaan in perpetuity (Genesis 17:1-14; Exodus 34:10-35).

Israel, of course, rejected the Messiah and turned away from God. But this does not mean God has rejected Israel. His promise to Israel remains valid today, as evidenced by the regathering of Israel in this century. (See Acts 2:22, 23; 4:10; 5:31; Romans 11; Genesis 17:8; Amos 9:11-15.)

Furthermore, God declared in the Abrahamic Covenant, "I will bless them that bless thee, and curse him that curseth thee" (Genesis 12:3). The fact is, every world power that has turned anti-Semitic has been judged by God. In the Bible we read of God's judgment upon the Assyrians, the Babylonians, the Amalekites, the Phoenicians, the Philistines, and the Syrians. In more recent times we can read about Spain, and most recently Nazi Germany. God has been faithful to his promise.

Christian attitudes toward Israel have generally fallen into two categories. On the one hand, some blame the Jews for their rejection of Christ and so become anti-Semitic. As we have seen above, this is clearly unscriptural and can lead to God's judgment.

On the other hand, many Christians seem to take the position that Israel can do no wrong, or at least cannot be criticized. That is not the meaning of Genesis 12:3. Jews, like all other people, are sinners; and today they are in rebellion against God. They are certainly capable of doing wrong, and when they do they should be criticized, as the prophets criticized them in the Old Testament.

But we must understand their unique circumstances. Israel is a small nation, surrounded by hostile Moslem powers. These Moslem nations, with few exceptions, do not recognize Israel's right to exist, loudly proclaim their intent to destroy Israel, and brag that they will "drive Israel into the sea." It is only natural that Israel should look after its own defense, even taking the initiative and becoming aggressive at times. The security of its people depends upon it. When terrorists and Palestinian guerrillas encamp just across the Lebanese border and use Lebanese territory as a base to launch mortar attacks upon Israel, it is not surprising that the Israelis would strike back—even launching preemptive attacks across the Lebanese border. We would do the same if terrorists launched similar attacks from the Canadian or Mexican borders.

We should not refrain from criticizing Israel when Israel is wrong. But God has ordained that Israel has a right to exist as a nation. He will bless our nation if we support Israel; and if we double-cross Israel, God will judge us.

Epilogue

"If thou art privy to thy country's fate, which happily, foreknowing may avoid, O speak—" (Horatio, speaking in Shakespeare's *Hamlet*, Act I, Scene 1)

Now that you have waded through twenty chapters, I have several brief closing admonitions.

First, like the Bereans of Acts 17:11, search the Scriptures daily to see whether these things are so. God's Word is inspired and infallible; my interpretation and application of God's Word is not. You may find, after studying the issues, that your conclusions are different from mine. If so, follow the Scriptures as you perceive them.

Second, dig more deeply than I have. On many issues I have merely scratched the surface. The Word of God has so much more to say than I have been able to cover.

Furthermore there are many issues I have not even mentioned. I have not discussed the energy crisis, environmental concerns, consumerism, product safety, race relations, or many other political issues that are of great concern to twentieth-century Christians. I have omitted these not because they are unimportant, but because of my limited knowledge in those areas, and because a book of this size can only cover so much. I urge you to explore the passages into which I have not ventured. And I will be interested in your conclusions.

Third, in James's words, I urge you to be doers of the Word, and not hearers only (1:22). Don't hide your light under a bundle; let it shine before the world. Be like salt that savors and lends flavor to your society. Use what you have learned to have an impact upon your community, your state, and your nation. (And if you have forgotten what you as a Christian can do, reread Chapter 10.)

Fourth, Christians will find that they disagree with one another from time to time. Let us do so vigorously, but let us also do so in Christian love.

Fifth, let us never forget that while reforming society is part of our calling as Christians, it is not a means of salvation. Personal trust in the Lord Jesus Christ is first and foundational. Social action is a result thereof, not a means thereto.

And finally, let us honor Jesus Christ as Lord of our lives, Lord of our minds, and Lord of our thoughts. Let his Word be the standard by which we judge.

In all thy ways acknowledge him, and he shall direct thy paths. (Proverbs 3:6)

Notes

Introduction

1. Stan Mooneyham, "United We Fall," *Liberty,* September/October 1980, p. 7.
2. Barry Goldwater, remarks on Senate floor, September 15, 1981, condensed in "Barry Goldwater on Religion and Politics," *Church and State,* Vol. 34, No. 9, October 1981, p. 11.

Chapter 1: Why Do We Need Government?

1. See John H. Hallowell, *Main Currents in Modern Political Thought* (New York: Holt, Rinehart & Winston, 1950, 1960), pp. 23, 27, 28.

Chapter 3: The Two Kingdoms: Church and State

1. Luther Hess Waring, *The Political Theories of Martin Luther* (Port Washington, N.Y.: Kennikat Press, 1910, 1968), p. 2.
2. Quoted in E. L. Hebden Taylor, *The Christian Philosophy of Law, Politics, and the State* (Nutley, N.J.: Craig Press, 1966), pp. 445, 446.
3. Reprinted in Ernest F. Henderson, *Select Historical Documents of the Middle Ages* (New York: Biblo & Tannen, 1965), p. 436.
4. W. Ullmann, "Donation of Constantine," *New Catholic Encyclopedia,* Vol. 4 (New York: McGraw-Hill, 1967), pp. 1000, 1001.

Chapter 4: Church and State in America: The First Amendment

1. 310 U.S. 296. I question whether the Fourteenth Amendment was ever legally ratified, and I also question whether its authors and supporters ever intended or even dreamed of the interpretation given to the Amendment by the Court in *Cantwell.* However, the decision is firmly entrenched in legal precedent now, and there is no point in arguing that issue here. The author gives the First Amendment much more thorough coverage in his book *The Christian Legal Advisor* (Milford, Mich.: Mott Media, 1984), Chapters 9-21.
2. 403 U.S. 602.
3. One such case, involving a Christian group called Cornerstone at the University of Missouri-Kansas City, went to the Supreme Court in 1981. The Court decided in favor of Cornerstone, but did so not on the basis of the free exercise clause, but on the basis of the free speech clause of the First Amendment. The Court's ruling indicates that religious speech must be afforded the same protection as other types of speech covered by the First Amendment.

4. John Whitehead, *The Separation Illusion: A Lawyer Examines the First Amendment* (Milford, MI: Mott Media, 1977), p. 89. Whitehead argues convincingly in light of other statements by Jefferson that Jefferson really meant "state" in a generic sense and that his true intent was to place a wall of separation between the federal government on the one hand, and the states and churches on the other.
5. *Journal of the House* (1789), p. 914; *Senate Journal* (1789), pp. 154, 155, 914, 915. Cited by Chester James Antieau, Arthur T. Downey, and Edward C. Roberts, *Freedom from Federal Establishment: Formation and Early History of the First Amendment Religious Clauses* (Milwaukee: Bruce, 1964), p. 131.
6. Quoted by Michael J. Malbin, *Religion and Politics: The Intention of the Authors of the First Amendment* (Washington, D.C.: American Enterprise Institute, 1978), p. 8.
7. Quoted by Rousas J. Rushdoony, *The Nature of the American System* (Fairfax, Va.: Thoburn Press, 1978), pp. 46, 47.
8. Rousas J. Rushdoony, *Law and Liberty* (Fairfax, Va.: Thoburn Press, 1971), p. 33.
9. 65 L.Ed. 2d 784.
10. 374 U.S. 203 (1963).
11. *Ibid.*

Chapter 5: Prayer

1. Wyatt Lipscomb and M. B. Dunn, *War in the Spiritual Realm* (Garland, Tex.: Support for Action, Inc., 1980), pp. 35-62.

Chapter 6: Obedience and Disobedience

1. Gene Fisher and Glen Chambers, *The Revolution Myth* (Greenville, S.C.: Bob Jones University Press, 1981), p. 1.
2. Rousas J. Rushdoony, *This Independent Republic* (Fairfax, Va.: Thoburn Press, 1978), p. 27.
3. Rousas J. Rushdoony, *The Nature of the American System* (Fairfax, Va.: Thoburn Press, 1978), p. 45.
4. Quoted by Jeremiah A. Denton, Jr., *When Hell Was in Session* (Clover, S.C.: Commission Press, 1976), p. 239.

Chapter 7: Taxation

1. Louis Matthews Sweat, "Tax, Taxing," *International Standard Bible Encyclopedia,* Vol. 5 (Grand Rapids, Mich.: Eerdmans, 1929, 1939), pp. 2918-2920.
2. Robert F. Sharpe, *Before You Give Another Dime* (Nashville: Thomas Nelson, 1979) is an excellent guide to estate planning and tax savings. See also my book *The Christian Legal Advisor* (Milford, Mich.: Mott Media, 1984), Chapters 26, 27.

Chapter 8: Patriotism

1. Paragraph 12, reprinted in *Humanist Manifestos I* and *II* (Buffalo, N.Y.: Prometheus Books, 1981), p. 21.

Chapter 9: Military Service

1. P. T. Ruinart, editor, *Acta Martyrum*, Samuel Kapustin, trans. Quoted in Albert Marrin, editor, *War and the Christian Conscience from Augustine to Martin Luther King, Jr.* (Chicago: Regnery, 1971), p. 41.
2. In *Medieval Epics*, W. S. Merwin, trans. (New York: Random House, 1963), pp. 152-157,
3. I treated this subject exhaustively in my Master's thesis at Dallas Theological Seminary, and this chapter is merely a brief summary of that thesis. The thesis consists of 170 pages and may be obtained through the Mosher Library at Dallas Theological Seminary, 3909 Swiss Ave., Dallas, Texas. It is titled "The Biblical View of War and Military Service" and was submitted in 1980.

4. C. N. Tokatloglou, "A Word Study—'Thou Shalt Not Murder,'" *Command*, Spring 1975 (17:1), pp. 14, 15. Cf. Francis Brown, S. R. Driver, and Charles A. Briggs, *A Hebrew and English Lexicon of the Old Testament* (Oxford: Clarendon Press, 1972), pp. 953, 954.

5. Walter Bauer, *A Greek-English Lexicon of the New Testament and Other Early Christian Literature*, William F. Arndt and F. Wilbur Gingrich, trans. (Chicago: University of Chicago Press, 1969), p. 803. Cf. Tokatloglou, "A Word Study."

6. "Matthew," *Interpreter's Bible*, Vol. 7 (New York: Abingdon Press, 1951), p. 301.

7. H. L. E. Luering, "Cheek," *International Standard Bible Encyclopedia*, Vol. 1 (Grand Rapids, Mich.: Eerdmans, 1929, 1939), p. 600.

8. R. C. H. Lenski, *The Interpretation of St. John's Gospel* (Minneapolis: Augsburg, 1936), pp. 205, 206.

9. Joseph H. Mayfield, "John," *Beacon Bible Commentary*, Vol. 7 (Kansas City, Mo.: Beacon Hill Press, 1969), p. 49.

10. Nor do Christ's words to Peter in this passage justify pacifism. Peter was ordered not to rebel against lawful government authority, and there was a special reason for not doing so in this instance: it was God's plan that Jesus should die for the sin of the world.

11. John Peter Lange, "Luke," *Lange's Commentary on the Whole Bible*, Vol. 8, Philip Schaff, trans. (Grand Rapids, Mich.: Zondervan, 1960), p. 343. Cf. Lenski, "Luke," *The Interpretation of St. Luke's Gospel* (Minneapolis: Augsburg, 1934), p. 1068.

12. Augustine, *Sermons*, 77:12. Quoted by R. C. Trench, *Notes on the Miracles of Our Lord* (Grand Rapids, Mich.: Baker), p. 243.

13. Some have argued that the expression is correctly translated "a son of God." But Colwell, Moule, Earle, Lange, and Lenski all agree that "the son of God" is correct. Lange describes this centurion as the third in "a triumvirate of believing soldiers, in the evangelic and apostolic histories." Lange, Vol. 8. pp. 381, 528; Vol. 18, p. 53; Lenski, "Luke," p. 1156; Ralph Earle, "Matthew," *Beacon Bible Commentary*, Vol. 6, p. 249.

14. Leon Wood, *A Survey of Israel's History* (Grand Rapids, Mich.: Zondervan, 1970), p. 170.

Chapter 10: Political Participation

1. Rousas J. Rushdoony, *The Biblical Philosophy of History* (Phillipsburg, N.J.: Presbyterian and Reformed Publishing Company, 1979), p. 16.

2. Mark Hatfield, "How Can a Christian Be in Politics?", Robert G. Clouse, Robert D. Linder and Richard V. Pierard, eds., *Protest and Politics: Christianity and Contemporary Affairs* (Greenwood, S.C.: Attic Press, 1968), pp. 13, 14.

3. Patrick J. Buchanan, *Moral Majority Report*, January 25, 1980.

4. Quoted by John Stormer, *The Death of a Nation* (Florissant, Mo.: Liberty Bell Press, 1968), p. 128.

Chapter 11: Left and Right

1. Quoted by Harry K. Girvetz, "Liberalism," *Encyclopedia Britannica*, Vol. 10 (Chicago: William Benton, 1978), p. 848.

2. Some have equated the divine covenant with the social contract. John Locke, for example, equated the social contract with the Noahic covenant. See John Locke, *Of Civil Government*, reprinted in Verna M. Hall, *The Christian History of the Constitution of the United States of America* (San Francisco: Foundation for American Christian Education, 1966, 1978), p. 112.

3. Thomas J. Dodd, *Freedom and Foreign Policy* (New York: McFadden, 1962), pp. 39, 40. Dodd relied upon documentation compiled by the Investigating Committee of Free Jurists in Berlin. Among those named therein were Dr. Kurt Schumann, president of the East German Supreme Court; Siegfried Dallmann, chairman of the Law Committee of the People's Chamber; and Hans W. Aust, chief editor of the official Communist theoretical periodical *German Foreign Policy*.

4. *Newsweek*, August 25, 1980, pp. 34, 35.
5. "ACU Senate Key Issues Index," *Battleline*, Vol. XV, No. 3 (May-June 1981), pp. 9-12.

Chapter 12: Liberty and Power
1. Whittaker Chambers, *Witness* (New York: Random House, 1952), p. 16.
2. Thomas Jefferson, first inaugural address, March 4, 1801. Reprinted in Saul K. Padover, *The Complete Jefferson: Containing His Major Writings, Published and Unpublished, Except His Letters* (New York: Duell, Sloan & Pearce, 1943), p. 385.
3. James Madison, "Federalist No. 51," *The Federalist Papers* (New York: Mentor, 1961), p. 322.
4. Quoted by Mark R. Rushdoony, "Human Nature and the Abuse of Power," *The Chalcedon Report*, March 1981 (No. 187), p. 1.
5. *Trop v. Dulles*, 356 U.S. 86.
6. Woodrow Wilson, *The New Freedom* (New York: n.p., 1914), pp. 44-48. Quoted by Richard Hofstadter, *Social Darwinism in American Thought* (New York: George Braziller, 1944, 1955), p. 3.

Chapter 13: Wealth and Poverty
1. "One More Plan to End Fraud in Welfare," *U.S. News & World Report*, January 9, 1978, p. 41.
2. Quoted in Lawrence D. Maloney and staff, "The Great National Rip-off," *U.S. News & World Report*, July 3, 1978, p. 27.
3. *Ibid.*
4. "Mess in Welfare—The Inside Story," *U.S. News & World Report*, February 20, 1978, p. 21.
5. Quoted in "Welfare Mess: Any Hope of Solution?", *U.S. News & World Report*, June 7, 1976, p. 33.
6. Kathleen Kroll, "A Worker: I Begrudge Living Less Well Than the Poor Do," *U.S. New & World Report*, March 30, 1981, p. 46.
7. Beth Macklin, "All-Lutheran Unit to Assess Federalism Effects," *Tulsa World*, February 21, 1982, p. B-2.
8. Beth Macklin, "Recession Readiness," *Tulsa World*, February 29, 1982, p. D-1.
9. "New York's Success Against Cheaters," *U.S. News & World Report*, July 3, 1978, p. 31.
10. "Did Reagan's Welfare Plan Work in California?," *U.S. News & World Report*, March 30, 1981, p. 23.
11. Michael Fries and C. Holland Taylor, *The Prosperity Handbook* (Oakland, Calif.: Communication, Inc., 1984), p. 443.
12. Quoted by Irving E. Howard, *The Moral Alternative to Socialism* (Chicago: Citizens Evaluation Institute, 1971), p. 109.
13. Quoted by Beth Macklin, "Don't Put Down Business!," *Tulsa World* March 21, 1982, p. B-2.

Chapter 14: The Family
1. J.D. Unwin, *Sex and Culture* (Oxford: Oxford University Press, 1934), pp. viii, 23, 340, 414, 431, 618, 619. Cited by O. R. Johnston, *Who Needs the Family?* (Downers Grove, Ill.: InterVarsity Press, 1979), pp. 43, 44.
2. Karl Marx, *The Communist Manifesto*, (1848, reprinted Chicago: Regnery, 1954), pp. 47, 48. Shortly after the Bolshevik Revolution in Russia, the New Communist rulers tried to abolish the family. They legalized abortion, changed marriage to mere civil registration, made divorce possible by simple declaration, and legalized incest, bigamy, and adultery. The result was social chaos, including delinquency violence, vandalism, and sadism by young children. As a result, in the 1930s the Communist rulers decided the Russian people weren't ready for the abolition of the

family yet, so they reluctantly returned to traditional family concepts. See Johnston, *Who Needs the Family?* pp. 28, 29.

3. Quoted by Alice Reynolds, Flower, *The Home, A Divine Sanctuary* (Springfield, Mo.: Gospel Publishing House, 1955), p. 5.
4. *Ibid.*, pp. 5, 6.
5. Tim LaHaye, *The Battle for the Family* (Old Tappan, N.J.: Fleming H. Revell, 1982), p. 142.
6. Quoted by Jerry Falwell, *Listen, America!* (Garden City, N.Y.: Doubleday, 1980), pp. 153, 154.
7. *Ibid.*, p. 153.
8. *Ibid.*
9. For example, see Britton Gildersleeve, "Doctor Urges 'Divorce' for Abused Children," *Tulsa World*, September 18, 1981.
10. Cited by Falwell, *Listen, America!*, p. 144.
11. *Ibid.*
12. Martin Guggenheim, "A Call to Abolish the Juvenile Justice System," *II Children's Rights, Report No. 9*, June 1978. Reprinted in Sanford J. Fox, *Modern Juvenile Justice: Cases and Materials* (St. Paul: West Publishing Company, 1981), pp. 50-53.

Chapter 15: Humanism in Government

1. This and the following quotations are taken from *Humanist Manifestos I and II* (Buffalo, N.Y.: Prometheus Books, 1973, 1978).
2. 370 U.S. 421 (1962).
3. Paul Blanshard, "Three Cheers for Our Secular State," *The Humanist State*, March/April 1976, p. 17,
4. Sheila Schwartz, "Adolescent Literature: Humanism Is Alive and Thriving in the Secondary School," *The Humanist*, January/February 1976. Quoted by Timothy D. Crater, "The Unproclaimed Priests of Public Education," *Christianity Today*, April 10, 1981, p. 46.
5. John Dumphy, *The Humanist*, January/February 1983, p. 26. Quoted in Cal Thomas, *Book Burning* (Westchester, Ill.: Crossway Books, 1983), p. 55.
6. *Memoirs of Stonewall Jackson* (Dayton: Morningside Bookshop, 1976), p. 131.
7. George Washington, *Daily Sacrifices*. Quoted in Peter Marshall and David Manuel, *The Light and the Glory* (Old Tappan, N.J.: Fleming H. Revell, 1977), pp. 284, 285.
8. 367 U.S. 488 (1961).

Chapter 16: Education

1. 333 U.S. 203 (1948).
2. Horace Mann, *Life and Works*, Vol. 2, pp. 46, 151. Quoted in R. J. Rushdoony, *The Messianic Character of American Education* (Nutley, N.J.: Craig Press, 1963), p. 28.
3. Horace Mann, *The Common School Journal*, January 1, 1841 (III:15). Quoted in *ibid.*, p. 29.
4. 159 Mass. 372, 34 N.E. 402 (1893).
5. Quoted by William Shirer, *The Rise and Fall of The Third Reich* (New York: Simon & Schuster, 1960), p. 249.
6. H. W. Koch, *Hitler Youth: The Duped Generation* (New York: Ballantine Books, 1971), p. 104.
7. DuPont de Nemours, *National Education in the United States of America* (Newark, Del.: The University of Delaware Press, 1923), pp. 3-5. Quoted in R. J. Rushdoony, *The Messianic Character of American Education*, pp. 329, 330.
8. "Daniel Webster on Education," discourse at Plymouth, December 22, 1820, see *The Works of Daniel Webster*, Vols. I and II, Boston, 1851. Reprinted in Verna M. Hall, *The Christian History of the American Revolution: Consider and Ponder* (San Francisco: Foundation for American Christian Education, 1976), p. 222.

9. Quoted in George W. Pierson, *Tocqueville in America* (Garden City, N.Y.: Anchor Books, 1959), pp. 293, 294.
10. Quoted in "Mediocrity in Education Turned Threat to Nation," *Tulsa Tribune*, May 3, 1983.
11. *Tulsa World*, April 4, 1981.
12. Raymond Moore, *School Can Wait* (Provo, Utah: Brigham Young University Press, 1979); *Better Late Than Early* (New York: Reader's Digest and McGraw-Hill, 1976); *Home Grown Kids: The Practical Handbook for Teaching Your Children at Home* (Waco, Tex.: Word Books, 1981); *Home-Spun Schools: Teaching Children at Home—What Parents Are Doing and How They Are Doing It* (Waco, Tex.: Word Books, 1982).
13. 351 N.E. 2d 750 (1976).
14. 589 S.W. 2d 877 (1979).
15. 382 A.2d 377 (1978).
16. 17 U.S. (4 Wheat.) 316, 4 L.Ed. 579 (1819).
17. Cited by Samuel Chester Parker, *A Textbook in the History of Modern Elementary Education* (Chicago: Ginn, 1912), p. 60.
18. Northwest Ordinance, Article III (1787). Cited by Leo Pfeffer, *Church, State and Freedom* (Boston: Beacon Press, 1953), p. 108.
19. John Dewey, *Characters and Events*, Vol. 2 (New York: Holt, 1929), p. 515.
20. Sidney Mead, *The Lively Experiment, The Shaping of Christianity in America* (New York: Harper & Row, 1963), p. 68. Quoted in Norman de Jung, *Christianity and Democracy* (Nutley, N.J.: The Craig Press, 1978), p. 158.
21. Martin Luther, *Luther's Works*, Vol. 6, Weimar edition.
22. 413 U.S. 756 (1973).
23. 421 U.S. 349 (1975).
24. 330 U.S. 1 (1947).
25. 103 S. Ct. 3062 (1983).
26. 440 F. Supp. 1284 (1977).
27. Quoted by Wendell R. Bird, "Freedom of Religion and Science Instruction in Public Schools," *Yale Law Journal*, January 1978 (Vol. 87, No. 3), p. 561.
28. 454 U.S. 263 (1981).
29. The use of Christmas carols in public school programs was upheld by the 8th Circuit U.S. Court of Appeals in *Florey v. Sioux Falls School District*, 619 F.2d 1311, cert. den. 499 U.S. 987 (1981). The use of Nativity scenes on government property is currently before the Supreme Court in *Lynch v. Donnelly*, 104 S. Ct. 1355 (1984).

Chapter 17: Censorship and Pornography

1. See Cal Thomas, *Book Burning* (Westchester, Ill.: Crossway Books, 1983), pp. 92, 93.
2. "Huck Suppressed at Twain School," *Tulsa Tribune*, April 7, 1982.
3. "Huck Finn Wins: Iowa School Panel Retains Twain Novel," *Tulsa Tribune*, February 17, 1982.
4. Thomas, *Book Burning*, pp. 64-70. See also Noel Epstein, "Censorship's No 4-Letter Word," *Tulsa World*, March 21, 1982.
5. Epstein, *ibid*.
6. Martin Mawyer, "Bible Club Ad Clipped from Yearbook," *Moral Majority Report*, July 1983, pp. 12, 13.
7. "Competency and Controversy: Issues and Ethics on the University/Pseudoscience Battlefield," *The Skeptical Inquirer*, Fall 1983 (Vol. 8), pp. 2-5.
8. Aldred de Grazia, *The Velikovsky Affair* (New Hyde Park, N.Y.: University Books, 1966). See also Fred Warshofsky, "Why the Sky Rained Fire: The Velikovsky Phenomenon," *Reader's Digest*, December 1975, pp. 220-240.
9. Quoted in *Moody Monthly*, September 1981, p. 123.
10. Thomas, *Book Burning*, p. 26.
11. Neil Gallagher, *How to Stop the Porno Plague* (Minneapolis, Minn.: Bethany Fellowship, 1977), pp. 14-24.

12. 172 F. 2d 788 (2d Cir. 1948), cert. denied 377 U.S. 938.
13. 413 U.S. 15 (1973).
14. 408 U.S. 229 (1972).
15. 427 U.S. 50 (1976).
16. 390 U.S. 629 (1968).
17. 102 S. Ct. 348 (1982).
18. Gallagher, *How to Stop the Porno Plague*, pp. 122, 131, 132.

Chapter 18: The Right to Life

1. I am endebted to the Rev. Bruce Einspahr of Columbia Bible Church, Pasco, Washington, whose typed message of November 1981 greatly helped me in exegeting the passages that follow.
2. An excellent analysis of this passage is found in "Miscarriage or Premature Birth: Additional Thoughts on Exodus 21:22-25," by H. Wayne House, *Westminster Theological Journal*, 41, Fall 1978, pp. 105-123. See also C. F. Keil and F. Delitzsch, *Commentary on the Old Testament*, Vol. 1, James Martin, trans. (Grand Rapids: Eerdmans, 1975), pp. 134, 135.
3. The above information is generally accepted medical fact. Specific sources include: Gary Bergel and C. Everett Koop, *When You Were Formed in Secret* (Elyria, Ohio: Intercessors for America, 1980), p. 6; C. Everett Koop, "The Right to Live," *Human Life Review*, Fall 1975, pp. 65-87; Allan C. Barnes, *Intrauterine Development* (Philadelphia: Lee Febiqer, 1968), p. 455; W. J. Hamilton and H. W. Mossman, *Human Embryology* (Baltimore: Williams and Wilkins, 1970), p. 188; A. W. Liley, as quoted by Senator James L. Buckley, "A Human Life Amendment," *Human Life Review*, Winter 1975, pp. 7-20; Trypena Humphrey, "The Development of Human Fetal Activity in Its Relation to Postnatal Behavior," *Advances in Child Development and Behavior*, Hayne W. Reese and Lewis P. Lipsitt, eds. (New York: Academy Press, 1975), pp. 12, 19; L. B. Arey, *Developmental Anatomy: A Textbook and Laboratory Manual of Embryology* (Philadelphia: W. B. Saunders, 1965), pp. 85-105; P. S. Timiras, *Developmental Physiology and Aging* (New York and London: Macmillan, 1972); David Granfeld, *The Abortion Decision* (Garden City, N.Y.: AA, 1969, 1971), pp. 15-28.
4. Burgel and Koop, *When You Were Formed*, pp. 1-17; Granfeld, *The Abortion Decision*, pp. 15-28, citing Dr. Paul E. Rockwell.
5. E. F. Diamond, "ISMS Symposium on Medical Implications under the Current Abortion Law in Illinois," *Illinois Medical Journal*, May 1967, p. 677.
6. B. M. Simms, "A District Attorney Looks at Abortion," *Child and Family*, Vol. 8, Spring 1969, pp. 176-180.
7. Dennis Horan, editor, *Abortion and Social Justice* (New York: Sheed and Ward, 1972), p. 48.
8. Otto Pollack and Alfred S. Friedman, eds., *Family Dynamics and Female Sexual Delinquency* (Palo Alto, Calif.: Sad Science and Behavior, 1969), p. 62.
9. 410 U.S. 113 (1973).
10. 60 U.S. 393, 19 Howard 393.
11. 10 Wheaton 66.
12. 428 U.S. 52 (1976).
13. 443 U.S. 622 (1979).
14. 450 U.S. 398 (1981).
15. 448 U.S. 297 (1980).
16. Franky Schaeffer, *A Time for Anger* (Westchester, Ill.: Crossway Books, 1982), pp. 72-74.
17. John Whitehead, *The Second American Revolution* (Elgin, Ill.: David C. Cook, 1982), p. 67.
18. Donald DeMarco, "On Human Experimentation," *The Christian Activist*, Spring 1984, p. 8.

19. Dr. Olga FairFax, "101 Uses for a Dead (or Alive) Baby," *A.L.L. About Issues,* January 1984, pp. 6-9. Published by the American Life Lobby, P.O. Box 490, Stafford, VA 22554.

20. Joseph Rebone with Dave Andrusko, "A Chronology of Infanticide: The Life and Death of Infant Doe," *National Right to Life News,* May 10, 1982, pp. 1, 11, 13.

21. Peter Singer, *Pediatrics,* Vol. 72, No. 1, July 1983, p. 138.

22. 355 A. 2d 647 (1976).

Chapter 19: Crime and Punishment

1. Horace Mann, *The Common School Journal,* January 1, 1841 (III:XV). Quoted in R. J. Rushdoony, *The Messianic Character of American Education* (Nutley, N.J.: Craig Press, 1963), p. 29.

2. John Eidsmoe, "Firearms Legislation—Commission Report," research paper for Legislation Seminar, University of Iowa College of Law, 1970, p. 22.

3. Gerhard Kittel, editor, *Theological Dictionary of the New Testament,* Vol. 4 (Grand Rapids, Mich.: Eerdmans, 1967), pp. 524-527.

4. Some might argue that the imposition of capital punishment for such "petty" offenses as blasphemy, witcraft, or idolatry is inconsistent with the principle. I suggest, however, that God's Word considers those offenses against God to be far more serious than we regard them today. The issue is not whether such offenses are deserving of death, but whether God has given such authority to the state in this age.

5. Charles W. Colson, "Is There a Better Way? A Perspective on American Prisons" (Washington, D.C.: Prison Fellowship, 1981), citing Thorsten Sellin, "The Origin of the Pennsylvania System of Prison Discipline," in George Killinger and Paul Cromwell, Jr., editors, *Penology: The Evolution of Corrections in America* (St. Paul, Minn.: West Publishing, 1973), pp. 13ff. See also David Rothman, "The Invention of the Penitentiary," *Criminal Law Bulletin,* September 1972 (Vol. 8), pp. 585, 586.

6. Colson, p. 11.

7. *Ibid.,* p. 13.

8. *Ibid.,* p. 11, citing Eugene Doleschal and Anne Newton, *International Rates of Imprisonment* (Hackensack, N.J.: National Council on Crime and Delinquency, 1979).

9. In no way do I wish to suggest that all or even most guards are brutal. Many prison personnel are highly competent and dedicated to their prisoners' welfare. My criticism is directed toward the prison system, not those who run it.

10. Colson, p. 12, citing *Crime in the United States* (Washington, D.C.: U.S. Government Printing Office, 1975), p. 44.

11. David Chilton, *Productive Christians in the Age of Guilt-Manipulators* (Tyler, Tex.: Institute for Christian Economics, 1981, 1982), p. 89.

12. *U.S. News and World Report,* November 1, 1982, p. 50.

13. "The Complex Minuet in Criminal Courts," *U.S. News and World Report,* November 1, 1982, p. 38.

14. *Ibid.,* p. 41.

15. For a more detailed discussion of the juvenile justice system, see John Eidsmoe, *The Christian Legal Advisor* (Milford, Mich.: Mott Media, 1984), Chapter 32.

Chapter 20: International Relations

1. Quoted by G. Edward Griffin, *The Fearful Master* (Los Angeles: Western Islands, 1964, 1965), p. iv.

2. *The Complete Works of Flavius Josephus* (Grand Rapids: Kregel, 1974), p. 30.

3. Griffin, *The Fearful Master,* p. 234.

4. Sergei Kourdakov, *The Persecutor* (Old Tappan, N.J.: Fleming H. Revell, 1973).

5. "The Testimony of Georgi Vins," Elkhart, Ind.: International Representation for the Council of Evangelical Baptist Churches of the Soviet Union.

6. Anita & Peter Deyneka, Jr., *A Song in Siberia*, (Elgin, Ill.: David C. Cook, 1977, 1979).

7. Alexander Solzhenitsyn, *The Gulag Archipelago* (New York: Harper and Row, 1973, 1974).

8. While Marx was officially an atheist, there is considerable reason to believe that under the atheist exterior, he was secretly a Satan worshiper. Richard Wurmbrand, in his book *Was Karl Marx a Satanist?* (Glendale, Calif.: Diane Books, 1976, 1979), raises this intriguing possibility, as does Sir Lionel A. Luckhoo, *The Devil and Karl Marx*. Wurmbrand points out numerous letters, plays, and poems written by Marx in which he uses satanist language. For example, in "The Player" he writes, "The hellish vapors rise and pell the grain, Till I go mad and my heart is utterly changed. See this sword? The prince of darkness sold it to me." Early in his life Marx had been a devoted Christian, but for some reason he turned against Christ and became his avowed enemy. As he writes to his father on November 7, 1937, "A curtain had fallen. My holy of holies was rent asunder and new gods had to be installed." And later he writes, "I wish to avenge myself against the One who rules above." He also writes in "The Pale Maiden," "Thus Heaven I've forfeited, I know it full well. My soul, once true to God, is chosen for hell." Marx's unusual beard and hairstyle were characteristic of the disciples of Joanna Southcott, a satanist priestess who considered herself in contact with the demon Shiloh. His son addressed him in correspondence as "my dear devil." Despite this and much other evidence, Wurmbrand acknowledges that his proof is not conclusive, and he encourages others to do further research into Marx's possible satanist connections.

9. Quoted by John H. Hallowell, *Main Currents in Modern Political Thought* (New York: Holt, Reinhart, and Winston, 1950, 1960), p. 402.

10. *The Correspondence of Marx and Engels* (New York: 1935), pp. 125, 126. Quoted by Richard Hofstadter, *Social Darwinism in American Thought* (New York: George Braziller, Inc., 1944, 1955), p. 3.

11. *Congressional Record*, Vol. 77, p. 1539. Quoted by Charles M. Crow, *In This Free Land* (Nashville: Abingdon Press, 1964), pp. 61, 62.

12. Whittaker Chambers, *Witness* (New York: Random House, 1952), pp. 9, 10. I regret that space does not permit me to quote the entire twenty-two pages of Chambers' "Introduction," which is the most profound and eloquent statement and refutation of Communist philosophy that I have ever read.

13. Quoted by J. Edgar Hoover, *Masters of Deceit* (New York: Holt, 1958, 1963), p. 301.

14. Dr. G. Stewart-Smith, *Defeat of Communism*. Cited by Eugene Lyons, *Workers' Paradise Lost* (New York: Paperback Library, 1967), pp. 354ff.

15. Quoted by Lyons, p. 377.

16. Karl Marx, *The Communist Manifesto* (1848, reprinted Chicago: Regnery, 1954), pp. 81, 82.

17. John A. Stormer, *The Death of a Nation* (Florissant, Mo.: Liberty Bell Press, 1968), p. 14.

18. Chambers, *Witness*, p. 8.

19. Charles C. Bonn, "The Next War: Mexico," *New Breed*, April 1983, pp. 18-21, 68.

20. "Grenada Indoctrination Amazes Experts," *Daily Oklahoman*, January 2, 1984.

21. It is said that a high-ranking Communist official once delivered an emotional harangue in which he declared that the Communists would eventually hang all the capitalists. A heckler from the audience, pointing out economic shortages in Communist nations, asked, "Where are you going to get the rope?" The speaker replied with great foresight, "The capitalists will sell it to us." Currently our government's policy is to encourage trade with Communist countries only in "nonstrategic" items. However, the distinction between strategic and nonstrategic is not easily maintained. For example, wheat can be compressed into ethyl alcohol, which is used in the production of TNT and atom bombs. And it is said that an army marches on its stomach; in time of war, nothing is more strategic than food.

22. William P. Hoar, "The Kremlin Arms for War," *Americanist Issues*, 1983, pp. 3, 4.

23. *The New Force,* Volume 2:6, 1983, p. 6.
24. Ernest Conine, "Soviet Way of Life: More Guns, Less Butter," *Tulsa World,* November 1, 1982.
25. *The New Force,* p. 6.
26. See *Americanist Issues,* 1983, p. 24.
27. *Ibid.*
28. Richard Wurmbrand, *The Wurmbrand Letters* (Pomona, Calif.: Cross Publications, Inc., 1967), p. 9.